THE SPIRIT IN THE WORLD

The Spirit in the World

EMERGING PENTECOSTAL THEOLOGIES
IN GLOBAL CONTEXTS

Edited by

Veli-Matti Kärkkäinen

WILLIAM B. EERDMANS PUBLISHING COMPANY
GRAND RAPIDS, MICHIGAN / CAMBRIDGE, U.K.

Published 2009 by
Wm. B. Eerdmans Publishing Co.
2140 Oak Industrial Drive N.E., Grand Rapids, Michigan 49505 /
P.O. Box 163, Cambridge CB3 9PU U.K.

Printed in the United States of America

14 13 12 11 10 09   7 6 5 4 3 2 1

Library of Congress Cataloging-in-Publication Data

The spirit in the world: emerging Pentecostal theologies in global contexts /
edited by Veli-Matti Kärkkäinen.
        p.   cm.
ISBN 978-0-8028-6281-5 (pbk.: alk. paper)
1. Pentecostal churches — Doctrines. 2. Pentecostalism.
I. Kärkkäinen, Veli-Matti.

BX8762.Z5S65   2009
230′.994 — dc22

                                    2009015432

www.eerdmans.com

Contents

Contents

Preface

This book is truly a unique contribution to an emerging worldwide Pentecostal theology. It does not merely offer a fascinating mixture of reports about developing Pentecostal churches in Africa, Asia, and Latin America, as well as theological reflections about new and astonishing experiences of the Spirit. It also expands our gaze to the activity of the Holy Spirit in nature, and in the different cultures and religions. Theologically, the Pentecostal movement has come of age! This is all the more remarkable since the Pentecostal movement is a revival and experiential religion that came into being without any fixed dogmas and without any tradition, simply with the open Bible in hand. But out of the new experiences of the Holy Spirit that are being made all over the world, beyond the frontiers and in the different cultures, the need for theological interpretations nevertheless emerges.

A new formation in Christianity is being heralded. In the ancient church of the Roman Empire we find a patriarchal form: God the Father is represented by the patriarchs, the pope, and the priests. With the Reformation, the Christocentric faith came into being: Jesus, the only begotten Son of God, is the firstborn of brothers and sisters. The church is a community of brothers and sisters. But since the seventeenth-century revival movements in Europe and America, a third image of this community has come to the fore ever more emphatically: there is one Spirit — but the Spirit has many gifts. There is one Spirit — and many spiritually endowed people with experiences of the Spirit. The church is a charismatic community. I have seen this image of the church with my own eyes in the Pentecostal churches in Korea and Nicaragua.

Pentecostal churches are not "sects," "steered by U.S. capital and the CIA." They have sprung up out of the ground everywhere, like mushrooms. They are an independent popular movement of the poor. They have something to say to the whole of Christendom on earth, and have liberating experiences to pass on to all men and women. So it is time to listen to their diverse theologies and to discuss them. But this book is not intended only for the theological public. It is also designed to serve theological clarification in the Pentecostal movement itself and to bring about a common, universal thrust.

A preface is not a review. Its purpose is to invite, not to criticize. So I shall first of all stress what seems to me important in these accounts of Pentecostal churches in the different countries. After that I shall say something about the Pentecostal theologies.

The Pentecostal churches emerged out of revival movements — and not just the well-known happenings in Azusa Street, Los Angeles, in 1906; almost at the same time they sprang up in Pyongyang, Korea, in Kerala, India, and in a number of places in Africa. Everywhere there were direct experiences of the Spirit shared by all the people involved. It was a truly democratic experience of the Spirit, without priests, tradition, and church order. This experience was called "baptism in the Spirit." But in this spiritual baptism a personal relationship to Jesus was born: Jesus lives — Jesus heals — Jesus comes: that was what Christoph Blumhardt taught at that time, in a South German revival movement; and it is that which distinguishes Pentecostalism from spiritism.

Pentecostal churches are termed experiential religion. Orthodoxy in the Spirit and orthopraxis in action is followed by an orthopathy in the feelings and motivations. The Pentecostal movement is everywhere a movement for healing. Not just in Third World countries but in the industrial societies too. Physical healing is linked with emotional, mental, and religious healing, its premise being a holistic view of the human being. That is both premodern and postmodern. Healing rooms and prayer mountains are part of it. Pentecostal worship shows an actively involved congregation in singing, hand-clapping, movement, and shout-out prayers. The congregation does not just consist of hearers of the Word or onlookers at the liturgy.

Pentecostal congregations in Latin America are the expression of a "religion of the poor." Pentecostal Christians come from below, and from the highways and byways. In Korea they come from the *minjung,* and experience liberation from *han* (pain and anger). This is not a religion *for* the people; it is a religion *of* the people. In Latin America it is true that there is a link between Pentecostal churches and the base communities of Catholic liberation theology. Whereas social-critical analyses explain why people sink into poverty, misery, and sickness, the experience of the Spirit enables people to emerge from social misery and to ascend the social ladder. However, in Korea I did not see the connection between the minjung congregations and the Pentecostal churches. It was only last year that Pastor Yonggi Cho, whom I revere and have often visited, proclaimed the year of "social salvation" and "the salvation of nature" for the Yoido Full Gospel Church. I wrote a contribution for his newspaper, welcoming this most warmly. In the German peace movement of the 1980s we felt the absence of the Pentecostal Christians to be a painful lack. They had not yet discovered for themselves the political charisma.

The Pentecostal churches will remain part of the Pentecostal movement. They participate in the movement of the Holy Spirit which "will be poured out upon all flesh." Pentecostalism is a missionary movement, with optimism, with the joy of the gospel, and without the judgmental spirit that condemns others.

The Pentecostal theologies must develop models with which to interpret the experiences of the Spirit and must open up new horizons, towards which the Spirit leads.

Experiences of the Holy Spirit in Jesus' name are not momentary experiences that come and go; they are the beginning of a permanent indwelling of the Spirit. Enthusiasm is an accompanying phenomenon; the essential is faithfulness and perseverance "to the end." A valuable feature of the present book is that its stress lies not on conversion but on deliverance. Experience of the Spirit is an inward liberation from dark and oppressive forces that torment the soul. Does the idea of "spiritual warfare" offer a good interpretative model? I do not think it does, for we are not engaged in a struggle with demonic forces and satanic powers in which the outcome is in doubt. With the apostle Paul we are singing "Death is swallowed up in victory. Death, where is thy sting? Hell, where is thy victory? Thanks be to God, who has given us the victory through our Lord Jesus Christ" (1 Cor. 15:55-57). The world of spirits and the victory of the Holy Spirit: that theological idea fits in with premodern notions about the world. We find it in Asia, Africa, and Latin America, but among us too. The world that consists of heaven, earth, and the underworld, the world of the spirits of our ancestors, of good and evil powers, witchdemonology, and the reverence for ancestors as well as the fear of them — that world accords well with the biblical world picture within which the history of Jesus and the activity of the Spirit are related. But it is this history and this activity that are important theologically, not the world pictures, which change. The mechanistic world picture with which some modern theologians have wanted to "demythologize" the Bible has long since given way to a picture of the world that is ecological and dynamic. The power that can liberate us from myths and powers proceeds from the Spirit of Jesus Christ, not from changes in the world picture.

The same applies to the experiences of healing in the Holy Spirit. They do not depend on an evanescent shamanistic view of the human being. They do accord well with psychosomatic healings. But they do not fit with the early modern view of the human being, the *homme machine* of La Mettrie and the computer picture of the body.

Dispensationalism was once a salvation-history model for interpreting the Pentecostal experiences of the Spirit. In this way these experiences were linked with apocalyptic expectations of an imminent end of the world. But I think it is better to associate them with a transforming eschatology of the coming kingdom. For the experiences of the Spirit are not just fire from heaven; they are also "the powers of the age to come" (Heb. 6:5), and so "the age to come" is a universe of charismatic forces of eternal life.

Finally, the problem of particular faith and universal grace awaits a theological solution. Bishop King (chapter 12) has offered a solution: The "religion of Christ" is universal and was there from the beginning; it appears, restricted in time and space, in "the Christian religion." So the Christian religion must always be related to the religion of Christ. It does not bring Christ to the peoples of the world, but discovers him among them, for he is already there. That is a good approach for interfaith dialogue. God's relationship to human beings is universal. In his love they are his children on earth, in the self-giving of Christ they are already reconciled; the seed of the Spirit who redeems is in them all. But the relationship of human beings to God is particular. When God's Spirit is experienced and faith is awakened, then they respond to God's relationship to them. Trusting in God's relationship to all human beings, believers understand their experience of the Spirit as the beginning and pledge of its outpouring "on all flesh." The experience is particular; the expectation is universal.

This book offers excellent contributions to interfaith dialogue, not merely on the levels of the world religions but also on the local levels of faith in the Spirit. But in the global context we still need to surmount terror, and still have to work for social justice too. Not least, we need a cosmic pneumatology for new ways of dealing with God's beloved earth.

JÜRGEN MOLTMANN
September 20, 2007
Tübingen
Translation by Margaret Kohl

Pentecostalism and Pentecostal Theology in the Third Millennium: Taking Stock of the Contemporary Global Situation

Veli-Matti Kärkkäinen

The Resurgence of an "Experientialist" Religion in the New Millennium

The Harvard theologian Harvey Cox, author of *The Secular City* at the height of the "secular decades" of the 1960s and 70s, has radically changed his views of the role of religion at the turn of the millennium. His highly acclaimed monograph that appeared in the mid-1990s, titled *Fire from Heaven*, argues that "*The Rise of Pentecostal Spirituality* . . . [means nothing less than] *the Reshaping of Religion in the Twenty-first Century.*" This dramatic development has to do with the demise of "scientific modernity and traditional religion," which for centuries "clashed over the privilege of being the ultimate source of meaning and value" but now "like tired boxers who have slugged away too long . . . have reached an exhausted stalemate."[1] Consequently, more and more people look for new options. In Cox's analysis, the two current contenders for souls are "fundamentalism" and "experientialism":

> Both present themselves as authentic links to the sacred past. Both embody efforts to reclaim what is valuable from previous ages in order to apply it to the present and future. Which of these two rivals eventually prevails will be decided in large measure by which one grasps the nature of the change we are living through. . . . Perhaps it has taken the very recent and unprecedented meeting of east and west to produce this new

1. Harvey Cox, *Fire from Heaven: The Rise of Pentecostal Spirituality and the Reshaping of Religion in the Twenty-first Century* (Reading, MA: Addison-Wesley, 1995), p. 299.

stage of consciousness. In any case, these thinkers find evidence for a new phase of history in virtually every field of human endeavor — in atonal and improvisational music, in the environmental movement, in new styles of painting and sculpture, in experimental architecture, and especially in poetry. I think one can also fit in pentecostalism.[2]

While one may want to debate how well — or how poorly — Pentecostalism fits in with "postmodernity,"[3] the main point of Cox's observation is well taken. While what he calls "experientialism," is "more disparate and inchoate, harder to describe than fundamentalism," it is on the rise not only in Christianity but also among other religions as, for example, ably documented in Seyed Hossein Nasr's *Islamic Spirituality: Manifestations*, which defines spirituality as the something that "is open to the transcendent dimension" and where the person "experiences ultimate reality." While focusing on the most likely candidate in Islam, Sufism, the principle has a wider application as well.[4]

A main reason why Pentecostal "experientialism" has drawn so great a following has to do with the fact that Pentecostalism

> has spoken to the spiritual emptiness of our time by reaching beyond the levels of creed and ceremony into the core of human religiousness, into what might be called "primal spirituality," that largely unprocessed nucleus of the psyche in which the unending struggle for a sense of purpose and significance goes on. Classical theologians have called it the "imago dei," the image of God in every person. Maybe the Pentecostals are referring to the same thing with different words. . . . My own conviction is that Pentecostals have touched so many people because they have indeed restored something.[5]

This openness to divine intervention, whether in terms of miracles such as healings or in terms of empowerment as in the daily exercise of

2. Cox, *Fire from Heaven*, pp. 300-301.
3. See further, Kenneth J. Archer, "Pentecostal Story: The Hermeneutical Filter for the Making of Meaning," *Pneuma: The Journal of the Society for Pentecostal Studies* 26, no. 1 (Spring 2004): 36-59; V.-M. Kärkkäinen, "'The Re-turn of Religion in the New Millennium': Pentecostalisms and Postmodernities," *Swedish Missiological Themes* 95, no. 4 (Fall 2007): 469-96.
4. Cited in Cox, *Fire from Heaven*, p. 309.
5. Cox, *Fire from Heaven*, p. 81.

spiritual gifts and charisms, undoubtedly is a key to the phenomenal spread of the Pentecostal/charismatic movements all around the world. The philosopher J. K. A. Smith rightly sees as highly significant theologically and spiritually Pentecostalism's "positioning of radical openness to God, and in particular, God doing something *differently* or *new.*" For him, one of the prime biblical examples is the narrative of Acts 2, namely

> Peter's courage and willingness to recognize in these "strange" phenomena the operation of the Spirit and declare it to be a work of God. . . . In postmodern terms, we might describe this as an openness to alterity or otherness. . . . Because of this, Pentecostal communities emphasize the continued ministry of the Spirit, including continuing revelation, prophecy, and the centrality of charismatic giftings in the ecclesial community. . . . Included in this ministry of the Spirit is a distinctive belief in the healing of the body as a central aspect of the work of the Atonement. This central belief is an indication of a Pentecostal deconstruction of fundamentalist dualisms. . . . The centrality of belief in physical healing is an indicator of this: it is a fundamental assertion of the value of embodiment and should constitute a radical critique of all dualisms, as does RO's [Radical Orthodoxy's] "incarnational" ontology. By affirming that God is concerned with the health of the body, we affirm materiality, embodiment, and the sensible world.[6]

Who Are the Pentecostals?

Who then are these contemporary "experientialists"? While nothing like a uniform definition of Pentecostalism exists, a helpful orientation to the myriads of movements known by that umbrella name is the terminology adopted by *The New International Dictionary of Pentecostal and Charismatic Movements.*[7] That typology lists, first, (classical) Pentecostal denominations such as Assemblies of God or Foursquare Gospel, owing their

6. James K. A. Smith, "What Hath Cambridge to Do with Azusa Street? Radical Orthodoxy and Pentecostal Theology in Conversation," *Pneuma: The Journal of the Society for Pentecostal Studies* 25, no. 1 (Spring 2003): 109-10, 112.

7. While canons are still in the making, this is the typology adopted in Stanley M. Burgess and Eduard M. van der Maas, eds., *The New International Dictionary of Pentecostal and Charismatic Movements,* rev. and expanded ed. (Grand Rapids: Zondervan, 2002).

existence to the famous Azusa Street revival; second, charismatic movements, Pentecostal-type spiritual movements within the established churches (the largest of which is the Roman Catholic Charismatic Renewal); and third, neo-charismatic movements, some of the most notable of which are the Vineyard Fellowship in the U.S.A., African Initiated Churches, and the China House Church movement, as well as an innumerable number of independent churches and groups all over the world). Numbers-wise, the charismatic movements (about 200 million) and neo-charismatics (200-300 million) well outnumber classical Pentecostals (75-125 million).

In this volume, the focus is on the first category, (classical) Pentecostalism. Yet even with regard to that, we need to be aware of a great diversity. The diversity arises in two dimensions: the cultural and the theologico-ecumenical. Pentecostalism, unlike any other contemporary religious movement, Christian or non-Christian, is spread across most cultures, linguistic barriers, and social locations.[8] Related to this is the theological and ecumenical diversity, which simply means that there are several more-or-less distinct Pentecostalisms. Thus, while speaking of Pentecostalisms would be a valid choice, for the sake of convenience usually the singular form is preferred. How different in ethos, manifestation, and to some extent in theology are, for example, Yoido Full Gospel Church in Seoul, Korea — the world's largest church, with more than one million adherents — from the African American (black) Pentecostal churches of the U.S. South, from the small Pentecostal congregations in any European country, and so on.

The question of what makes Pentecostalism Pentecostalism — in other words, what is its identity? — is a notoriously difficult one.[9] Unlike, say, Lutheranism or Roman Catholicism, Pentecostal identity is not based on creeds or shared history. Nor can Pentecostal identity be based on ecclesiastical structures, since you can find the whole repertoire: from most local-church autonomous models (Scandinavia) to Congregationalist

8. The diversity is well documented. For an up-to-date account, see e.g., the annual statistic lists in the January issue of *International Bulletin of Missionary Research* compiled by David B. Barrett and Todd M. Johnson.

9. For starters, see V.-M. Kärkkäinen, "Free Churches, Ecumenism and Pentecostalism," in V.-M. Kärkkäinen, *Toward a Pneumatological Theology: Pentecostal and Ecumenical Perspectives on Ecclesiology, Soteriology, and Theology of Mission,* ed. Amos Yong (Lanham, MD: University Press of America, 2002), pp. 53-64.

(Continental Europe and England) to Presbyterian (White Pentecostals in the U.S.A.) to episcopal (black Pentecostals in the U.S.A. and elsewhere) to other types.

Let me operate with the concept that I think most theological observers of Pentecostalisms would endorse, namely its distinctive, Christ-centered charismatic spirituality going back to the classical Full Gospel template in which Jesus is perceived as Savior, Sanctifier, Healer, Baptizer with the Spirit, and the Soon-returning King.[10] Spirituality, thus, is the key to "defining" Pentecostal identity.[11]

Behind Pentecostal spirituality is the "Pentecostal Story as a Hermeneutical Narrative Tradition." As the Pentecostal theologian Kenneth J. Archer puts it:

> The Pentecostal community is a distinct coherent narrative tradition within Christianity. Pentecostal communities are bound together by their charismatic experiences and common story. The Pentecostal narrative tradition is one embodiment of the Christian metanarrative. Yet, because the Pentecostal community understands itself to be a restorational movement, it has argued that it is the best representation or embodiment of Christianity in the world today. This may sound triumphalist; yet, Pentecostals, like all restorational narrative traditions of

10. A definitive study of the main motifs of "Full Gospel" is Donald W. Dayton, *Theological Roots of Pentecostalism* (Grand Rapids: Zondervan, 1987). For a fine account of key themes and orientations in Pentecostal spirituality, see Russell P. Spittler, "Spirituality, Pentecostal and Charismatic," in Burgess and van der Maas, *New International Dictionary of Pentecostal and Charismatic Movements*, pp. 1096-1102.

11. No one else has argued so forcefully and convincingly for the primacy of spirituality as the way to define Pentecostalisms as Walter J. Hollenweger, the most noted theological observer of the movements. Hollenweger for decades has insisted that it was the early years of the emerging Pentecostal movement that gave the movement its *prodigium*. The first decade of the movement, says Hollenweger, forms the heart, not the infancy, of Pentecostal spirituality. Walter J. Hollenweger, *The Pentecostals* (Peabody, MA: Hendrickson, 1988), p. 551. So also Steven J. Land, *Pentecostal Spirituality: A Passion for the Kingdom* (Sheffield: Sheffield Academic Press, 1993), pp. 14, 47. Features such as orality of liturgy, narrativity of theology and witness, maximum participation at the level of reflection, prayer, and decision-making in a community characterized by inclusion and reconciliation, inclusion of dreams and visions into personal and public forms of worship, and a holistic understanding of the body-mind relationship reflected in the ministry of healing by prayer, were formative at the movement's inception. Hollenweger, "After Twenty Years' Research on Pentecostalism," *International Review of Missions* 75 (January 1986): 6.

Christianity, desire to be both an authentic continuation of New Testament Christianity and a faithful representation of New Testament Christianity in the present societies in which they exist. Of course, the understanding of what was and should be New Testament Christianity is based upon a Pentecostal understanding. Moral reasoning, which includes biblical-theological interpretation, is contextualized in the narrative tradition of the Pentecostal community. Pentecostals will engage Scripture, do theology, and reflect upon reality from their own contextualized communities and narrative tradition.[12]

The Emergence of Pentecostal Theological Reflection at the Global Level

For many decades the Pentecostal movement — which recently celebrated its first centenary, reflecting on the global significance of the humble beginnings on Azusa Street in Los Angeles in 1906 — was known merely for its aggressive evangelistic and missionary work, enthusiastic charismatic spirituality, and lay-led, nonacademic way of proclaiming the gospel. Academia and Azusa Street seemed to be at odds with each other — or at least living in different worlds.

During the past two decades or so, Pentecostal theology has emerged and is about to establish its place among other traditions. A younger generation of Pentecostal theologians, many of them educated in some of the best theological schools and thus knowledgeable of wider Christian tradition, have done some exciting work in reflecting theologically on the Pentecostal "experientialism," the significance of charisms in the community, the conditions and unique features of missions work and social concern, and so forth. Pentecostal theologians have also offered reflections on the relation of Pentecostal spirituality to social and cultural context now that Pentecostal movements can be found among all cultures. Some recent attempts have even been made to explore the relationship between Pentecostalism and other religions.

The present volume is a tribute to and an up-to-date assessment of

12. Archer, "Pentecostal Story," pp. 40-42. This sounds very postmodern — McIntyrean, and indeed it is. Interestingly enough, a key resource for Archer's construal of Pentecostalism is Alasdair McIntyre's insights into the importance of narrative and tradition(s) for community formation.

these contemporary exciting developments in Pentecostal theological reflection coming from an esteemed group of Pentecostal academicians from all around the world. This book was suggested by the organizers of an international symposium titled "Spirit in the World: The Dynamics of Pentecostal Growth and Experience," held October 5-7, 2006, at the University of Southern California (USC Los Angeles), hosted by the Center for Religion and Civic Culture of USC and sponsored by the John Templeton Foundation. The book project was subsequently sponsored financially by the Templeton Foundation.

The symposium gathered scholars from around the world to discuss the implications of Pentecostal growth worldwide, including the "Ten Country Survey of Global Pentecostalism" by the Pew Forum on Religion and Public Life. The symposium inspired two book ideas, the present one and another one currently in the making, under the tentative title *Spirit and Power: The Global Impact of Pentecostalism*, edited by Professor Anthea Butler of Rochester University, Dr. Kimon Sargeant, vice president of the John Templeton Foundation, and Professor Donald Miller of USC, a noted researcher of Pentecostalism. While *Spirit and Power* focuses on the extent of and reasons for the worldwide growth of Pentecostalism as well as its social, political, and economic growth, the present volume concentrates on theological issues.

The contributors to this volume come both from the presenters at the USC conference and some other leading Pentecostal theologians from different locations and contexts. They represent four continents, men and women, and different Pentecostal traditions. Thematically, this volume is divided into three main sections:

I. "The Spirit Among the People": Pentecostal Theology and Spiritual (em)Power(ment)
II. "The Spirit Among Cultures": Pentecostal Theology and Cultural Diversity
III. "The Spirit Among Religions": Pentecostal Theology and Religious Plurality

While the stated focus of the present book is constructive theology, many of the writers also engage theological reflection from an interdisciplinary perspective, in keeping with the diverse nature of the Pentecostal experience and phenomena. Thus, among the contributions are discussions that engage sociological (Poloma), cultural (Kalu, Crumbley), his-

torical (Paulson), missiological (Ma, Petersen), and religious (Yong) studies, among others, from a theological perspective.

Pentecostal Theology and Spiritual (em)Power(ment)

In Part I, with the focus on Pentecostal Theology and Spiritual (em)Pow-
er(ment), the first essay is written by a leading constructive Pentecostal
systematic theologian, Frank D. Macchia, who for years has developed
constructive Pentecostal theology through the lens of Spirit baptism and
spiritual gifts, especially *glossolalia,* speaking in tongues, the most cher-
ished charism among Pentecostals. Macchia tackles foundational issues
such as whether Pentecostalism globally has a theologically distinctive
message and if so, what that possibly might be. And: What have been the
major trajectories among Pentecostal theologians globally? While Pentecostal theology is more than Spirit baptism, that question has been — and
in Macchia's estimation — continues to be the key issue.

One of the charisms along with speaking in tongues that has caught
the attention of both insiders and outsiders to Pentecostalism has to do
with physical healing, the topic of Margaret Poloma's discussion. In light
of the role of healing in Christian history and contemporary society,
Poloma offers an exciting theological and sociological investigation into
the distinctive features of healing among Pentecostals based on their
worldview and spirituality, as well as how Pentecostal healing practice and
theology might relate to current medical practice and philosophy. Wearing
the two hats of both sociologist of religion and theologian, Poloma also
brings to the task her wide field research results in various locations in
North America.

While for outsiders the empowerment by the Spirit has mainly to do
with the individual believer's life, both global Pentecostal experience and
emerging theological reflection argue that it has everything to do with
communities and social issues as well. This is what the Korean Wonsuk
Ma, with more than twenty years of experience as a missionary theologian
in the Philippines, discusses in his "When the Poor Are Fired Up." In keeping with the narrative and oral theology of Pentecostalism, Ma offers representative examples from various locations in the world, both East and
West, going all the way to the beginnings at Azusa Street, of the implications for social concern of the baptism in the Spirit.

The same kind of topic is discussed by Doug Petersen, a leading Pentecostal theologian of social concern who has decades-long experience doing social work in Latin America. Looking at the ways Pentecostals read the Bible and understand the theology of Spirit baptism and the kingdom of God, Petersen offers an exciting interpretation of Pentecostalism's desire as the "popular movement" in Latin America to shape their "moral imagination" in search of justice and righteousness, whether at the personal or communal level. Like Ma, he also offers concrete case studies to make the theological reflection more pointed.

Pentecostal Theology and Cultural Diversity

Part II, which is focused on the Pentecostal engagement with cultural diversity, opens with Paulson Pulikottil's postcolonial reading of the history and current identity of one of the oldest Pentecostal movements in his homeland, India. In keeping with the postcolonial approach that lays special emphasis on locality and historical particularity, Pulikottil argues — against "Western" readings of Indian Pentecostal phenomena — that the first Pentecostals in Kerala, India, were steeped in their "Syrianness," the Syrian Christian influence of their context. Pulikottil reflects theologically on the reasons why this Indian Christian identity brought the fledgling movement into conflict with the Eurocentric approach of missionaries, and what might be the lessons for today.

Another example of Pentecostalism's engagement with Asian cultures comes from the pen of the Korean theologian Koo Dong Yun, who now teaches in the United States. While the term *minjung* has usually been related merely to Korean liberation theology, Yun shows its wider application to any liberation movement "from below." In a surprising move, he contends that the Azusa Revival can be considered "a black *minjung* movement." The African Americans at the Azusa Street revival experienced racial discrimination and economic exploitation by the ruling classes and thus exemplified a people on the margins. Yong considers implications of this for Pentecostalism in the contexts of his homeland, Korea, and in India.

Black culture has always been part of Pentecostalism, if for no other reason then because the first preacher at Azusa Street was a former Methodist pastor, the African American William J. Seymour. Not surprisingly then, by far the largest Pentecostal denomination in the United States,

Veli-Matti Kärkkäinen

much bigger than any single white movement, is the black Church of God in Christ. Like several other writers in this volume, Deidre Helen Crumbley, herself an African American female scholar, wears two hats, that of an ethnographer and theologian. Reflecting on her long-term ethnographic research — which, like the postcolonial approach, focuses on particularity — on both sides of the Atlantic, namely among African Instituted Churches and a black inner-city church in the northeastern United States, Crumbley reflects on gender and power issues. She looks for theological reasons for the fact that while in that particular African church women are fully excluded, in the American black church they have access to offices and power.

The African cultural context is also the focus of the discussion by the Nigerian Ogbu U. Kalu, a prolific author who unexpectedly passed away a few months after having finished this essay. In recent decades, Africa has become the most Christianized continent, with an explosive Pentecostal/charismatic growth. Against the typical tendency to attribute the growth of Pentecostalism to urbanization factors, the main thesis of Kalu's chapter is that it is rather the symbols and worldviews of indigenous African religions and cultures that help explain the phenomenon. Reconstructing an African worldview with its hierarchy of deities and spirit beings, combined with results of local ethnographic investigations, leads Kalu to offer a fresh theological interpretation of Pentecostalism and its potential as well as challenges in that context.

Pentecostal Theology and Religious Plurality

While Pentecostals are famous — or in the eyes of many, infamous — for their aggressive missionary work among the nations, it is a much less known fact that several constructive Pentecostal theologians have engaged both the theology-of-religions discourse and particular interfaith issues. A Pentecostal response to religious plurality and pluralisms is emerging, and some of the most current developments are being presented in the third part of this volume.

The purpose of the first essay, by the editor of this volume, is to offer a broad overview and critical assessment of the distinctive nature of Pentecostal pneumatology (the doctrine of the Holy Spirit) in the matrix of contemporary theologies of the Spirit in general and theology-of-religions conversations in particular. One of the many challenges in presenting Pen-

xxii

tecostal pneumatology is that it is debatable whether there is *the* Pentecostal doctrine of the Spirit — or if it is the case, the diversity and plurality reign even there, at the heart of Pentecostal theology. Having located Pentecostal reflections on the Spirit in the contemporary pneumatological renaissance, the author takes a critical look at the perceived difficulties and challenges for Pentecostals as they attempt to offer a response to religions and to the understanding of the role of the Spirit among religions.

Three case studies in the Pentecostal engagement with religions and the theology of religions follow. Again, going back to the African context, the chapter written by the Ghanaian Opoku Onyinah looks at the Pentecostal response to witchcraft. Against earlier interpretations, a number of scholars are arguing that witchcraft in Africa, rather than belonging to "traditional" cultures alone, is part of the continent's modernity. All religions in the African context have given their response to the phenomenon — except for the "enlightened" Christianity from Europe and North America. African Pentecostalism as well as the rest of African Christianity has taken up the challenge and developed "deliverance" models based on a distinctive theology and spirituality. Similarly to Poloma and Kalu, Onyinah's theological reflection is enriched and challenged by a field study as well.

Another case study in the emerging Pentecostal engagement with religions comes from the Chinese-Malaysian Amos Yong, who moved to live — and is now teaching — in the United States. His reflection on Buddhist-Pentecostal encounter begins with the obvious question, "What has Azusa Street to do with the Bo Tree?" Against contrary suspicions, Yong suggests they have a lot to do with each other. Based on his wide knowledge of religions, Yong, the leading Pentecostal pneumatologist of religions, both takes stock of encounters between these two movements and proposes common themes, both in terms of similarities and differences, including the most foundational one, namely, the relationship between the Buddhist core concept of *anatman* (literally: no-self) and the Pentecostal concept of *pneuma* (the Spirit).

The last case study in this final part of the volume is offered by another Pentecostal theologian who in recent years has worked in the area of the theology of religions, Tony Richie. He discusses implications for the theology of religions found in the theology and faith of a Pentecostal pioneer of the first generation, Joseph Hillary King, the founder and early leader of the Pentecostal Holiness Church. In Richie's careful reading of

King's writings, the bishop exemplified a "guarded and graced optimism" toward other religions, while at the same time not being naïve about the weaknesses and errors. Taking his lead from this pioneer's legacy, Richie suggests for Pentecostals an "optimistic" yet not uncritical approach to religions, and urges them to continue painstaking and careful reflection on the topic on the basis of their distinctive theology and spirituality.

The preface to this collection of essays was graciously authored by the leading living constructive theologian Jürgen Moltmann, Emeritus Professor of Systematic Theology at the University of Tübingen. Not only is he known for his groundbreaking work in the area of pneumatology with his seminal work from 1992, *The Spirit of Life: A Universal Affirmation,*[13] but also for training a number of theologians from a Pentecostal background. No other "mainstream" theologian at the global level has had such a wide engagement with Pentecostal/charismatic movements in terms of lectureships, academic symposia, and writings. The willingness of Professor Moltmann to write the preface is a great tribute to the growing cadre of Pentecostal theologians and to their constructive work.

This manuscript was edited carefully and with great skill by Susan Carlson Wood of Fuller School of Theology's Faculty Publications Services. Throughout the years, Susan has worked untiringly and patiently with a number of my books and other writings. She deserves a big "thank you."

---

13. Trans. Margaret Kohl (Minneapolis: Fortress, 1992).

PART I

"The Spirit Among the People":
Pentecostal Theology and Spiritual (em)Power(ment)

CHAPTER 1

Baptized in the Spirit:
Towards a Global Theology of Spirit Baptism

Frank D. Macchia

Introduction

There can be no question but that research in the area of global Pentecostalism has tended to be dominated by historical and sociological investigations supported by concerns over ethos or other phenomenological
issues. Such research has yielded and continues to yield helpful insights
into the values, community involvement, and political orientations of
Pentecostal churches. Less attention, however, has been paid to the larger
trends taking shape in the growing effort to define Pentecostal "theology."
Such research is important, since, as George Lindbeck has shown, a community of faith is shaped in significant measure by its doctrinal concerns
and theological thinking. A study that concentrates on current trends in
Pentecostal theology can only serve to enhance our appreciation for the
depth and richness of Pentecostalism as a movement of Christian faith
and life.

Our task is difficult, since Pentecostalism globally is a very diverse
movement. So let me ask right from the start: Does Pentecostalism globally
have a chief theological distinctive or a theologically distinctive message?
If so, how have Pentecostal theologians over the past several decades developed this message? What have been the major trajectories among Pentecostal theologians globally? Finally, how may we bring these lines of
thought and research together in a way that implicitly invites many different Pentecostals to the table in conversation? I cannot explore all of these
questions in the context of this brief paper, but I will try to give some indi-

cation of the broad lines of inquiry that have dominated discussions over Pentecostal theology.

I will begin with the doctrinal issue with which Pentecostals were arguably most preoccupied in the early decades of the movement and beyond, namely, the baptism in the Holy Spirit.

The Indwelling Spirit: The Early Concern over Spirit Baptism

The dominant theological concern of Pentecostalism in the early decades of the movement was an experience called the "baptism in the Holy Spirit," especially as accompanied by speaking in tongues and other extraordinary gifts of the Spirit, such as those mentioned in Acts and 1 Corinthians 12–14. The dominant focus was on the divine calling for humanity to bear the divine Spirit, or the *inhabitatio Dei,* the indwelling of God through the reception of the Spirit. From where did this focus on Spirit baptism arise?

The Holiness Movement took from Wesley the desire to achieve "entire sanctification" in this life. Wesley regarded the achievement of entire sanctification as a lengthy, even lifelong, quest. Under the influence of American revivalism, however, this quest for Christian perfection (including the eradication of the compulsion to sin) was reduced in the Holiness Movement to a crisis experience following soon after conversion to Christ. Entire sanctification was a "baptism in the Spirit" as an extraordinary endowment expected to be received soon after the born-again experience.[1]

The earliest Pentecostals accepted this twofold initiation to the sanctified life (regeneration and entire sanctification) but decided that entire sanctification was not a Spirit baptism, since sanctification (unlike Spirit baptism) was to be regarded as an element of Christ's redeeming work. Spirit baptism was rather an endowment of the Spirit as power for service, a power that opened the believer up to multiple extraordinary gifts of the Spirit. Most early Pentecostals did not deny that the Spirit was active in Christ's redemptive work, but they tended to appropriate to the Spirit the missionary empowerment and charismatic enrichment of the church. They thus added a third element to the experiences of regeneration and

1. This is the main thesis of Melvin E. Dieter, *The Holiness Revival of the Nineteenth Century,* 2nd ed. (Metuchen, NJ: Scarecrow Press, 1996).

entire sanctification, namely, an empowerment for witness or a "filling" with the Spirit for a charismatically enriched witness. It was this third element that they designated the "baptism in the Holy Spirit."

What was unique about the Pentecostal movement theologically, however, was not just the addition of a third element to one's journey into the life of the Spirit. It was also in the shift in accent from the effects of the Spirit's work (whether it be regeneration, sanctification, or charismatic enrichment) to the indwelling of the Spirit as the chief goal of life with God. Holiness advocates did indeed focus on sanctification as the work of the Spirit (as a Spirit baptism). Donald W. Dayton has documented how the Holiness movement had turned to the work of the Spirit and to terminology drawn from the Book of Acts to describe the event of sanctification.[2] However, the Pentecostals made Spirit indwelling the major emphasis. While Holiness advocates used Spirit indwelling to explain sanctification, the Pentecostals used sanctification to help explain Spirit indwelling and infilling. Though Pentecostals had a strong Jesus piety, their theological interest centered on the indwelling Spirit. Throughout their early writings, they never tired of telling their readers how one proceeds through various stages to possess the Spirit in fullness, or to be possessed by the Spirit to overflowing.

An example is the following description by Pentecostal founder, William J. Seymour, concerning how the sinner becomes the habitation of God:

> The Lord has mercy on him for Christ's sake and puts eternal life in his soul, pardoning him of his sins, washing away his guilty pollution, and he stands before God justified as though he had never sinned. . . . Then there remains that old original sin. . . . Jesus takes that soul that has eternal life in it and presents it to God for thorough cleansing and purging from all Adamic sin. . . . Now he is on the altar for the fire of God to fall, which is the baptism with the Holy Ghost. It is the free gift upon the sanctified, cleansed heart.[3]

For Seymour, the journey toward Spirit filling began with the entry of "eternal life" within and spiritual rebirth, which Seymour identified as jus-

---

2. Donald W. Dayton, *Theological Roots of Pentecostalism* (Peabody, MA: Hendrickson, 1991), pp. 87-88.

3. William Seymour, "The Way into the Holiest," *The Apostolic Faith* 1, no. 2 (October 1906): 4.

Frank D. Macchia

tification. Then comes the eradication of Adam's sin, which Seymour understood as the uprooting of the inherited power of the sinful nature over sinners. The human vessel is then prepared for Spirit filling and empowerment. The penultimate fulfillment of the Spirit's work in the life of the believer is Spirit filling or Spirit baptism. Important to note, however, is that this filling turns into a flowing river or a spreading flame as Spirit-filled believers share the goodness of God with others. As important as Spirit baptism was to the early Pentecostals, more was needed. This focus on the indwelling Spirit needed to be integrated into the Pentecostal emphasis on the victory of Christ in his life, death, and resurrection and on the future eschatological fulfillment of the reign of God on earth. The Christological issue would surface with great force in the work of the Pentecostal preacher William J. Durham.

Durham soon challenged the three-step journey towards full possession of the Spirit advocated by early, Wesleyan Pentecostals of justification/regeneration, entire sanctification, and Spirit baptism (filling). Durham took the Pentecostal accent on Jesus' atonement (including his death and resurrection) and used it to challenge the belief that one must be sanctified through a two-step process of justification/regeneration and entire sanctification. Since Christ's "finished work" on the cross and in the resurrection is sufficient to save us completely, one must be regenerated and entirely sanctified at the moment of faith in Christ. The believer would for Durham reaffirm and even grow deeper in the sanctified life, but both the cleansing of sin and the removal of the root of sin's dominion over a believer's life occur at the moment of faith in Christ. One Durham scholar appropriately called Durham's position "single-work perfectionism."[4] Rather than emphasizing the stages in the Spirit that one takes to achieve the fullness of the divine indwelling, Durham accented the achievement of this fullness through union with Christ by faith. Most Pentecostals from a Wesleyan background criticized Durham for advocating a Spirit baptism without the needed preparation of entire sanctification (these critics did not regard regeneration as sufficient for entire sanctification).

Oddly, Durham did not include Spirit filling or Spirit baptism within the fullness that is achieved through incorporation into Christ and his fin-

---

4. Thomas George Farkas, *William H. Durham and the Sanctification Controversy in Early American Pentecostalism, 1906-1916* (Ph.D. diss., Southern Baptist Theological Seminary, Louisville, KY, 1993), p. 21.

6

ished work. The reason for this may be found in the fact that most Pentecostals did not formally regard Spirit baptism as an element of Christ's saving work, but rather as the fulfillment of that work that remains nevertheless distinct from it. The early Pentecostal belief in glossolalia as evidence of Spirit baptism (Acts 2:4) helped to keep Spirit baptism distinct from initiation to Christ. After all, it is one thing to limit the revival of the Spirit's fullness and power to the glossolalics, but quite another to limit salvation to them! But the Oneness Pentecostals (known for their denial of the classic doctrine of the Trinity) who came from Durham's wing of the Pentecostal movement (and currently represent about one-fifth of global Pentecostalism) did take Durham's position in this direction. The Oneness Pentecostals regard Spirit filling as the crowning moment of a conversion or initiation complex that involves faith, repentance, and water baptism in Jesus' name. Trinitarian Pentecostals who have their origins in Durham's movement maintained Durham's distinction between initiation to Christ (understood as Spirit indwelling) and Spirit filling (which is a richer experience of the Spirit). None of the Pentecostals coming out of Durham's movement, however, kept his idea of entire sanctification at the moment of rebirth.

Though Durham's single-work perfectionism did not survive (due in part to his untimely death), he helped the Pentecostal movement wed its central focus on the indwelling Spirit with a needed external focus on the person and work of Christ for our salvation. Pentecostals struggled to make sense of this connection between Christ and the experience of the indwelling Spirit and were not in agreement over how the connection was to be understood. But they left future generations with the creative task of doing so. The task is important, since the Pentecostal emphasis on the indwelling Spirit and our participation in Christ's person and work through consecration and mission have ecumenical relevance in an era in which discussions over soteriology are attempting to move beyond the impasse between the anthropocentric Catholic emphasis on graced human cooperation with God and the theocentric but lifeless declaration of righteousness in Christ. The indwelling Spirit is both the life from which human participation in God is graced and the means by which declarations of life in the midst of death may be heard and embraced as something real.[5]

---

5. See my forthcoming book, *Justified in the Spirit: Towards a Trinitarian Soteriology* (Grand Rapids: Eerdmans). Other Pentecostals have shown a similar concern to connect justification to the Spirit: Veli-Matti Kärkkäinen, *One with God: Salvation as Deification and*

The ecumenical relevance of the early Pentecostal accent on Spirit baptism requires discernment, especially since Pentecostal theology has globally become quite diverse. Let us look at some of the diversity that has characterized Pentecostal theology.

Pentecostal Theological Diversity

As already indicated, early Pentecostal theology was diverse. There were four developments worth mentioning here that complicated the early history of Pentecostal theology and added considerable variety to how Spirit baptism was understood among Pentecostals. First, though many early Pentecostals sharply distinguished Spirit baptism from sanctification in polemics against the Holiness Movement, they tended when away from these polemics to speak of Spirit baptism as a sanctifying experience of the love of God poured into our hearts, using Romans 5:5 as their proof text.[6] One early Pentecostal author even wrote:

> There is no difference in quality between the baptism in the Holy Ghost and sanctification. They are both holiness. Sanctification is the Lord Jesus Christ crowned in your heart and the baptism in the Holy Spirit is His power upon you. It is all holiness. It makes you more like Jesus.[7]

As a consequence of this trend, Singaporean Pentecostal pastor David Lim even speaks of Spirit baptism as "vocational sanctification."[8]

Second, it was not entirely clear as to whether entire sanctification occurred at the new birth (Durham), at a point distinct from new birth (most Holiness Pentecostals), or as a lifelong process that is never fully achieved in this life (most spiritual heirs of Durham's stream of the Pentecostal movement).

Justification (Collegeville, MN: Liturgical Press, 2004) and Steven Studebaker, "Pentecostal Soteriology and Pneumatology," *Journal of Pentecostal Theology* 11, no. 2 (2003): 248-70.

6. E.g., E. N. Bell, "The Believers in Sanctification," *Christian Evangel*, September 19, 1914, p. 3. See my discussion of this with other examples from early Pentecostal literature in Frank D. Macchia, *Baptized in the Spirit: A Global Pentecostal Theology* (Grand Rapids: Zondervan, 2006), pp. 80-82.

7. Author unknown, "The Baptism with the Holy Ghost," *The Apostolic Faith* 1, no. 11 (Oct. to Jan. 1908): 4.

8. Shared with me in personal conversation.

Third, the steps involved in one's journey toward full possession of the Spirit were not entirely clear. Does one go through regeneration, entire sanctification, and Spirit baptism as distinct stages (the Holiness Pentecostals), does entire sanctification occur at regeneration as preparation for Spirit baptism (Durham), are regeneration and Spirit baptism distinct stages toward Spirit fullness (with sanctification viewed as a lifelong journey rising from regeneration, but not as an event distinct from conversion [most Trinitarian Pentecostals from Durham's movement]), or is Spirit baptism to be viewed as regeneration, the crowning moment of conversion/initiation, while sanctification progresses throughout life (most Oneness Pentecostals)?

Even the Oneness Pentecostals, who regarded Spirit baptism as intimately connected to water baptism as part of a conversion-initiation complex, have not held to a single view of Spirit baptism, since some have conceived of the relationship to water baptism more loosely than others.[9] Furthermore, some Trinitarian Pentecostal groups (e.g., in Chile and Germany) have identified Spirit baptism as Christian regeneration, separate from water baptism.

Fourth, the doctrine of speaking in tongues as initial evidence of Spirit baptism has been variously interpreted among Pentecostals. Many early Pentecostals considered tongues the means by which the world would be evangelized (through *xenolalia,* unlearned, miraculously spoken foreign languages). This passion soon waned (understandably). Others considered tongues an in-depth praise or groaning in the Spirit opened up through Spirit baptism. Some Pentecostals outside of U.S. Pentecostal denominations do not regard tongues as necessary to Spirit baptism. Even within the United States, where the doctrine of tongues as evidence of Spirit baptism has strongest support, various understandings of the doctrine may be found. For example, the prominent pastor Jack Hayford, of the International Church of the Foursquare Gospel, has written of Spirit baptism as opening up the capacity or privilege of in-depth prayer in tongues but refused to see tongues as absolutely necessary to the Spirit baptismal experience.[10] Pentecostal founder William J. Seymour viewed tongues as the

---

9. See Thomas Fudge, *Christianity without the Cross: A History of Salvation in Oneness Pentecostalism* (Parkland, FL: Universal Publishers, 2003).

10. Jack Hayford, *The Beauty of Spiritual Language: My Journey Toward the Heart of God* (Dallas: Word, 1992), pp. 89-107.

Bible evidence that the powerful experiences of the Spirit among Pentecostals are bringing together people from all races and nations to share the goodness of God with the world, a view shared by others in the early days of the movement.[11] More recently, Murray Dempster has written of tongues as the chief sign that God is breaking down barriers between people, the renewal of language signifying the creation of a new humanity in Christ.[12] I would regard tongues speech as the first "ecumenical language" of the church, in that it calls into question the adequacy of human speech to capture the divine mystery and lodges an implicit protest against any effort to make one language or cultural expression determinative for how the gospel is to be understood or witnessed to in the world. The Pentecostal doctrine of tongues as symbolic of Spirit baptism implies that the Spirit's redemptive and empowering work is to be experienced and expressed in a vast diversity of tongues that groan for the redemption to come (Rom. 8:26), revealing the ultimate inadequacy of human thought and speech to express the divine mystery. Many Pentecostals today who lift up glossolalia as a mark of the experience of Spirit baptism, however, have lost touch with this early ecumenical (and I hasten to add, Lukan) perspective concerning glossolalia. How "glossocentric" Spirit baptism is in our understanding of the experience and how the connection between Spirit baptism and tongues speech is to be defined is by no means settled among Pentecostals globally.

In general, this diversity of viewpoints concerning Spirit baptism opens up the question as to what purpose it serves to speak of Spirit baptism as the dominant Pentecostal theological distinctive if there has been little agreement as to what the doctrine might mean within the broader context of the Christian life. Whether the issue is sanctification, conversion-initiation, or tongues as evidence, Spirit baptism has been interpreted in various ways within Pentecostalism.

Diversity of Pentecostal theology also means that Spirit baptism is not the only distinctive doctrine of the Pentecostal movement historically or globally. Divine healing and the second coming of Jesus have also received a great deal of emphasis among Pentecostal groups. Divine healing was

11. William J. Seymour, "The Same Old Way," *The Apostolic Faith*, September 1906, p. 3. See also T. Hezmalhalch, "Among the Indians at Needles, California," *The Apostolic Faith*, January 1907, p. 3.

12. Murray Dempster, "The Church's Moral Witness: A Study of Glossolalia in Luke's Theology of Acts," *Paraclete* 23 (1989): 1-7.

waning at the turn of the twentieth century among evangelical and Holiness churches right about the time that the Pentecostal movement spread. One is tempted to conclude that Pentecostalism spread in part as a haven for those passionate about healing. The healing doctrine also reveals the somewhat "material" understanding of salvation among Pentecostals. Salvation is not only of the soul but also for general well-being in this life. This assumption is widespread among Pentecostals today globally, leading increasing numbers toward an exaggerated "health and wealth" gospel that promises prosperity and good health to all of the redeemed. Though this trend seems extreme to many, it is rooted in an impulse that is quite distinctively Pentecostal.

Furthermore, the premillennialist (especially dispensationalist) second coming doctrine that became popular among evangelical churches (especially among Baptists and Presbyterians) near the turn of the twentieth century had a tremendous influence on early Pentecostals and, to an extent, on Pentecostalism down through the decades that followed. Though early Pentecostals were more concerned with transforming the world through witness and missions than predicting the time of Christ's return, they shared the fervency for Christ's soon return with their early evangelical peers. They were convinced that the Pentecostal revival was ushering in the latter days. The urgency for missions gripped them deeply, since the gospel was to go out to all the earth before Christ returned.

The question raised by the importance that topics like healing and eschatology played in Pentecostal experience and belief has to do with whether or not there is a distinctive message among Pentecostals that is coherent — are we left with a cafeteria of doctrinal emphases among Pentecostals that were variously interpreted? Due in part to the diversity of belief that has been discovered by Pentecostal scholarship, Spirit baptism no longer enjoys the attention it once warranted among theological spokespersons of the Pentecostal movement. Not since Harold Hunter's and Howard Ervin's books on Spirit baptism written nearly three decades ago has there been a constructive effort at elaborating on the doctrine by a Pentecostal systematic theologian. This trend occasioned the writing of my recent book, in which I attempted to write a Pentecostal theology with Spirit baptism as the dominant metaphor.[13]

13. H. D. Hunter, *Spirit Baptism: A Pentecostal Alternative* (Lanham, MD: University Press of America, 1983); H. M. Ervin, *Conversion-Initiation and the Baptism in the Holy*

Both issues, the diversity of viewpoints concerning Spirit baptism and the diverse range of doctrines emphasized among Pentecostals, raise the question as to whether there is a Pentecostal movement to speak of. Are we forced to refer to various "Pentecostalisms" rather to "Pentecostalism" in the singular? This question is profoundly theological as well as phenomenological. If the Lutherans had justification, the Calvinists election, and the Wesleyans sanctification, what did the Pentecostals have? Is there a theological distinctive typical of global Pentecostalism?

Answer One: Experience and Oral Theology

Walter J. Hollenweger's research revealed a vast doctrinal diversity among Pentecostals worldwide and even within the United States, both now and from the beginning of the movement. His classic, *The Pentecostals,* fell like a bombshell in the late sixties and early seventies upon geographically sheltered Pentecostal groups surprised by the doctrinal diversity of the movement globally.[14] In essence, Hollenweger sought coherence in what is distinctive to Pentecostalism, not in a point or points of doctrine (since for him no such coherence exists) but rather in experience and how this is expressed. I will explain.

Hollenweger not only diversified the doctrinal distinctives of Pentecostal theology, he shifted what was most distinctive about Pentecostal theology from doctrinal points to religious experience and how this was expressed orally and narratively. He wrote that "talk of 'the doctrine' of the Pentecostal churches is highly problematical. What unites the Pentecostal churches is not a doctrine but an experience and this can be interpreted and substantiated in many different ways."[15] Hollenweger thus sought to describe Pentecostal distinctives experientially and in terms of how Pentecostals bring their experiences to expression orally. He wrote in another context concerning the diversity of Pentecostal theologies, "A description of these theologies cannot

Spirit: A Critique of James D. G. Dunn, Baptism in the Holy Spirit (Peabody, MA: Hendrickson, 1984). See also my book *Baptized in the Spirit: A Global Pentecostal Theology* (Grand Rapids: Zondervan, 2006).

14. Walter J. Hollenweger, *The Pentecostals,* 2nd ed. (Peabody, MA: Hendrickson, 1988).

15. Walter J. Hollenweger, "From Azusa Street to the Toronto Phenomenon," in *Pentecostal Movements as Ecumenical Challenge,* ed. Jürgen Moltmann and Karl-Josef Kuschel, Concilium 3 (London: SCM Press, 1996), p. 7.

begin with their concepts. I have rather to choose another way and describe how they are conceived, carried and might finally be born."

Specifically, Hollenweger was taken with the typically non-Western ways in which Pentecostals experienced God and expressed theological truth, namely, through visions, bodily healing, and stories rather than primarily through rational discourse and abstract propositions. This shift in focus from doctrine to experience and theological method made Spirit baptism seem like an accident of history, a holdover from the Holiness Movement that is not at all significant to what is most distinctive about Pentecostal theology. The narrow and ecumenically irrelevant understanding of Pentecostalism as a revivalist "tongues movement" was replaced in Hollenweger's work with a Pentecostalism that seemed ecumenically relevant, at the forefront of a way of doing theology that is not burdened with post-Enlightenment standards of rational discourse. His school of thought, connected still to the University of Birmingham, has produced a long line of researchers into Pentecostal narrative and oral approaches to theology in various contexts of the Two-Thirds World.

While recognizing the value of Hollenweger's approach to Pentecostal theology, it is also important to note that doctrinal issues cannot be so easily detached from the symbolic framework that shapes how a movement experiences God and expresses theological truth, as George Lindbeck has shown us.[16] Furthermore, Spirit baptism is not only a doctrine but a metaphor that can function imaginatively in ways other than doctrinal conceptualization. Of course, we cannot deny that there was doctrinal diversity early on and historically among Pentecostals globally. But this diversity does not necessarily mean that there was not some kind of coherent, doctrinal vision typical of Pentecostal thinking. It is to this issue that we now turn.

Answer Two: Towards Doctrinal Coherence

Donald W. Dayton and D. William Faupel accepted the fact that Pentecostals were diverse doctrinally and, therefore, not just concerned about Spirit baptism. Dayton and Faupel, however, were not willing to forsake the possibility of a conceptually coherent doctrinal distinctive throughout global

16. George Lindbeck, *The Nature of Doctrine: Religion and Theology in a Post-Liberal Age* (Philadelphia: Westminster Press, 1984).

Pentecostalism. They both in their own way showed that there was a theologically coherent understanding of God's redemptive work through Christ and the Holy Spirit in early Pentecostal theology that remained typical of the movement. Dayton showed that early Pentecostal theology advocated a fourfold devotion to Jesus as Savior, Spirit Baptizer, Healer, and Coming King.[17] D. William Faupel highlighted the final element of this fourfold gospel as that which was decisive, namely, the eschatological.[18] Pentecostalism was mainly about the latter rain of the Spirit to restore the gifts and power of Pentecost to the church in order to empower global mission before Christ's soon return. Pentecostals viewed the church as a "missionary fellowship," which (as Grant Wacker noted) was "riding the crest of the wave of history" toward the end of the latter days of the Spirit.

Steven J. Land's seminal effort at writing a Pentecostal theology follows Faupel's shift of emphasis from Spirit baptism to eschatology within the context of the fourfold gospel. Interestingly, Land's *Pentecostal Spirituality* devotes no more than a few pages to Spirit baptism, marking a significant departure from past Pentecostal theological polemics.[19] He explicitly takes issue with Dale Bruner's description of Pentecostal theology as "pneumato-baptistocentric" (Spirit baptism centered). Land regards Bruner's description as "missing the point altogether" concerning what is really distinctive about Pentecostal theology, which is in Land's view the sanctification of the affections as part of an eschatological passion for the kingdom of God yet to come.[20] Through the work of Dayton, Faupel, and Land, the fourfold gospel and eschatology had virtually replaced the concentrated focus on Spirit baptism as the dominant theological distinctive of Pentecostalism.

The Current State of Pentecostal Theology: Spirit Baptism Rediscovered?

For many, we can no longer return to the old assumption that Pentecostalism is *only* about "Spirit baptism." We have arrived rather at two options

17. Dayton, *Theological Roots of Pentecostalism*.

18. William Faupel, *The Everlasting Gospel: The Significance of Eschatology in the Development of Pentecostal Thought* (Sheffield: Sheffield Academic Press, 1996).

19. J. Land, *Pentecostal Spirituality: A Passion for the Kingdom* (Sheffield: Sheffield Academic Press, 1993).

20. Land, *Pentecostal Spirituality*, pp. 62-63.

concerning that which is most distinctive to Pentecostal theology. Either we follow Hollenweger in positing a theologically diverse Pentecostal movement united principally by a holistic experience of the Spirit and an oral or narrative way of doing theology or we assume a distinctive doctrinal coherence to Pentecostal theology that revolves around the fourfold gospel (following Dayton) or around an eschatological fervency for the soon return of Christ that involves principally the sanctification of the affections but also Spirit baptism (empowerment), healing, and missionary zeal (following Faupel and Land). Either way, Spirit baptism has largely lost its role in the scholarship as the dominant theological concern of the Pentecostal movement. Just when the Pentecostals effectively raised the issue of Spirit baptism to the level of theological discussion and debate, they seem to be backing away from the importance that the doctrine has held for them historically and globally.

In reflecting on this situation in the scholarship, it seems to me that theological diversity within Pentecostalism, though significant, should not be used to eclipse what Pentecostals typically hold in common concerning Spirit baptism. There are Pentecostal theologians who wish to recapture the Pentecostal focus on Spirit baptism but to develop it beyond the narrow confines of post-conversion empowerment for service. Singaporean theologian Simon Chan, for example, notes that Pentecostals are not in agreement over the details of their distinctive beliefs, but nevertheless, "what comes through over and over again in their discussions and writings is a certain kind of spiritual experience of an intense, direct, and overwhelming nature centering on the person of Christ which they schematize as 'baptism in the Holy Spirit.'"[21] Chan believes that an expansion of the boundaries of Spirit baptism to involve the entire life and mission of the church can help Pentecostals develop an ecumenically relevant theology. Rather than view pneumatology individualistically, Chan wishes to see the Spirit as the ecclesial Spirit who comes to us in the life and worship (including the sacraments) of the church.

Korean theologian Koo Dong Yun agrees with Chan that Spirit baptism is the dominant theological concern of Pentecostals, noting that "out of a number of intriguing characteristics of the Pentecostal-charismatic movement, 'Baptism in the Holy Spirit' (also known as Spirit Baptism)

---

21. Simon Chan, *Pentecostal Theology and the Christian Spiritual Tradition* (Sheffield: Sheffield Academic Press, 2003), p. 7.

represents the most distinctive doctrine."[22] But Yun prefers, in distinction from Chan's focus on church traditioning, to see the Pentecostal theological concern over Spirit baptism as "pragmatic," open to a number of horizons of meaning.[23]

There has recently been a tendency to draw from Faupel and Land to reinterpret Spirit baptism in the context of the expansively eschatological work of the Spirit. In distinction from Faupel and Land, however, those following this trend have attempted to show that the turn to eschatology does not necessarily mean the displacement of Spirit baptism as the dominant metaphor of Pentecostal theology. Narciso Dionson, for example, notes that Spirit baptism as an eschatological reality spans the entire experience of the Christian, from new birth to resurrection. He adds that "we no longer have to be drawn into the debate whether the purpose of Spirit baptism is soteriological or missiological, whether it is conversion-initiation or second stage blessing."[24] Similarly, for Amos Yong, the Pentecostal focus on salvation "in the Spirit" opens up the possibility that God's presence and activity may be experienced outside of the boundaries within which Christ is explicitly honored as Lord.[25] Pentecostal theology is "global" in the sense that it has a pneumatological center that offers "breathing room" for a vast diversity of theological voices.

My own effort in the direction of reinterpreting the metaphor of Spirit baptism has focused on five important details concerning the use of the Spirit baptismal metaphor in the New Testament.[26] First, Pentecostalism has without a doubt placed Spirit baptism on the table as a legitimate theological emphasis. They did this drawing from Holiness and revivalist forebears. But the recent monographs that have highlighted Spirit baptism as a new point of emphasis for Christian theology were written consciously in response to the Pentecostal message.[27] This distinctly "Pentecostal" focus on Spirit bap-

---

22. Koo Dong Yun, *Baptism in the Holy Spirit: An Ecumenical Theology of Spirit Baptism* (Lanham, MD: University Press of America, 2003), p. 12.

23. Yun, *Baptism in the Holy Spirit*, p. 155.

24. Narciso C. Dionson, "The Doctrine of the Baptism in the Holy Spirit: From a Pentecostal Pastor's Uneasy Chair," *Asian Journal of Pentecostal Studies* 2 (1999): 238.

25. See, for example, Amos Yong, *The Spirit Poured Out on All Flesh: Pentecostalism and the Possibility of Global Theology* (Grand Rapids: Baker Academic, 2005).

26. The following points are taken from my recent book *Baptized in the Spirit*, and will be elaborated on in my forthcoming book, *Justified in the Spirit*.

27. For example, James D. G. Dunn, *Baptism in the Holy Spirit*, Studies in Biblical The-

tism places "new life" through the indwelling Spirit at the center of the church's message. Pietistic streams of thought that are represented so forcefully in the global Pentecostal movement have created a vision of the Christian life that is not distant from God, dominated by legal metaphors or anthropocentric concerns with graced human cooperation with God.

The focus has been on the healing and transforming presence of the Spirit within to shape humanity eventually into the image of Christ and into a temple for God's indwelling presence. As Jürgen Moltmann has noted, a Pentecostal theology of life encourages all to "experience the abundant, full, healed and redeemed life with all of our senses."[28] Juan Sepulveda, writing from a Chilean Pentecostal background, has seen the center of the Pentecostal attachment to Spirit baptism as representing a unique accent on new life in the Spirit rather than on tongues per se.[29] In an era in which people are wary of organized religion but thirsty to experience life in the midst of (and in opposition to) death, disease, and social oppression, a Christian message that centers on new life in the Spirit in hope for the breaking in of the kingdom of righteousness can seem both biblically accountable and ecumenically relevant.

Second, the Spirit baptism metaphor in the scriptures is fluid, referring to judgment (Matt. 3:12), cleansing (Acts 15:8-9), empowerment (Acts 1:8), incorporation into the life of the church (1 Cor. 12:13), and the final new creation (Acts 2:17-21). The metaphor is eschatological in the broadest sense of the term. It is developed primarily in the context of the kingdom of God (Matt. 3:2, 11-12; Acts 1:3-8) but also involves the role of the Spirit in communion, both with God and one another (cf. 1 Cor. 12:13; Eph. 5:18). The location of Spirit baptism primarily in the context of the kingdom serves to liberate debates over Spirit baptism from the impasses of competing ecclesiologies and corresponding notions of Christian initiation (Word, sacramental, Holiness, charismatic) and allows for an expansive notion of the metaphor that involves significant insights from them all. The church, though significant to Spirit baptism, is also relativized by the

ology, Second Series, 15 (London: SCM Press, 1970), p. 229; and Kilian McDonnell and George T. Montague, *Christian Initiation and Baptism in the Holy Spirit: Evidence from the First Eight Centuries* (Collegeville, MN: Liturgical Press, 1991).

28. Jürgen Moltmann, "A Pentecostal Theology of Life," *Journal of Pentecostal Theology* 9 (October 1996): 4.

29. Juan Sepulveda, "Born Again: Baptism and the Spirit: A Pentecostal Perspective," in Moltmann and Kuschel, eds., *Pentecostal Movements as an Ecumenical Challenge*, pp. 104-9.

Frank D. Macchia

overarching work of the Spirit in the world to turn the creation into the consecrated dwelling place of God.

Third, Spirit baptism is the most unique Christological claim made of Jesus in the New Testament. The Jewish messianic expectations assumed that the messiah would uniquely *bear,* or be *anointed by* the Spirit (cf. Isa. 61:1-3). It was assumed also that the messiah's coming would occasion a new era of the Spirit, but no specific link was forged between the messiah as the Spirit bearer and the new era of the Spirit to explain how one would necessitate the other. The New Testament's proclamation of Christ addresses this issue directly. All four Gospels begin by lifting up Jesus as the Baptizer in the Spirit in order to explain how his anointing would lead to a new era of the Spirit for everyone. So Luke testifies that from the exalted position at the right hand of the Father Jesus poured out the Spirit (Acts 2:33). Jesus is raised from the dead as a "life-giving spirit" (1 Cor. 15:45). He even "breathed" the Spirit on his disciples, recalling God's act of breathing the Spirit into Adam (John 20:22; Gen. 2:7). It was Jesus' role in imparting the Spirit that eventually caused the church to assume that Jesus was identifiable with God, for, as St. Augustine noted concerning Christ, "how much must he who gives God be God!" (*De Trinitate* 15.46).

Fourth, much of the New Testament develops its doctrines of Christ, atonement, election, and church in the light of the astounding fact that the ceremonially unclean Gentiles received the Spirit. How can the Gentiles, cursed under the law, receive the Holy Spirit, the blessing of the new age? Paul reasons that Christ himself was cursed under the law on the cross but vindicated in the Spirit in resurrection "in order that in Christ Jesus the blessing of Abraham might come to the Gentiles, so that we might receive the promise of the Holy Spirit by faith" (Gal. 3:13-14). Both Jews and Gentiles were seen as "sinners" cursed under the law so that they might all be justified the same way in the Spirit of the cursed (crucified) and Spirit-vindicated (resurrected) Jesus (Gal. 2:15-16; cf. Rom. 1:4; 4:25; 1 Tim. 3:16). Spirit baptism, the reception of the indwelling Spirit, was the context from which much of the theologizing of the New Testament took place, including the Pauline teaching on justification by faith (Gal. 3:1-14). Though the term "Spirit baptism" is not everywhere used in the New Testament, the substance of the metaphor is arguably one of the most important theological concerns of the New Testament. The Pentecostal movement has been at the forefront of drawing the church's attention to this fact.

18

Fifth, the uniquely Pentecostal attention to charismatic enrichment in ministry and mission allows Spirit baptism to define the church in ways that liberate it from juridical and hierarchical notions which center the ministry in the clergy. If the church in its totality is constituted directly by the outpouring of the Spirit, the ministry cannot be confined to the clergy. Neither can the Spirit be imparted through the narrow portals of ordained clergy (as Miroslav Volf has pointed out[30]). Though there is in existence ministries of oversight, these ministries are gifts of the Spirit among other gifts, for all believers are bearers of the Spirit and ministers of grace (Eph. 4:7-16; 1 Cor. 12:12-18), as Miroslav Volf and Veli-Matti Kärkkäinen have shown.[31] The universal priesthood of believers cannot be confined to the priestly function of parents in the home but must shape fundamentally the life of the congregation in its public services and mission in the world. The church must burst forth with signs of grace in an increasingly graceless world, offering many the fountain of life in the Spirit. If one of the chief ends of humanity is to bear the divine Spirit as the first fruits of the new creation in Christ, then the church must find Spirit baptism to be at the heart of its vision of itself.

As William Seymour noted of humanity:

> The Lord has mercy on him for Christ's sake and puts eternal life in his soul, pardoning him of his sins, washing away his guilty pollution, and he stands before God justified as though he had never sinned. . . . Then there remains that old original sin. . . . Jesus takes that soul that has eternal life in it and presents it to God for thorough cleansing and purging from all Adamic sin. . . . Now he is on the altar for the fire of God to fall, which is the baptism with the Holy Ghost. It is the free gift upon the sanctified, cleansed heart.[32]

For the Pentecostal, the journey of the human race is meant to be such a journey toward bearing the divine Spirit in loyalty to Christ and as a source for liberating existence in the world in relation to others. Though

---

30. Miroslav Volf, *After Our Likeness: The Church as the Image of the Trinity* (Grand Rapids: Eerdmans, 1998), p. 152.

31. Volf, *After Our Likeness*, p. 152; Veli-Matti Kärkkäinen, "Pentecostalism and the Claim for Apostolicity: An Essay in Ecumenical Ecclesiology," *Ecumenical Review of Theology* 25 (2001): 323-36.

32. Seymour, "The Way into the Holiest," p. 4.

not necessarily following distinct stages as Seymour implied, the journey towards the Spirit will take one through many dimensions of new life and horizons of meaning, all of them Christoformistic and directed to the new creation yet to come. While recognizing Pentecostal diversity, I would like to place this focus on the table as the crown jewel among the various points of emphasis for the future of Pentecostal theology.

CHAPTER 2

Divine Healing, Religious Revivals, and Contemporary Pentecostalism: A North American Perspective

Margaret M. Poloma

Introduction

There is a strong link between religious revivalism and divine healing in religious history, with the practice of divine healing tending to decline as its charismatic moment morphs into religious doctrine and ritual. This "routinization of charisma" (to use a Weberian term) can be observed as healing moved away from its experiential roots to assume institutional form as religious doctrine and ritual throughout the two millennia of Christian history.[1] Despite the darkness of rationality's limitations that threatened to engulf the experiential light of the Spirit, periodically fresh revival fires would rekindle the light with a flame from reported miraculous cures. The restoration of Christian healing beliefs, practices, and experiences has come in waves throughout modern history, ebbing and flowing seemingly as the Spirit wills. Of particular importance for the revitalization of divine healing in modern America are the waves of revival that have revitalized, popularized, and democratized this spiritual gift over the past one hundred-odd years within Pentecostalism.

Although divine healing can be found throughout Christian history, most Christian groups that were open to its experience and practice did not make it a central tenet of faith. It was not until the twentieth-century Azusa Street revival (1906-1909) and the rise of Pentecostalism that divine

---

1. F. S. MacNutt, *The Nearly Perfect Crime: How the Church Almost Killed the Ministry of Healing* (Grand Rapids: Chosen Books, 2005).

healing once again assumed a central role in orthodox Christian practice to match its role in the early church.[2] A cursory view of religious history, however, will demonstrate that charisma routinizes quickly. It would take several major waves of revival during Pentecostalism's one-hundred-year history to counter routinization's ongoing corrosive effects.

This presentation will deal with three main topics relevant to Pentecostal and neo-Pentecostal belief, ritual, and experience of divine healing. First, we will present an abridged history of Christian divine healing to place the topic of revivalism and healing within a larger historical context; next, we will discuss the holistic worldview inherent in Pentecostal teachings about divine healing and their relationship to the larger American culture; and finally, we will offer a modest attempt to construct a tentative bridge between Pentecostal healing and modern scientific thought.

Divine Healing in Historical Context

Divine healing was an integral part of the ministry of Jesus of Nazareth and of the early Christian church. It is not without significance that nearly one-fifth of the Gospels is devoted to accounts of healing, and the Acts of the Apostles (a biblical account of the history of early Christendom) includes many stories of miraculous healings. Divine healing had remained (more or less) a normative expectation in the early church for nearly three centuries.[3] It was with the increased institutionalization of Christianity and the eventual development of an Aristotelian-based theology dichotomizing body and soul that divine healing was downplayed in favor of secularized medicine.

While Catholicism left room for faith healing in its folk religion of pilgrimages and apparitions, a rationalized Protestantism in its uneasy dance with the Enlightenment inherited a theology in which faith healing was re-

2. As Grant Wacker has astutely noted, "Divine healing was as old as Christianity itself, but the distinctive form that it took in American radical evangelical circles . . . departed from historic Christian doctrine (which had enjoined elders to anoint and pray for the sick) by insisting that Christ's atonement on the cross provided healing for the body just as it provided healing for the soul." See G. Wacker, *Heaven Below* (Cambridge, MA: Harvard University Press, 2001), p. 3.

3. For further discussion see M. Kelsey, *Healing and Christianity* (New York: Harper & Row, 1973); and MacNutt, *The Nearly Perfect Crime.*

garded as little more than superstition. Theologians may have acknowledged that miraculous healing occurred in Jesus' ministry and could be found among early Christians to jumpstart Christianity, but such "signs and wonders" were no longer regarded as normative experiences. Impacted by the Enlightenment, Catholics and Protestants alike (in both liberal and conservative dress) came to share a common skepticism about so-called faith healing at the onset of the twentieth century.

Rumors of divine healing, however, could be heard from time to time in new religious groups that encouraged its belief and practice. One of the earliest American groups to advocate healing was the Society of Friends, with George Fox (the founder of the Quakers) having a significant healing ministry. It was not unusual for American religious movements birthed in the fervor of revivalism (including the Quakers, Shakers, Mormons, Noyesites, and Adventists) to encourage the practice of healing prayer.[4] Wesleyan revivals of the late nineteenth century added a theological rationale to the experiential base that served to restore divine healing as a normative Christian belief and practice. In the Wesleyan Holiness movement, a direct antecedent to the Pentecostal revivals of the twentieth century, leaders began to link a doctrine of Christian perfectionism with divine healing, teaching that "Christ's atonement provided not only for justification but also for the purification of the human nature from sin." According to some perfectionist theology, this purification would "eliminate illness."[5] During the same time period that the New Religious Thought Movement with Mary Baker Eddy (Christian Science), Charles and Myrtle Fillmore (Unity School of Christianity), and Ernest Holmes (The Church of Religious Science) was promoting metaphysical Christian healing,[6] the disciples of a more orthodox Holiness movement were reporting miraculous healings that occurred during religious revivals. Nineteenth-century healing revivals led by Maria Woodworth-Etter, John Alexander Dowie, and lesser-known personalities set the stage for Pente-

---

4. R. A. N. Kydd, "Healing in the Christian Church," in *The New International Dictionary of Pentecostal and Charismatic Movements*, ed. Stanley M. Burgess and Eduard M. van der Maas, rev. and expanded ed. (Grand Rapids: Zondervan, 2002), pp. 698-711.

5. F. C. Chappell, "Healing Movements," in *Dictionary of Pentecostal and Charismatic Movements*, ed. S. M. Burgess and G. B. McGee (Grand Rapids: Regency Reference Library, 1988), pp. 353-74, 357.

6. See F. C. Darling, *The Restoration of Christian Healing: New Freedom in the Church Since the Reformation* (Boulder, CO: Vista Publications, 1992).

costal healing ministries that would grow in number throughout the twentieth century.

One of the best-known and controversial historical figures in the proto-Pentecostal healing movement is John Alexander Dowie (1847-1907), founder of the Christian Catholic Church and the utopian religious community of Zion City in Illinois. The 1893 Chicago World's Fair provided a public forum for Dowie to practice his healing powers in meetings he conducted across the street from popular attractions. His healing ministry flourished in part due to countless testimonies of healing that reportedly took place as a result of his prayer. Dowie's restorationist vision for Christianity, however, lost ground to his critics, and he died in 1907, rejected by many who had acclaimed him. With his combative style, Dowie had alienated even other believers who practiced divine healing. His vision of a pristine Christianity left no room for the medical profession, and he barred its practitioners from entering his Zion City. Anyone who sought Dowie's prayers for healing was required to relinquish all medical treatment, relying solely on the power of faith to heal.[7]

Although Dowie died during the height of the Azusa Street revival that birthed Pentecostalism, he is commonly seen as an important forerunner of the Pentecostal movement. Dowie's ministry established what he called "healing homes" to replace hospitals — places where those with severe illnesses came to reside and to receive prayer until they were totally healed (or died). Dowie became a mentor to John G. Lake, who today is heralded as the father of the contemporary healing rooms movement. Following the remarkable healing of his wife from tuberculosis after Dowie prayed for her, Lake joined Dowie's ministry and served as an elder in the Zion Catholic Apostolic Church.[8]

Eight years into his healing ministry with Dowie, Lake experienced a spiritual breakthrough that many in the Holiness movement would call a "second blessing" and contemporary Pentecostals would call "Spirit baptism." As a friend and he were praying for healing for a woman in a wheel chair, Lake felt as if he had "passed under a shower of warm tropical rain, which was not falling on me but through me. My spirit and soul and body,

---

7. E. L. Blumhofer, "Dowie, John Alexander," in Burgess and van der Maas, eds., *The New International Dictionary of Pentecostal and Charismatic Movements*, pp. 586-87.

8. J. R. Ziegler, "Lake, John Graham," in Burgess and van der Maas, eds., *The New International Dictionary of Pentecostal and Charismatic Movements*, p. 828.

under this influence was soothed into such a deep calm as I had never known." Lake believed he heard the Spirit speak to him telling him that he was now "baptized in the Holy Spirit." Nearly immediately Lake, his prayer partner, and the woman all began to experience the "rush of power" that they attributed to the Spirit of God.

Shortly after this perceived anointing (and after Dowie's death in 1907), Lake and his family set out for mission fields in Africa. His wife's untimely death in 1908 shortly after they arrived in Africa failed to dampen Lake's belief in healing. After returning to the United States in 1913, Lake opened Dowie-like healing rooms in Spokane and Portland, with a vision to establish chains of healing rooms across the United States. He put together a team of men and women whom he called "healing technicians" who ministered from a suite of rooms in downtown Spokane from 1914 to 1920. Five years after establishing the Spokane Divine Healing Rooms, Lake described the work of the "competent staff of ministers" as follows:

> They believed in the Lord as the present, perfect Healer, and ministered the Spirit of God to the sick through prayer and the laying on of hands. The records show that we ministered up to 200 persons a day; that of these, 176 were non-church members. The knowledge of and faith in Jesus Christ as the Healer has gripped the world outside the present Church societies, and the number of those who believe are increasing with such rapidity that in a short time they may become a majority in many communities.[9]

When Lake died of a stroke in 1935 the unfulfilled vision of establishing a nationwide chain of healing rooms seemed to die with him. The dream was to be revived in the late twentieth century through the ministry and work of Cal Pierce, a retired real estate developer from Redding, California, who felt the call of God to "redig the ancient wells" in Spokane.

Although healing had been and remained a central belief and practice for Pentecostal believers throughout the twentieth century, the revitalization of dynamic healing practices was often associated with famous healing evangelists — well-known "anointed" men and women like William Branham (1909-65), Kathryn Kuhlman (1907-76), Oral Roberts (1918-),

9. J. G. Lake, *The John G. Lake Sermons on Dominion over Demons, Disease and Death,* ed. G. Lindsay (Dallas: Christ for the Nations Inc., 2002 [1949]), p. 7.

and Benny Hinn (1952-) — rather than ordinary believers. In teaching common men and women to function as healers, Lake's healing rooms and its contemporary counterparts (found in Cal Pierce's 450-plus members of the International Healing Rooms Association) demonstrate that the practice of divine healing is not the sole property of a few healing evangelists.

Worthy of at least passing note in this greatly abridged history of Pentecostal healing is John G. Wimber, founder of the Association of Vineyard Churches. Perhaps no single individual did more to promote this democratized belief in divine healing that paved the way for the contemporary healing rooms movement during the last decades of the twentieth century than did Wimber. From the mid-1980s until his death in 1998, Wimber conducted many well-attended conferences in both North America and abroad on healing that taught attendees how to pray for divine healing. It was in Wimberite circles during the 1990s that revival fires first ignited to energize the rebirth of John G. Lake's vision of a chain of healing rooms not only across the nation but also around the globe.[10]

Although names of healing evangelists like Benny Hinn and Oral Roberts are familiar to many Americans, the practice of divine healing has come to rest more with those who operate in Wimber style "to equip all believers to exercise divine powers." The International Healing Rooms Association is but one vehicle for this popularization and democratization of divine healing that can move the belief and practice beyond its contemporary Pentecostal origins.[11] Teaching about and the normative practice of divine healing can be found within most Pentecostal congregations as well as within parachurch ministries. While there always seems to be room for the person with a seemingly special gift of healing to establish his or her own healing ministry, ministries that "teach and equip" ordinary believers are growing in both popularity and numbers.

---

10. See M. M. Poloma, "Old Wine, New Wineskins: The Rise of Healing Rooms in Revival Pentecostalism," *Pneuma: The Journal of the Society for Pentecostal Studies* 28 (Spring 2006): 59-71; M. Poloma, *Main Street Mystics* (Walnut Creek, CA: AltaMira Press, 2003), esp. pp. 200, 213.

11. Anyone, regardless of religious belief, can come to the healing rooms for prayer free of charge. Other parachurch organizations (such as the evangelist Randy Clark's "Global Awakening") operate schools to teach the principles and practices of divine healing in the field of missionary activity, where healings are said to be far more commonplace than in North America.

Prayer for divine healing, notes Allan Anderson, "is perhaps the most universal characteristic of the many varieties of Pentecostalism and perhaps the main reason for its growth in the developing world."[12] To understand Pentecostalism, it is imperative to wrestle with its understanding of healing. Although doctrinally speaking, some Pentecostals have made speaking in tongues (glossolalia) its main distinctive, it is healing that increasingly has assumed a central role in the Pentecostal alternative worldview.

Pentecostal Worldview and Components of Divine Healing

Consistent with most other contemporary spiritual healing practices, healing for Pentecostal Christians involves more than curing physical ailments. Recognizing the intricate interweaving of soul, mind, body, and spirit, this perspective places a personal relationship with God at the center of its beliefs and practices. Healing, as understood by those involved in the Spirit movement, is somewhat different from a common use of the term where it is often equated with "curing" medical maladies. A Pentecostal understanding of healing differs from a mechanistic medical model in two important ways: (1) in its understanding of "healing" as a juxtaposition of the ordinary and the sacred and (2) in its holistic approach to healing that reflects soul, spirit, mind, and body.

Healing and the Sacred

As Meredith McGuire observed in her study of Catholic charismatics, a medically diagnosable condition is not necessary for the reporting of a healing experience.[13] Pentecostal healing involves, first and foremost, a spiritual experience, with "the key criterion of healing" being the "process of becoming closer to the Lord." Establishing a vertical relationship with God is the base for healing of self as well as for healing horizontal relationships with

12. Allan Anderson, *An Introduction to Pentecostalism* (Cambridge: Cambridge University Press, 2004), p. 30.

13. Meredith McGuire, *Ritual Healing in Suburban America* (New Brunswick, NJ: Rutgers University Press, 1988), p. 43.

family, friends, and co-workers. When relationships are in good order, personal healing of a person's spirit, mind, and body is expected to follow. Although healing tends to accompany revivals, it is not surprising that experiencing of the presence of God has been the focal point of religious revival meetings, with a corresponding emphasis on the need for personal holiness and spiritual healing of personal relationships with God.

McGuire's observation about how neo-Pentecostal healing is centered in a personal relationship with the sacred resonates with other theological and anthropological discussions of religious healing. Philip Hefner, for example, speaks of a "double entendre" in his discussion of the Christian scriptures on healing as he notes the interface of concepts like healing or curing, serving and caring for, and restoration to wholeness and their relationship to the sacred:

> Three terms are important for interpreting the texts in the Christian New Testament that are most relevant to our theme. The terms (from the Greek) are *hiamoai*, "heal or cure"; *therapeuo*, "to serve or care for"; and *sothesomai*, "make whole." These terms all share the character of the double entendre, that is, they refer to curing, caring, and wholeness as purely physical but also at the same time spiritually transcendent.[14]

According to Hefner, the "double entendre of the physical and the transcendent occurs not only in the sacred texts, but also in Christian practice and belief."[15] In the Christian theology and practice of healing there is thus a juxtaposition of the spiritual and sensate as "the sensate deals with what *is*" and "the spiritual deals with what *could be*."[16]

In emphasizing a transcendent sacred, Pentecostals, like many others who practice forms of religious healing, demonstrate the central belief in what Koss-Chioino, Philip Hefner, and others have termed "spiritual transformation" as a basic component for holistic healing. While these authors speak in terms of "spiritual transformation," Pentecostals and neo-Pentecostals, however, are more likely to speak more specifically about

---

14. Philip Hefner, "Spiritual Transformation and Healing: An Encounter with the Sacred," in *Spiritual Transformation and Healing: Anthropological, Theological, Neuroscientific, and Clinical Perspectives*, ed. J. D. Koss-Chioino and P. Hefner (Lanham, MD: AltaMira Press, 2006), p. 120.

15. Hefner, "Spiritual Transformation and Healing," p. 123.

16. Hefner, "Spiritual Transformation and Healing," p. 124.

spiritual, inner, and emotional healing (as well as deliverance from demonic strongholds, healing broken relationships, and forgiveness) as being important components for receiving and retaining any physical cure that may occur as a result of prayer. It is within this multifaceted understanding of healing and wholeness — "whether or not the sufferer's symptoms remain"[17] — that divine healing is said to occur.

In sum, for Pentecostals, the very heart of the healing process has always been a person's relationship with God, a stance that reflects the common etymological root enjoyed by holiness and health.[18] Pentecostals and their neo-Pentecostal descendents believe that salvation (the "first blessing") is the primary form of healing. It is through an acceptance of the grace of salvation and forgiveness of sin that one comes into a right relationship with God and embarks on a lifelong journey toward holiness. Many believe that just as salvation is accepted "by faith," physical healing is also available "by faith" through the atonement provided by Jesus' suffering, crucifixion, and resurrection.

The basic relationship between the atonement, spiritual empowerment (provided by the "second blessing" of Spirit baptism), and healing can be found in the populist theologies of early Pentecostals. This theology, however, was relatively underdeveloped, rooted in a simplistic restoration model of the early apostolic church in which divine healing (not scientific medicine) was reportedly a normative experience.[19] For many, if not most, early Pentecostals there was an unbridgeable divide between divine healing and medical science, a chasm that can be spanned through teachings and practices reflecting a contemporary holistic approach to health and healing.

17. J. D. Koss-Chioino, "Spiritual Transformation and Radical Empathy in Ritual Healing and Therapeutic Relationships," in Koss-Chioino and Hefner, eds., *Spiritual Transformation and Healing,* p. 47. See also T. J. Csordos, *The Sacred Self: A Cultural Phenomenology of Charismatic Healing* (Berkeley: University of California Press, 1994).

18. See H. Newton Malony, *Wholeness and Holiness: Readings in the Psychology/Theology of Mental Health* (Grand Rapids: Baker Book House, 1983).

19. See E. L. Blumhofer, *The Assemblies of God: A Chapter in the Story of American Pentecostalism* (Springfield, MO: Gospel Publishing House, 1989).

Healing, Holiness, and Wholeness

A second issue, and one related to Hefner's "double entendre" that characterizes a Pentecostal understanding of healing, is its reluctance to equate healing with mechanistic "curing" of physical ailments. Although contemporary Pentecostals tend to have a more nuanced theology of healing and its relationship to modern medicine than did their forebears, they share with their ancestors the profession that it is God who is always the healer. God can use physicians as well as "Doctor Jesus," but those committed to divine healing are likely to seek Dr. Jesus and prayer as first try, only then to seek help from modern medicine. Whether a healing is due directly to prayer, scientific medicine, or alternative health and healing practices, Pentecostals are quick to give all the credit to God, even if a physician or holistic health practice is involved in the cure.

American Pentecostals of the twenty-first century thus reflect a holistic stance on healing (physical, mental, and emotional) that is shared with many other complementary healing practices. For Pentecostals, as for other practitioners of alternative healing, it is impossible to separate physical health from spiritual well-being. Where Pentecostals may differ from others involved in alternative healing practices is in their understanding of "spiritual healing" and their primary concern about eternal salvation for the soul that has here-and-now consequences. A central role is played by an ongoing pursuit of an ever-more-intimate relationship with God that builds on the born-again experience — a relationship believed to be essential for emotional and mental well-being and for sound social relationships. Unlike the earlier Pentecostal thinking on divine healing, contemporary Pentecostal healing is increasingly a process with horizontal, vertical, and personal axes. Although the vertical relationship with the divine remains pivotal, relationships with others as well as self-acceptance are also seen to impact health and wellness.

Thus perhaps the most significant form of healing to enter the Pentecostal model of healing is what has been called "inner" or "emotional healing," a practice that reflects the influence of twentieth-century psychology reflected in popular culture.[20] Inner healing has been conceptualized by

---

20. Although inner or emotional healing was not a component of the early Pentecostal model, it has a long and steady tradition in the Pentecostal and neo-Pentecostal literature. For one of the earliest prominent works on the topic, see Agnes Sanford, *The Healing Light*

Pentecostals in at least two interrelated ways: (1) as personal healing of "wounded" self-perceptions (e.g., increased self-acceptance and decreased self-denunciation) and (2) as healing of relationships with others (e.g., forgiveness and reconciliation). An important key to the process expressed in different words and rituals is said to involve the "healing of memories" from hurtful and abusive treatment from others. Healing of relationships also includes the person's relationship with God, where wounding from an abusive or uncaring father may have distorted the personal image of God.

Both spiritual healing and inner healing reflect a transcendent quality of human beings that goes beyond the individual body or mind. These forms of healing are interrelated with healing of clinically diagnosed mental problems and physical maladies. Past hurts, unforgiveness, and emotional pain are believed to impact both mental and physical health. A failure to forgive wrongs, ruptured family relationships, and unrepented injuries done to another all may "block" the reception of a proffered healing grace for physical cures as well as relief from mental and emotional distress.

Meredith McGuire's pioneering qualitative work on Catholic charismatic (neo-Pentecostal) healing practices suggests that the beliefs about divine healing can be quite complex.[21] As already noted, it is clear that healing is not limited to "curing" of physical ailments but rather represents an array of facets that center around perceived experiences of the divine. It involves a holistic perspective that posits an image of a person as an interconnection of the spiritual, emotional, mental, and physical. It was McGuire's thick description that provided a model used by the author to frame a quantitative analysis of survey data collected from one of the epicenters of the 1990s revivals in which experiencing the "Father's love and giving it away" was the primary motif. The findings from this analysis of 918 respondents will serve as a base to discuss the third topic of this presentation, namely, the relationship between Pentecostal healing practices and scientific research on spirituality and health. Once regarded as incompatible, Pentecostal practices of healing and modern medicine are increasingly recognized as complementary means of health maintenance by both believers and nonbelievers.

(Plainfield, NJ: Logos International, 1947); for more recent examples, see also Charles Kraft, *Deep Wounds, Deep Healing* (Ann Arbor, MI: Servant Publications, 1993); and John and Mark Sanford, *Deliverance and Inner Healing* (Grand Rapids: Chosen Books, 1992).

21. McGuire, *Ritual Healing.*

Margaret M. Poloma

Integrating Faith Healing and Medical Science

This final section offers a modest attempt to construct a bridge between the Pentecostal belief and practice of divine healing and modern scientific thought. The exercise will be filtered through research data collected in 1995 and 1997 from pilgrims to the so-called "Toronto Blessing." In January 1994 a revival broke out at the then Toronto Airport Vineyard (renamed the Toronto Airport Christian Fellowship in 1996), sparks from which spread the revival around the globe. Although it was a palpable sense of God's immanent presence and love that drew thousands of pilgrims to the Toronto church, the revival made secular news largely because of the unusual physical manifestations experienced by those who came seeking the Blessing. As happened with revivals that preceded it, pilgrims began to report various forms of healing — spiritual, relational, emotional, psychological, and at times physical cures. Questions on healing and revival experiences were included in a survey conducted in 1995 by the author and in the follow-up survey of 1997.[22] Each of the component parts was evaluated in light of McGuire's implicit healing model in which spiritual healing is the pivotal variable, related to emotional responses to prayer and revival ritual and a catalyst for inner, mental, and physical healing.[23]

Of particular relevance for this discussion was the nightly prayer offered by prayer teams for each pilgrim following the three-hour (or longer) revival service, which included vivacious singing and dancing, and listening to testimonies and preaching, with opportunities for cathartic responses throughout the service. The individual prayer that followed each service came to be regarded as the time during which the Blessing was most likely to be bestowed. As the music began to play at the end of the formal service, people gathered in the assigned locations in the large auditorium to await individual prayer. Many appeared to be in an altered state of consciousness, lost in quiet worship as they waited for a prayer team to come by and pray with them, while others were in various modes of so-

22. For detailed reports of the survey findings, see M. M. Poloma, *The Toronto Report* (Wiltshire, UK: Terra Nova Publications, 1996); M. M. Poloma, "Inspecting the Fruit of the 'Toronto Blessing': A Sociological Assessment," *Pneuma: The Journal for the Society for Pentecostal Studies* 20 (1998): 43-70.
23. A full report of this study can be found in Margaret M. Poloma and Lynette F. Hoelter, "The 'Toronto Blessing': A Holistic Model of Healing," *Journal for the Scientific Study of Religion* 37, no. 2 (1998): 267-72.

matic manifestations. The prayer teams were often said to act as spiritual midwives, to assist in the "birth" of the "new work" that God had begun. The prayer offered by these teams was simple, with commonly used phrases being "Bless her, Lord," "Another drink (of the Holy Spirit)," "Increase," "Peace," "More fire," or "Fill him, Lord" that blended into a kind of ordered chaos where music offered a backdrop for the laughter and tears, jerking and shaking, pounding of feet against the floor, or silent "resting in the Spirit" by those already lying on the floor. The ritual embodied a sense of a Durkheimian "collective effervescence" reflected in the communal experiences that are simultaneously also individualistic. The more individualistic nature could be found in the various and sundry somatic manifestations that could be seen around the room.

The somatic manifestations — shaking, laughing, jerking, crying, and even occasional "animal sounds" of barking or roaring — were in evidence throughout the more formal ritual time, but usually increased in intensity during the time of individual prayer. This array of unusual physical manifestations has accompanied other early American revivals, including the First Great Awakening, the Methodist revivals, and the Azusa Street revival that birthed Pentecostalism.[24] One person might have been convulsing with laughter, another shaking uncontrollably, a third screaming as if in deep pain, still another sobbing quietly, while still others lay motionless on the floor, seemingly in the deepest peaceful rest.

The manifestations were commonly regarded as a kind of sacrament — signs that God was at work within those for whom the prayer was being offered. The primary "work" that was believed to be underway was one of holistic healing. This healing included experiences of drawing closer to God, God's forgiveness, forgiving others who have inflicted pain, improved personal relations, healing of emotional hurts, and sometimes reports of dramatic physical and mental healing.

An overwhelming majority of the 918 survey respondents reported that the revival was a catalyst in deepening their relationship with God. They claimed they were more in love with Jesus than ever before (92%) and that they had come to know the Father's love in a new way during their revival visits (90%). The renewal and its enhancement of intimacy with

24. For an excellent discussion of experiencing religion and explaining its experience (from Wesley to James), see Ann Taves, *Fits, Trances and Visions* (Princeton, NJ: Princeton University Press, 1999).

the divine was accompanied by receiving a "fresh sense of God's forgiveness," a new "recognition of my sinful condition," and for some "deliverance from Satan's strongholds on my life." The vast majority experienced at least one of the fourteen manifestations listed on the survey, with the most common being resting or being "slain in the spirit" (45%), deep weeping (32%), and holy laughter (32%), with uncontrolled jerking (23%), deep repeated bending from the waist (29%), and being "drunk in the spirit" (27%) also occurring with great frequency. The controversial animal sounds were reported by some 12% and the old Pentecostal practice of "holy rolling" by 13%.[25] Eighty percent of the respondents claimed to experience an inner or emotional healing, 22% a healing of a physical disorder, and 6% a healing from a clinically diagnosed mental disorder.

In sum, analysis of the survey data confirmed the narrative accounts heard in countless testimonials, that prayer received during the revival was a healing balm. Receiving prayer from prayer teams serving the pilgrims who came to Toronto was positively related to reported positive emotional responses to revival experiences and to experiencing a wide array of physical manifestations. Prayer, positive emotional responses, and physical manifestations all had a direct effect on spiritual healing (i.e., experiencing God's forgiveness and deliverance from demonic bondage), although not necessarily a direct effect on other forms of healing. Spiritual healing proved to be a kind of linchpin, positively affected by the emotional and somatic responses to revival experiences; and spiritual healing, in turn, was the best predictor of reported inner, mental, and physical healing.

The following is a short summary of the detailed findings reported elsewhere, which presented the statistical evidence and discussed the "Toronto Blessing" in relation to the Pentecostal holistic model of healing:

> The results of our analyses support the need to employ a holistic model when studying Christian healing. At the center of the model is a relationship — namely a relationship with the divine — that must be in "right order" before other forms of healing ordinarily can take place. Becoming aware of one's sinful condition, deliverance from demonic strongholds, and receiving a fresh sense of forgiveness are all means of deepening this relationship with God. . . . Without fail, measures of

25. For further details see M. M. Poloma, "The 'Toronto Blessing' in Postmodern Society: Manifestations, Metaphor and Myth," in *The Globalization of Pentecostalism,* ed. M. W. Dempster, B. D. Klaus, and D. Petersen (Carlisle, CA: Regnum, 1999), pp. 363-85.

spiritual healing were significantly related to measures of inner, mental, and physical healing in our analysis. These associations held even when ritual, experience of bodily manifestations, and positive emotional responses were held constant.

The model confirms the interdependence of divine and human relationships as perceived by Pentecostal believers. Inner healing is understood to involve healing of distorted self-perceptions, the forgiving of wrongs inflicted by others, and experiencing a release from the bondage of hurtful memories of personal injury. It includes growing in a healthy love of self as well as a love of neighbor. . . . The control variables representing ritual, bodily manifestations, and emotional responses also speak to the need for a holistic model in understanding Pentecostal healing. All were related to the "linchpin" of spiritual healing. The "Toronto Blessing" has provided a place and ritual where bodily and emotional responses are accepted and even encouraged. These soma-emotional responses appear to have similarities to many reports found in both psychoanalytic and shamanic healing literature, suggesting the significant role that "primal responses" may have in the healing process.[26]

What Does This Mean? Summary and Conclusions

At this stage in the presentation some may be asking the same question the "amazed and perplexed" bystanders to the first Pentecost asked about glossolalia: "What does this mean?" (Others may be standing with the skeptics and saying, "She's had too much wine.") What I would like to do in closing is to note a few links between emerging bodies of literature that might cast additional light on the components of healing introduced in this paper. Although a foundation for and a more detailed discussion has been presented elsewhere, I will close with a few suggestive links for exploring divine healing from a scientific perspective.[27]

I want to begin this section with a general observation from the history of Christianity and its relationship to divine healing noted by Francis MacNutt, a trained Catholic theologian who has been a leader in the Christian healing movement for over four decades. MacNutt writes, in his

26. Poloma and Hoelter, "The 'Toronto Blessing,'" p. 269.
27. See Poloma, *Main Street Mystics.*

most recent book, *The Nearly Perfect Crime: How the Church Almost Killed the Ministry of Healing:*

> The Church's original healing ministry was so strong and vital, so clearly a part of the Gospel, that the crime could not take place at once. It took time — nearly two thousand years. Still the enemies of healing succeeded so well that by 1970 an accepted spiritual author could claim that "miracles are merely a holdover from the age of pre-scientific explanation, an anachronism which persists only in those moldering ivory towers which continue to exist."[28]

In short, the practice of divine healing went from playing a central role in early pre-Constantinian Christianity when the movement was in its charismatic moment, to having lost increasing ground to secularized medicine of various forms and practices throughout subsequent history. With the success of Enlightenment thought, Christian healing was for the most part eclipsed and then denigrated by the rise of a mechanistic model of healing found in modern medicine. Pentecostalism initially represented a twentieth-century protest against modernity, including modern medicine, but as the century wore on, Pentecostalism's anti-medical stance softened to embrace both divine healing and modern medicine. The rise in popularity of alternative healing practices in the last quarter of the twentieth century shared the same fertile cultural ground as did more accommodative forms of Pentecostal and neo-Pentecostal healing practices. Although those who teach about Pentecostal healing often vehemently deny it is a form of alternative medicine, from a social scientific perspective it fits into this genre, albeit with important distinctions that must be kept in mind. Roy Lawrence expresses this significant difference in light of his understanding of Jesus' powerful healing ministry, a ministry that involved both physical healing and spiritual transformation: "In a nutshell, Christian healing is practicing the presence of Jesus and expecting him to be 'the same' — no more and no less."[29]

Hefner's "double entendre between the physical and the sacred" thus must be taken seriously for an understanding of Pentecostal healing. Any

---

28. MacNutt, *The Nearly Perfect Crime*, p. 16, including a citation by the then-popular Catholic spiritual author Louis Evely.

29. Roy Lawrence, *The Practice of Christian Healing* (Downers Grove, IL: InterVarsity Press, 1996).

research that proposes to study Pentecostal healing from a medical or scientific perspective must also incorporate its holistic stance that includes not only the interconnection of the body and mind, but also a sense of the sacred that is "embodied" in believers. In attempting such research it would be wise to note the following observation of Kenneth Pargament:

> It is important to stress that the reality of the sacred cannot be determined from a social-scientific perspective. We have no tools to measure God, nor can we assess the authenticity of miraculous healings. However, we can study perceptions of sacredness and their implications for people's lives. In fact, there is growing evidence that people who see the world through a sacred lens experience life quite differently than do their more secular counterparts.[30]

As we have attempted to demonstrate in this presentation, Pentecostals do experience life through different lenses than do non-Pentecostals, and perceptions of their experiences of the sacred (particularly in revivalistic settings) do make a difference in healing and wholeness. Our preliminary research, with its account of open display of seemingly bizarre bodily manifestations and wide range of emotional responses at revival services, serves as a fresh reminder that believers are not merely disembodied spirits, but that they experience a material world as well as perceptions of a nonmaterial world in their bodies as well as spirits. While on one level it is possible to reduce this experience of the nonmaterial as some form of unknown energy[31] (an exercise that might serve some heuristic purposes), it would not capture adequately the personalized "energy" (i.e., love energy) experienced by Pentecostals that is central to their understanding of healing.[32]

Having made these general observations, I would contend that Pentecostal healing is far from ethereal, with indicators of the experience of the sacred that are available for scientific study. We have seen how somatic manifestations and the positive emotional responses linked to them by re-

---

30. Kenneth J. Pargament, "The Meaning of Spiritual Transformation," in Koss-Chioino and Hefner, eds., *Spiritual Transformation and Healing*, p. 14.

31. See, for example, C. Norman Shealy, *Sacred Healing: The Curing Power of Energy and Spirituality* (Boston: Element Books, 1999).

32. For a sociological discussion of the concept of "love energy," see Pitirim A. Sorokin's classic work *The Ways and Power of Love* (Philadelphia: Templeton Foundation Press, 2002 [1954]).

spondents point to a role that both may play as indirect agents of the healing process. The somatic responses appear to be similar to some bodily reactions observed by some in psychotherapy (albeit with differences that should not be swept away without careful inspection). As McGuire has observed, Christian groups frequently cited "emotional causes . . . usually concomitant with spiritual causes" as factors in illness. She suggests a parallel between Christian reference to emotional aspects of illness as "memories" that needed healing and "psychoanalytic notions of repressed emotional responses."[33]

Another important key for understanding aspects of embodiment and emotional response is music. Music has always played a significant role in Pentecostal ritual, and its role in healing has been noted by worship leaders. Andy Park, for example, a well-known musician and composer of music used in Toronto-like revival services, discussed the interface of grace and music in the healing process when he wrote: "From as early as the time of King David, we see music employed as a healing balm for the human soul. As David played his harp, evil spirits were driven away from Saul. This wasn't music alone — it was the anointing of the Holy Spirit."[34] Musicology, as I have discussed elsewhere, may hold important insights for understanding the role music plays in the culture that develops around healing rituals and revivals.[35]

Also related to issues of embodiment and emotional response is the role of catharsis in healing rituals and the process of healing. As Nichols and Zax have noted, catharsis has two dimensions related by separate components: the intellectual recall of forgotten material and the "physical discharge of emotion in tears, laughter, or angry telling."[36] While "intellectual recall" is commonly featured in religious rituals, there is often little space for "physical discharge." The revival ambiance of the Toronto Blessing gave pilgrims space to dance out (literally and metaphorically) their intense religious experiences.

---

33. McGuire, *Ritual Healing*, p. 50. Koss-Chioino ("Spiritual Transformation and Radical Empathy," p. 37) also made a similar observation in her discussion of "radical empathy" and healing, where "bodily and psychic incorporation of spirits or God(s) or other extraordinary beings . . . are directly associated with being healed, whether or not all of the sufferer's symptoms remain."

34. Cited in Poloma, *Main Street Mystics*, p. 107.

35. Poloma, *Main Street Mystics*, pp. 39-53.

36. Cited in Poloma, *Main Street Mystics*, p. 109.

Divine healing is much more than simply a set of beliefs and rituals, but rather it is woven into the very warp and woof of the Pentecostal worldview. It occurs in a context, as suggested by Hefner's "double entendre," in which believers accept the reality of a parallel but transcendent spiritual world. They are aware of the sensate or "what is," but they are also in tune with the spiritual or "what can be." This spiritual world of possibilities is accessed through a personal relationship with God that begins when the believer is "born again" and enhanced through the experience of "the baptism with the Holy Spirit." As such, innovative methods and measures are required to incorporate this sense of the holy and the world of spiritual possibilities into research on healing.

As Philip Hefner has argued effectively,

> This field of research cannot attain maturity until it fashions methodologies sophisticated enough to encompass both the unmanageable element of the holy and the reductionist techniques that can provide knowledge about human perceptions of sacredness and their implications for people's lives.[37]

This conference on "The Spirit in the World" is an important step toward this important goal.

---

37. Hefner, "Spiritual Transformation and Healing," p. 132.

CHAPTER 3

"When the Poor Are Fired Up": The Role of Pneumatology in Pentecostal/Charismatic Mission

Wonsuk Ma

As We Begin

During the one hundred years of the modern Pentecostal-charismatic movement, it has had an impact in many ways on Christianity in general, but its role in mission is extremely significant. The explosive growth of churches, particularly in the non-Western continents, is but one example. As discussed below, several important roles of the Holy Spirit are evident in the mission practices of Pentecostal-charismatic believers.

However, before we take this journey of discovery, it will be helpful to clarify several issues. The first is the complexity of Pentecostal-charismatic Christianity in the world today. Many have argued that the "fountainhead" of the movement is found in North America at the turn of the twentieth century, especially in the Azusa Street Mission (1906-1909) under the leadership of the African American preacher William J. Seymour. However, more evidence has been presented to contest this theory, with India and Korea being examples. Also, the stunning "discoveries" of the so-called indigenous Pentecostals from Africa and Asia appear to support the theory of "multiple fountainheads" for the origin of Pentecostal-charismatic Christianity.[1] In fact, we may be arriving at the notion that "the church is charismatic" after all, from its inception.

---

1. For a good review, see Hwa Yung, "Endued with Power: The Pentecostal-Charismatic Renewal and the Asian Church in the Twenty-first Century," *Asian Journal of Pentecostal Studies* (2003): 63-82.

As I try to represent this fastest-growing segment of Christendom, I do so with evident limitations. First, Pentecostal/charismatic Christianity is not homogenous. It encompasses classical (or denominational) Pentecostals, charismatic (or neo-) Pentecostals, and indigenous (or neo-charismatic) Pentecostals. The last category is particularly problematic because of its diversity and also because some groups in this classification advocate questionable doctrines with which orthodox Christians are not comfortable. This gives rise to the possibility of having groups that may be "more Pentecostal, but less Christian." Second, the pneumatology of groups broadly classified as Pentecostal or charismatic is not "standardized." For example, while classical Pentecostals feature a unique experience called "baptism in the Holy Spirit," many other groups may not necessarily subscribe to such a doctrinal statement but are, nonetheless, open to the supernatural work of the Holy Spirit. The rapid growth and vast diversity of this movement also pose a challenge in defining the parameters of the movement. Nevertheless, as I attempt to represent this loosely identified group of Christians all over the world, here is a minimal working definition for our discussion: "Segments of Christianity that believe and experience the dynamic work of the Holy Spirit, including supernatural demonstrations of God's power and spiritual gifts, with consequent dynamic and participatory worship and zeal for evangelism."[2]

My reflection comes with two main points: Pentecostal-charismatics represent the "poor," for whom poverty and sickness are a part of their lives, and the core of Pentecostal-charismatic pneumatology is "empowerment" for witness.

The Spirit and the Poor: "Religion *of* the Poor"

Early Pentecostals at the turn of the twentieth century were "poor" in many ways. Most participants of the Azusa Street revival came from the lower socio-economic bracket of society. Urban African Americans and ethnic immigrants, with "sprinkles of whites," made up this controversial epicenter of one of the most significant revivals in modern church history.[3] Prac-

---

2. Wonsuk Ma, "Asian Pentecostalism: A Religion Whose Only Limit Is the Sky," *Journal of Beliefs and Values* 25, no. 2 (August 2004): 192.

3. E.g., William W. Menzies and Robert P. Menzies, *Spirit and Power: Foundation of*

tically marginalized by the society, and sometimes by established churches, they understood themselves to be the eager recipients of the Messiah's message of hope, who came "to preach good news to the poor" under the anointing of the Holy Spirit (Luke 4:18).[4] These socially "dislocated" found such strong solidarity among themselves, courageously going against commonly accepted social norms such as racial segregation, that they forged a social and spiritual culture where the hopeless found a space to experience God's grace and power. This "haven for the disinherited" created a powerful drawing force to make Pentecostal Christianity a "religion of the poor."[5] The context of "poor," as the socio-spiritual context of Pentecostal-charismatic Christianity, has left several unique contributions.

This characterization is important in that Pentecostalism is a religion *of* the poor, not *for* the poor. Marginalized by existing churches, this group of people coming from the lower socio-economic strata found themselves to be the main players in the church. Their "primal spirituality" is expressed in the participatory and expressive worship as well as testimony times. The very fact that the Holy Spirit chose to visit them through powerful experiences such as healings, baptism in the Spirit, prophecy, and miracles, as well as drastic conversion experiences, was in itself a social uplift.

As observed in many non-Western continents such as Latin America and Asia, Pentecostal believers have achieved socially upward mobility, and this has been viewed as God's special blessing. This is also the reason why Pentecostal mission has been traditionally focused on evangelism (the spiritually lost) and care for the poor and marginalized. In many cultures where women are considered not appropriate for ministry, the Pentecostal faith has brought "liberation" for them. One such example is the cell system of David Yonggi Cho of Korea. In this highly male-dominant society, Cho organized, trained, and empowered women laity to exercise their ministry gifts over vast numbers of cell groups of the Yoido Full Gospel Church.

Pentecostal Experience: A Call to Evangelical Dialogue (Grand Rapids: Zondervan, 2000), p. 22, argues: "The uniqueness of the modern Pentecostal revival lies in its very survival — surviving long enough to gain a hearing in the larger church world and to emerge as a significant component of the Christian world."

4. Scripture quotations are from the New International Version.

5. David Martin, *Pentecostalism: The World Their Parish* (Oxford: Blackwell, 2002), p. 4. Also Robert M. Anderson, *Vision of the Disinherited: The Making of American Pentecostalism* (Peabody, MA: Hendrickson, 1992).

The Immanence of God

The "outpouring" of the Holy Spirit in the early twentieth century brought several powerful paradigm shifts. First, their self-understanding changed drastically: from being marginalized to being conspicuously "called" for God's ministry. Second, it was also seen as a strong eschatological sign for the immediate return of the Lord, and this brought urgency to their divine call to minister. Third, this "apostolic" movement had a strong restorational expectation in the early years. Having inherited the Holiness spiritual traditions, supernatural interventions of God, such as healings and miracles, were regularly expected. Even if "classical Pentecostalism" began in North America, its beliefs exhibited a strikingly holistic worldview in which the supernatural world intersects with the natural world on a daily basis.[6] Fourth, the unique experience of baptism in the Holy Spirit and other supernatural manifestations made this religion a religion of experience.

This emphasis on God's immanence (closeness) and the unique religious worldview strongly suggests its potential for explosive growth in the non-Western world, and that is exactly what we have had in the past one hundred years. Testimonies of healings, exorcisms, miracles, and the like are heard daily. Unlike many other Christian traditions, Pentecostal/charismatic spirituality includes the real level of daily human existence, including particularly physical and material aspects, as well as spiritual dimensions. This is a "religion with flesh and bones,"[7] and compares well with many church traditions where the Holy Spirit and his work are moved to ethical, moral, and spiritual levels, quickly bypassing the physical and material dimensions.

When They Are "Fired Up" for Service

There are several important studies enumerating distinct characteristics of Pentecostal mission. One of them, for example, is by Allan Anderson, a

6. Among others, this may come under the category of the "Black Root" of Pentecostalism. Walter J. Hollenweger, *Pentecostalism: Origins and Developments Worldwide* (Peabody, MA: Hendrickson, 1997), pp. 18-24.

7. Wonsuk Ma and Julie C. Ma, "Jesus Christ in Asia: Our Journey with Him as Pentecostal Believers," *International Review of Mission* 94 (October 2005): 493-506.

South African Pentecostal missiologist. His list includes (1) pneumato-centric mission, (2) dynamic mission praxis, (3) evangelism, with a central missiological thrust, (4) contextualization of leadership, (5) mobilization in mission, and (6) a contextual missiology.[8] In order to highlight several important characteristics of the work of the Holy Spirit in Pentecostal mission, I will select several models, including two individuals and several organizations. Not all may overtly identify themselves as "Pentecostal," but either their link with Pentecostal Christianity or their unique practices reflect its influence. As any real case is a complex matter, duplication of certain elements is unavoidable.

The Holy Spirit as the Initiator of Mission: "One-Way Ticket Missionaries"

The distinct missionary nature of Pentecostal experiences, particularly baptism in the Spirit, is well attested in the stream of missionaries who went out of and were influenced by the Azusa Street Mission. Gary McGee argues that within five years of the Pentecostal revival in Los Angeles, at least two hundred Pentecostal missionaries from North America served in various parts of the world.[9] Reinforced by eschatological urgency, many Pentecostal believers, often not properly trained, clergy as well as laity, men as well as women, young as well as old, devoted their lives to evangelism. Vinson Synan termed them "missionaries of the one-way ticket," with several useful examples.[10] According to him, they were "evangelists and missionaries who went out with little or no institutional or financial support."[11] However, in my opinion, the most crucial genius of this new breed of missionaries lies in their expectation of not returning home in their lifetime, but of working "to the end of their lives" in mission fields. There is no doubt that their shared eschatological urgency

---

8. Allan Anderson, "Towards a Pentecostal Missiology for the Majority World," *Asian Journal of Pentecostal Studies* 8, no. 1 (2005): 29-47.

9. Gary B. McGee, "Mission, Overseas (N. American Pentecostal)," in *The New International Dictionary of Pentecostal and Charismatic Movements,* ed. Stanley M. Burgess and Eduard M. van der Maas, rev. and expanded ed. (Grand Rapids: Zondervan, 2002), p. 888.

10. Vinson Synan, *The Spirit Said "Grow": The Astounding Worldwide Expansion of Pentecostal and Charismatic Churches* (Monrovia, CA: MARC, 1992), pp. 39-48.

11. Synan, *The Spirit Said "Grow,"* p. 39.

must have contributed to this determination, but equally powerful was their passion for the lost.

Synan has several powerful examples, many of whom indeed never returned home, but planted a seed that now blossoms powerfully: Ivan Efimovich Veronaev, who introduced the Pentecostal message to his homeland, Russia; Willis Collins Hoover, the father of Chilean Pentecostalism; and Daniel Berg and Gunnar Vingren, who began the Brazilian Pentecostal movement. Lillian Trasher (1888-1961), a Spirit-filled twenty-three-year-old believer, broke her engagement and sailed to Egypt. There she founded the very first orphanage in the country and once cared for 1,200 orphans, widows, single mothers, and blind women.[12] Although she received a heroic welcome in her brief 1955 visit to the States after twenty-five years of ministry without furlough, she was no doubt a missionary with a one-way ticket. She and many early Pentecostal missionaries and evangelists exhibited a lifestyle of commitment to mission that is uniquely Pentecostal.

"Prophethood of All Believers": Youth with a Mission (YWAM)

Established by a Pentecostal minister in 1960, this powerful mission group has mobilized Christian youth for mission all over the globe. Loren Cunningham, the founder, once saw "waves on a map" which "turned into young people, going to every continent, sharing the good news about Jesus."[13] YWAM's ministry is focused on evangelism, training, and mercy ministry with 900 bases (or centers) in over 140 countries, with a staff of over 11,000.[14]

The most significant "Pentecostal" tradition observed in YWAM is the "liberation" of ministry from elite clergy to the hands of every believer. For Pentecostals, one of the most important passages is Acts 1:8, "But you will receive power when the Holy Spirit comes on you; and you will be my wit-

12. The entire issue of *Assemblies of God Heritage* 4, no. 4 (Winter 1984/85) is on Trasher's life and ministry. This volume is available at http://www.agheritage.org/pdf2/Heritage/Winter-1984-1985.pdf#Page7 (checked July 26, 2005).

13. "History of YWAM," http://www.ywam.org/contents/abo_his_introhistory.htm (2004; accessed April 27, 2005).

14. "Introducing YWAM," http://www.ywam.org/contents/abo_introduction.htm (2004; accessed April 27, 2005).

nesses in Jerusalem, and in all Judea and Samaria, and to the ends of the earth." The coming of the Holy Spirit (or "baptism in the Spirit" as they call it) is for empowerment, and empowerment is for witnessing. Cunningham had difficulty in convincing his own Pentecostal denominational leadership to envision mobilizing youth for mission. Its training program practically aims to turn the "ministered" to the "ministering" believers. The life-changing testimonies of participants are heard almost daily. In order to be a "missionary" in this organization, what is required is one's willingness to give time and talent in mission, be it a week or a year. Now, this tradition of "democratization of ministry" is being expressed in various creative ways in many parts of the world. In the academic realm, a new expression has been suggested: "prophethood of all believers," possibly an active move from the traditional notion of "priesthood of all believers."[15]

"God of Healing and Miracle": David Yonggi Cho

Perhaps best known as the pastor of the largest single congregation in the world, Yoido Full Gospel Church, Cho has changed millions of lives throughout his forty-five years of ministry. He was born in 1936 and grew up in Korea under an oppressive colonial rule, went through the difficulties of war, and spent a hopeless youth, with a deadly terminal case of tuberculosis.[16] His encounter with Christianity, particularly a Pentecostal type, is described as follows:

> On what was thought to be his deathbed he was visited by a Christian girl who was a friend of his sister. His Buddhist parents had forbidden her to visit their home, but she persisted and gave Cho a Bible, preaching the gospel to him. Soon Cho became a Christian and his health began to improve dramatically.[17]

15. Earlier used in James Luther Adams, ed., *The Prophethood of All Believers* (Boston: Beacon, 1986), the expression is recently appropriated to Pentecostal beliefs by Roger Stronstad, *The Prophethood of All Believers: A Study in Luke's Charismatic Theology* (Sheffield: Sheffield Academic Press, 1999).

16. Among many biographies of Cho, see Nell L. Kennedy, *Dream Your Way to Success: The Story of Dr. Yonggi Cho and Korea* (Plainfield, NJ: Logos International, 1980).

17. Young-hoon Lee, "The Life and Ministry of David Yonggi Cho and the Yoido Full Gospel Church," *Asian Journal of Pentecostal Studies* 7, no. 1 (2004): 4.

His radical experience of God's love and power through healing made him an evangelist of a "good God" who heals and blesses those who seek him. Coming from a Buddhist religious tradition and extremely poor social conditions, his message has been consistently about a God who loves and cares for the daily needs of his people. Stories of God's miraculous healing, blessing, and restoration (of families, relationships, and the like) filled the pages of the *Shinang-gye (World of Faith)*, once the most popular monthly magazine (both religious and secular) in the country. It impacted not only Christians, but also the entire society, as the magazine was read in schools, military camps, prisons, etc.[18] Now he terms this a "ministry of hope."

His ministry and theology demonstrate a holistic worldview, including the physical and material aspects of human life, as much as the spiritual level. A bowl of rice and healing of terminal diseases in a poverty-stricken society are as important as the matter of sin and salvation. In the "majority world," if the most powerful and loving God cannot heal a person, he is not as useful as the ancestor spirits on whom many have been relying for such needs. God is expected to be the savior, not only after this life, but also during this earthly existence. This is where the work of the Holy Spirit comes in with "signs and wonders." Often the demonstration of God's power through the Holy Spirit triggers a "people's movement" or conversion by groups. This partly explains the phenomenal growth of the Pentecostal-charismatic churches all over the world.

Priority of Inner Change and Evangelism: Teen Challenge

Established by a North American Pentecostal minister, David Wilkerson, in 1958,[19] this drug rehabilitation program has become the "oldest, largest and most successful program of its kind in the world," with over 170 centers in the United States and 250 worldwide.[20] The "National Institute on

18. Myung Soo Park, "Korean Pentecostal Spirituality as Manifested in the Testimonies of Members of Yoido Full Gospel Church," *Asian Journal of Pentecostal Studies* 7, no. 1 (2004): 35-56.

19. David Wilkerson, *The Cross and the Switchblade* (New York: B. Geis Associates, 1963), details the story of Teen Challenge.

20. "About Us," http://www.teenchallenge.com/index.cfm?infoID=1&centerID=1194 (2005; accessed April 27, 2005).

Drug Abuse Report," found at the same website, argues that the drug reha-bilitation programs of Teen Challenge records a 70 percent success rate, while most secular programs reach a 1-15 percent success rate.[21] The pro-grams include residential rehabilitation facilities, seminars among youth for education and prevention, and others. The residential program in-volves a strong spiritual component, which underlines the theological as-sumption that any transformation of a society begins with individuals, and a change in a person begins with his or her inner (in this case, spiri-tual) being. This inner change involves not only a conversion experience, but also an encounter with God's reality, often through baptism in the Holy Spirit. For instance, the first entry in the testimony section reads, "John Melendez was spiritually lost and confused on the streets of New York, as a teen and young man."[22] As human suffering begins with a spiri-tual loss, the restoration should also begin with the spiritual component of a human being.

The practice of Teen Challenge epitomizes two Pentecostal values. The first is the primacy of evangelism as a Pentecostal mission focus. Driven partly by the eschatological conviction that the Holy Spirit was poured upon them for the last-minute harvest before the return of the Lord, many committed their lives to "reaching the lost." They were church planters and evangelists. Everything they did, be it mercy ministry or training, was to achieve the ultimate goal of evangelism and church planting.

The second is the Pentecostal pattern of social ministry. Many of the social ministries were to care for the "poor," such as girls' and boys' homes in India, orphanages in Egypt and many other countries, educational pro-grams in Latin America, feeding and educational programs in India, voca-tional training schools in Korea, etc. This value is aptly expressed in a well-known statement: when asked by a fellow Christian in Latin America if there are any social programs among Pentecostals, the answer was, "We are social programs!" Although this "care for victims" is not enough to remove structural evil in this world, Pentecostals have taken as their paradigm the ministry of Jesus found in Luke 4:18-19.

---

21. "National Institute on Drug Abuse Report," http://www.teenchallenge.com/index .cfm?studiesID=3 (accessed April 27, 2005).

22. "Can a Drug Addict Really Change?" http://www.teenchallenge.com/index .cfm?testimonyID=1 (2005; accessed April 27, 2005).

Empowered for Witness: Brother Badol's Story[23]

Brother Badol, as we call him, was a young man who lived in Papasok, a village of the Kankana-ey tribe, deep in the mountains of the northern Philippines. Reachable only by foot, this totally isolated community had served ancestor spirits and many gods for generations. About twenty grass-roofed houses welcome rare visitors, who upon reaching them are exhausted from the long mountain hike.

Badol and his wife lost their two young children on the same day. A simple fever took both lives. As advised by village elders, Badol offered animal sacrifices to appease the angry ancestor spirit who took them. During this time, a Christian worker visited his community once in a while and introduced a God who made pine trees, pigs, and humans. He told them that this God loves everyone dearly, and that he also hears prayers, even if there is no animal offering.

Badol and his wife soon had two new children, but they too died young, following another epidemic that took many lives in the village. He decided to try this new God, who seemed to be quite different from the spirits he had served. Of course, this was never easy, as the entire village expected him to be punished by the spirits, but they still began their strange new worship in their house. Very soon, a neighbor quietly asked him if this new God could heal his dying child. Badol laid his hand upon the motionless baby and prayed in the name of Jesus who had given life to her. The next Sunday, the entire family, with the now recovered baby, joined the "church." Badol believed that the Holy Spirit came not only to save him from darkness, but also to empower him so that he could share the gospel with effectiveness. In fact, the villagers regularly asked him to pray for the sick, and most of them were healed miraculously.

About fifteen years later, everyone in Papasok serves this new God who can heal the sick. Badol and his wife had ten more children and none died. He visited nearby villages and shared this good and powerful God with them. Because of this missionary work, seven villages have their own churches.

This story from our place of ministry epitomizes millions of Pente-

23. The full text is available in Julie C. Ma, *Mission Possible: The Biblical Strategy for Reaching the Lost* (Oxford: Regnum International; Baguio, Philippines: APTS Press, 2005), pp. 18-22.

costal-charismatic believers all over the world who are never properly recognized as "ministers" or "missionaries," and yet are faithfully and powerfully carrying out God's call for mission. The coming of the Holy Spirit as promised in Acts 1:8 has been understood as "Pentecostal missiology": The Spirit calls, empowers, and sends his people to the ends of the earth to be his witnesses. The Holy Spirit, whom they experienced through healings, miracles, and empowerment, is also expected to perform miracles and healings. Even the promise of the Lord for supernatural power as recorded in Mark 16:15-18 is understood in the context of mission:

> He said to them, "Go into all the world and preach the good news to all creation. Whoever believes and is baptized will be saved, but whoever does not believe will be condemned. And these signs will accompany those who believe: In my name they will drive out demons; they will speak in new tongues; they will pick up snakes with their hands; and when they drink deadly poison, it will not hurt them at all; they will place their hands on sick people, and they will get well."

"The Spirit Who Makes Us One": Azusa Street Mission

Among the many challenging traditions observed in this renewal movement, the work of the Holy Spirit to remove human barriers is distinct. This incredible anti-cultural phenomenon against the social norm of that day appeared on two fronts. The first was the multiracial composition of the mission. Under the leadership of an African American Holiness preacher, the twelve leaders were an equal mixture of black and white. An observer, who happened to be Seymour's teacher, reported the eruption of this spiritual movement with a distasteful flavor:

> Men and women, whites and blacks, knelt together or fell across one another; frequently a white woman, perhaps of wealth and culture, could be seen thrown back in the arms of a big "buck nigger," and held tightly thus as she shivered and shook in freak imitation of Pentecost. Horrible, awful shame! Many of the missions on the Pacific coast are permeated with this foolishness, and in fact, it follows the Azuza [*sic*] work everywhere.[24]

24. Charles F. Parham, "Free-Love," *The Apostolic Faith* [Baxter Springs, KS] 1, no. 10 (December 1912): 4-5.

However, this congregation where "the 'color' line is washed by the blood"[25] is a powerful demonstration of what the Holy Spirit can do in a complex and troubled world. The other was the ecumenical nature of the mission. The participants of the Azusa Street revival came from a variety of Christian traditions. Stories abound about how a visitor, theologically suspicious, was overwhelmed by the presence of the Holy Spirit and ecclesial differences suddenly disappeared. This ecumenical potential was again presented during the charismatic renewal when "Spirit-filled" members of various churches (often from mainline churches, including the Roman Catholic Church) were able to celebrate common faith with genuine Christian love and appreciation.

However, this unique demonstration of the Spirit's work was short-lived, at least in the Azusa Street revival. Soon various Pentecostal denominations were organized, often along racial lines. Also, the ever-increasing number of Pentecostal-charismatic congregations from splits remains as a testimony against its spiritual tradition. However, the recent spread of the "Pentecostal" practices (or culture) in singing and worship has reminded us of its potential to bring a divided humanity (including the church) together through the Holy Spirit.

In Conclusion

This short presentation is purposefully brief and incorporates narratives (to be truthful to the Pentecostal testimonies). The role of Pentecostal-charismatic churches and believers in fulfilling God's mission will become increasingly important in the coming years. Particularly significant will be the role of the non-Western churches, which I represent, with their explosive growth and increasing challenges. This will require the active exchange of experiences with the members of the world church.

The highlighted strengths are shared, not to argue that the Pentecostals have at last found the secret formula for world evangelization, but to humbly present to the church community at large that the Lord has brought this movement with its unique set of gifts to the body of Christ, particularly in fulfilling God's mission mandate. The one-hundred-year

25. Frank Bartleman, *Azusa Street,* foreword by Vinson Synan (Plainfield, NJ: Logos International, 1980), p. 54.

history of the Pentecostal-charismatic movement is an unfortunate combination of the Spirit's empowerment and human shortcomings, and we Pentecostals know this all too well.

As a "new kid on the block," Pentecostals have much to learn from the historic churches with their rich histories and traditions. At the same time, the rise of such new movements (particularly the renewal type) in itself serves as God's reminder to his people of his missionary mandate to the world. If the Pentecostal-charismatic movement can serve this purpose by strengthening and renewing the body of Christ through its healing and restorational potential, its primary historical calling is fulfilled. May this be the case by the help of the Spirit. Thus, come, Holy Spirit, and empower us for your mission!

CHAPTER 4

A Moral Imagination: Pentecostals and Social Concern in Latin America

Douglas Petersen

Discrimination, neglect, and economic disparity are the norm within most Latin American countries. The masses still struggle to obtain their daily bread. Globalization and authoritarian power structures have eliminated lesser groups from participation. In these hostile environments, Pentecostal groups have exploded from a not-so-long-ago "brush-arbor" handful to the most extensive network of popularly directed associations outside the Roman Catholic Church. These social networks of largely autonomous local congregations, numbering fifty million members and adherents, are not merely at the margins, but at the vanguard of a clamor for a more rewarding, secure future.

As the dust settles on this phenomenon, it is apparent, however, that the majority of Latin Americans still struggle for social and economic survival. In the face of a systematic structural injustice that sustains unacceptable conditions, Pentecostals are confronted with a myriad of novel and complex challenges requiring equally novel solutions that are innovative and workable. Even though this army of compassionate workers may be sufficiently motivated to remain in the trenches and reach the hurting and marginalized around them, more than ever before and especially given their spectacular growth, Pentecostals will need an inspired moral imagination if they wish to be effective agents of social transformation at the macro level.

The thesis of this chapter is that Pentecostals, accustomed to the supernatural and equipped with the empowering presence of the Spirit, would enhance the effectiveness of their social action programs by encouraging the development of the skills, approaches, and methods that are necessary for moral imagination and organizational creativity to flourish. A moral imagination, guided by the Spirit, would provide a platform from which Pentecostals could develop effective strategies that are innovative and entrepreneurial.

Challenges and Opportunities

Expressions of social concerns are found in all types of Pentecostal churches. In general, however, while literature on Pentecostalism is growing, the movement's popular appeal and dynamic social processes have been probed only on the surface. Lacking has been on-the-ground scholarly investigations that could produce the empirical data to establish even a tentative basis for definitions, quantification, and description of Pentecostal social program functions and resources. However, recent field research by Donald Miller and Tetsunao Yamamori, focusing upon an expanse of Pentecostal social programs, will go a long way to fill that vacuum.[1] Over a four-year period, Miller and Yamamori visited dozens of social ministry projects and interviewed hundreds of leaders in twenty countries and four continents. Assessing social programs without imposing restrictive and inflexible categories, they accepted at face value and as normative the stories of spiritual experience and claims of the supernatural. Miller and Yamamori lay emphasis on claims that Pentecostals are not on a "social strike" and that a vibrant social dynamic plays an integral part in Pentecostal expressions.

While such studies highlight a veritable multiplication of social endeavors, it is equally clear from even a cursory review that mere involvement in social action programs does not automatically inspire Pentecostals to make a corresponding commitment to sociological or theological reflection. Pentecostal experience is not self-interpreting, and thoughtful analysis to accompany actions is often slow to develop. Too often, their social action strategies lack intentionality or a systematic set of coherent and integrated components that would empower them or the persons they serve to become more effective agents of social transformation.

---

1. Donald E. Miller and Tetsunao Yamamori, *Pentecostalism and Social Transformation: A Global Analysis* (Berkeley: University of California Press, 2007).

The task for Pentecostal groups is to establish an "essential connectedness" between their experience of Spirit baptism and the practice of social action. To respond effectively to the extreme needs that surround them, Pentecostals would do well to focus on the formulation of a social doctrine that enables them to evaluate their own actions and stimulate new thinking, a redefinition of methods, and out-of-the-box social action strategies.[2] Furthermore, a systematic focus would also help Pentecostals, for example, to move beyond the parameters of conventional social action strategies and create a type of social program that is not solely dependent upon economic or political means. The effectiveness of their social strategies is often limited or paralyzed because local congregations lack even modest economic resources and the most humble traditional and/or institutional social programs are still costly to operate. Churches may be comprised (and usually are) of the very people they desire to help. If the delivery of social action strategies requires substantial monies, entire networks can be sidelined. In a noisy, alienated world, the marginalized — especially children and young people — are seeking identity, meaning, acceptance, relationships, and a sense of community. They yearn for more than economic assistance.

Strategically located among the most needy, with an emphasis upon personal participation, supernatural experience, and divine empowerment, Pentecostals are ideally positioned to engage a moral imagination that focuses on issues of personal dignity and interrelational skills that are not costly to develop. Clearly, the exponential growth of this religious and social phenomenon has created new responsibilities, new challenges, and new opportunities. Indeed, a moral imagination that would include Spirit baptism as an empowering focus in pursuit of justice could be a unique contribution of the Pentecostal tradition to evangelical social praxis.

The Components of a Moral Imagination

Despite complaints that Pentecostals have neglected "the here and now" for the "sweet by and by," the fact is that the explosive growth of Pente-

---

2. Murray W. Dempster has done the most comprehensive work at connecting a Pentecostal social ethic to Spirit baptism. See "The Structure of Christian Ethics Informed by Pentecostal Experience: Soundings in the Moral Significance of Glossolalia," in *The Spirit and Spirituality*, ed. Wonsuk Ma and Robert P. Menzies (New York: T. & T. Clark International, 2004), pp. 108-40.

costalism among the destitute and vulnerable has created a viable force that can address the contemporary situation facing millions of its adherents. In the midst of grinding poverty and a context dominated by a global market economy that offers prosperity to few, Pentecostals should break out of the box of conventional thinking that tends to hold them hostage — theologically and strategically — and resort to their strengths.

Pentecostals thrive in the chaotic and disorderly paradigm shifts within modern Latin American culture and religion. They are comfortable operating independently of institutional, authoritative, and monolithic ecclesial power, and seldom hesitate to utilize resourcefully every means of communication and technology (sometimes to the extreme). Pentecostals are inclined, when the odds seemed stacked against them, to depend upon the inspiration of the Spirit to spark creative ideas that produce methods and strategies that work. In the midst of a social and economic nightmare that is daily fare for their brothers and sisters, Latin American Pentecostals, regardless of resources or lack thereof, should do everything possible to foster a moral imagination.

Certainly, being imaginative is nothing new for most Pentecostals. However, practicing a moral imagination is more than coming up with a few inspired ideas. A moral imagination is comprised of, indeed links together, a set of distinct parts. Being morally imaginative means embracing a systematic and entrepreneurial approach that links a creative problem-solving process to desired outcomes.[3] With an experiential starting point that takes seriously spiritual discernment, the supernatural, and divine empowerment, it is the imagining of a preferred future undergirded by social and theological reflection, a resolve to overcome emerging obstacles, the creation of new possibilities and solutions, and the selection from those options of a dynamic social action alternative. A moral imagination, then, driven by a vision of the future, links together and integrates the steps of the decision-making process with an aim to achieve the desired outcome.[4] A moral imagination is an imaginative rationality that is insightful, critical, exploratory, and transformative.[5]

---

3. P. F. Drucker, *Innovation and Entrepreneurship: Practice and Principles* (New York: Harper & Row, 1985), p. 19.

4. Here I borrow this framework from Patricia H. Werhane, *Moral Imagination and Management Decision Making* (New York: Oxford University Press, 1999).

5. Mark Johnson, *Moral Imagination* (Chicago: University of Chicago Press, 1993), p. 202.

Pentecostalism — by its democratization of religious life, promise of physical and social healing, compassion for the socially alienated, and practice of Spirit empowerment — has the ingredients for a powerful moral imagination that can address the concerns of the disinherited, frustrated, and assertive persons who in large part make up the movement. For the Pentecostal community of faith, a moral imagination saturated with spiritual discernment and supernatural empowerment becomes a powerful tool for creative thinking and action to practice all that "Jesus said or did."

When engaging a moral imagination that is undergirded by biblical foundations, Pentecostals draw on a rich tradition of evangelical scholarship: that theological reflection must begin with an understanding of God's self-revelatory nature and character; that Israel's socio-ethical actions were to demonstrate this theocentric nature and character; that the concept of the kingdom of God, implicit in the Old Testament and explicit in the person and teachings of Jesus in the New Testament, is the unifying theme that provides a description of what life would look like under God's redemptive reign; and that life in the kingdom of God is characterized by the ethics of justice, mercy, love, and peace as its principal moral features. This ethical construct served as the moral foundation of the primitive Christian church. In the Acts account, for example, gender distinctions of male and female were challenged by the empowerment of the Spirit. Economic distinctions between rich and poor and cultural distinctions between Jew and Gentile were leveled out by the power of the Spirit.[6]

The coming of the Spirit at Pentecost and its contemporary application through the experience of Spirit baptism integrate the ethical character of God's reign into a Pentecostal moral imagination. If the Pentecostal experience of Spirit baptism is basically one for empowerment, then the task of a Pentecostal theology is to demonstrate the centrality of the experience as a key pattern to open the way to discuss how these ethical demands are actualized and become operative in the power of the Spirit. The aspect of a moral imagination that makes it Pentecostal is the work of Spirit baptism. The actualization of this empowerment in the experience of contemporary Latin American Pentecostals provides an integral contex-

---

6. For a further development of a theological ethic of social concern in similar contexts, see Douglas Petersen, *Not by Might Nor by Power* (Oxford/Irvine: Regnum Books, 1996), pp. 186-226.

tual framework for the practice of a moral imagination that is uniquely Pentecostal.

When Latin American Pentecostals read the Bible (a common reading), for example, there is an inherent consistency in the interplay of linking their Pentecostal worldview (pre-understanding) and the reality of daily circumstances with their subsequent biblical interpretation and application.[7] They have at their core a supernatural worldview perspective that is both overtly expressed and instilled in teachings and sermons. This worldview is codified through religious symbols and practices such as *glossolalia* and healings, supernatural interventions, participative worship, and expressions in music. They approach the scriptures with a pre-understanding that they are participants in God's unfolding drama. The biblical narratives of sorrow and pain, or of power and justice, are interpreted theologically into the concrete realities of their daily spiritual, social, or physical contexts. Their interaction with the text is sharpened further by a personal sense that, in spite of their circumstances, the Holy Spirit has bestowed upon them an "enduement of power." They are God's instruments even if their contextual reality systematically may deny them access to basic human rights, marginalize them to huge slums and shantytowns, or refuse them access to political and social opportunity.

Consciously or not, Pentecostals read and interpret the biblical text through the lens of their own contextual realities. By moving back and forth interpretively between the world of the biblical text and the realities of the world where they live, they interpret the "meaning or significance of the text" that emerges from this process into a practical application to their actual life context and for the local community of faith. This praxis theology — reflecting, adapting, and appropriating the Scripture into new and refreshing perspectives that are framed by their historical context and empowered by the Spirit — provides a dynamic hermeneutic that enables Pentecostals to practice a dynamic moral imagination, "doing theology from the bottom up."

Certainly, as Latin American Pentecostals seek programs of social con-

7. The distinction between a Latin American evangelical and Pentecostal is almost indiscernible, especially in their supernatural worldview. Evangelicals, while differing on certain nuances of Spirit baptism, share more common than uncommon ground with Pentecostals. Undoubtedly, there would be disagreements from either perspective, but we can hardly tell the difference. It is important to note that Pentecostals in Latin America are seldom referred to, or refer to themselves, as Pentecostals, but rather as *evangélicos.*

cern and justice, it is vital that they maintain a healthy tension — an essential connectedness — between their Pentecostal pre-understanding of the common reading of the biblical text and their social action strategies. However, when critical theological reflection is informed by a Pentecostal worldview and done from within the cultural contexts where the movement is flourishing, new possibilities emerge that could be socially transformative.

Some Western conservative theologians may be haunted in this process by a style of postmodern theological thought that pursues questions of regional fragmentation, shifting contextual purpose, and subjective meaning. But can there be creative and dynamic theological reflection concerning problems like poverty, sickness, oppression, and marginalization, if rules and procedures about what is permissible hold the theological process hostage?

Theologians throughout history, including paradigm pioneers like St. Augustine or Martin Luther as well as more recent figures such as Karl Barth, rose to the challenges of their times in a variety of complex and sophisticated ways. They were able to "think outside the box" — seeking a basis for biblical understandings and applications in common human needs, in feelings, in reason, and in the notion of transcendence. Their theological contributions remain influential today and are still the subject of current debates. For that reason alone, the process discussed in this essay is worth the risk to anyone who is serious about hearing "theology in a new key," to borrow McAfee Brown's phrase.

Latin American Pentecostals, whose experiences and contexts parallel the accounts in the Acts of the Apostles, when practicing a moral imagination open the door of possibility for a dynamic equivalent experience similar to those in the early church. A moral imagination — a fresh "praxis of faith" — freed from the traditionally articulated scientific/theological ideas of an academic-bound theological system, could produce an exciting new paradigm for the community of faith everywhere. Indeed, it is the sound of an evangelical/Pentecostal moral theology with a Latin accent!

Practicing a Moral Imagination

This section presents two levels of a Pentecostal moral imagination at work. At the first level of a moral imagination, the leadership of social ac-

tion programs should imagine an outcome where participants are personally empowered to "function effectively" within the infrastructure of everyday civil life, with the capacity to access available resources (and
entitlements) and to create and influence social relationships. In short,
empowerment is the acquisition of personal and interpersonal skills that
equip participants "to act efficaciously" in that what they have learned
leads to action.[8]

On the second and more corporate level, the leadership of social action programs should imagine an outcome where their social delivery
agencies and networks, together with the participants as well as themselves, are empowered to corporately influence, change, or transform unjust social and structural dimensions or at a minimum create new alternatives to them. Moving beyond envisioning a future of empowered
participants who can now access the accouterments of civil society (clearly,
no small thing), this second level of a moral imagination, more complex
and more profound than the first, envisions what could happen when Pentecostal social concern programs and networks activate their moral imagination in pursuit of creative solutions to what appears to be an impossible
challenge — the chiasmic discrepancies in power relationships in social
and political structures.

Level One: Moral Imagination and Personal Empowerment

Unlike most unaffiliated Latin Americans, Pentecostals are able to create
communities (the local church) that provide not only social recognition,
but also offer members a platform of opportunities to develop interpersonal and life and leadership skills, essential components of individual empowerment.[9]

If new converts' experience is, on the one hand, intensely personal,
spiritual, mystical, and eternal; on the other hand, it is corporate and practical, permeated with opportunities that empower them to function effectively in the here and now. The local church provides a safe place where

8. The discussion of the concept of empowerment theory and practice — individually
and corporately — is an important debate, but for now is outside the scope of the immediate argument.

9. This section follows an earlier chapter I wrote in *Not by Might*, pp. 121-45.

people can find security, acceptance, wholeness, recognition, and even the rights and privileges of membership. Personal discipline, acceptable conduct, and accountability provide basic rules of pedagogic importance. New converts typically find themselves involved in a great deal of structured activity. They must accept individual responsibility for their actions and exhibit willingness to contribute or sacrifice for the common good of the community.

Regardless of age, ethnicity, social status, or gender, everyone is offered opportunities. For example, women — often marginalized within traditional society and seldom given opportunity to develop the skills required to negotiate civil society — are admitted to leadership ranks at almost every level within the local church, including in many countries the right to occupy the office of pastor. Some observers have tended to see Pentecostal churches as essentially a protest mounted by women in what could be considered a response to social class or ethnic disqualification. As David Martin notes, "Women are among the 'voiceless' given a new tongue in the circle of Pentecostal communication."[10] For many Pentecostal women, their decision to convert has resulted in a sense of self-esteem and equality that has permitted them to gain control of their domestic affairs.[11] The husband's moral deviations are no longer seen as the inevitable foibles of *machismo*.[12] Instead of being dependent upon his desires, a wife senses a divine confidence and authority to speak to her husband when she believes his behavior is contrary to God's laws.[13] Interpersonal skills learned in the context of congregational responsibilities transfer to familial relationships in the home and to leadership options and social functions within the community.

In sum, when the local church enables people to take part in the larger social and economic struggles for a better life and more secure future by engaging a moral imagination that generates decision-making strategies to

10. David Martin, *Tongues of Fire* (Oxford: Blackwell, 1990), p. 180.
11. John Burdick, "Rethinking the Study of Social Movements," in *The Making of Social Movements in Latin America*, ed. Arturo Escobar and Sonia Alvarez (Boulder, CO: Westview Press, 1992), p. 177.
12. Cornelia Butler Flora, "Pentecostal Women in Colombia," in *The Journal of Interamerican Studies and World Affairs* 17 (November 1975): 412-13. The best book on Pentecostals and *machismo* is Elizabeth Brusco, *The Reformation of Machismo* (Austin: University of Texas Press, 1995).
13. Flora, "Pentecostal Women in Colombia," pp. 412-13.

develop self-esteem, provide hope, and equip participants with skills applicable to the social system, participants are empowered to "act efficaciously," acquiring a potential to be significant agents of spiritual and social change.

Level Two: A Moral Imagination, Corporate Action, and Alternative Structures

The emergence of Pentecostals as a popular social movement — exhibiting horizontal networks, fellowship, and reciprocity — enables participants to move beyond only the personal-empowerment concerns of the first level. At this second level, Pentecostals can now imagine a future of "what ought to be," in contrast to the way they functioned as recently as two decades ago. United by a shared worldview that expects God to be involved in everything they do and working collectively through their networks to explore possibilities of what life should be like, they have acquired the institutional strength to address corporately the human needs of the societies in which they live. Pentecostals can be agents of social transformation for large numbers of Latin Americans by offering innovative solutions that contribute to the resolution of difficulties or even by creating their own social alternatives within civil society.

Pentecostals — their social capital and networks — represent the most independent, self-initiated popular movement to be found in Latin America today.[14] Their networks possess features and functions similar to a popular social movement.[15] It is helpful here to view this emerging popular social movement through the lens of Robert Putnam's theory of "social capital." Putnam defines social capital as "trust, norms, and networks that improve the efficiency of society by facilitating coordinated actions."[16] The central premise of social capital theory is that the "value" of social net-

14. Edward L. Cleary and Hannah Stewart-Gambino, eds., *Power, Pentecostals, and Politics* (Boulder, CO: Westview Press, 1997), p. 231.

15. I define a popular social movement as a group with high levels of popular participation, working together in religious or socio-economic contexts, usually resistant to the status quo, and determined by their actions to alter existing situations and create for themselves free social space.

16. Robert D. Putnam, *Making Democracy Work* (Princeton: Princeton University Press, 1993), p. 167.

works, if focused, can lead to the formation of an empowered civic society able to bring about structural change. The civic virtue that results from these horizontal linkages is at its best when networks are tightly knit together by mutual obligation and shared concerns.

A moral imagination requires an honest and fresh assessment of "what is" — to assess realistically the breadth and depth of the obstacles encountered by Pentecostals to find their place at the political table. Social capital arguments should not be idealized, and cannot be analyzed in isolation or independent from the hard realities of the broader socioeconomic institutional context in which they are imbedded. The complex political realities of emerging democracies in Latin America are fraught with problems, and the political agenda has not moved much beyond "the minimum rules of the democratic game" (the voter gets to cast a ballot). There is neither coherent accountability nor consistent avenues for representation.

However, if hopes for bona fide democracy are viewed from a popular Pentecostal perspective — the urban poor, peasants, women, indigenous groups, and ethnic minorities — then there is more "bad news than good news." Aside from members casting their vote at the ballot box, in many Latin American contexts social capital is simply not enough to gain access to national levels of decision-making.

The "bad news" reality for the overwhelming numbers of Pentecostals is immobilization of essential democratic evolutionary processes. Existing but flawed historical structures, paralyzed by ideology that perceives the economic markets and "economic consumption" to be the new panacea, impedes the democratic process. The dark side of globalization and technological diversification, shaping new "absolutist" entities that are seldom responsive or accountable to the citizenry, erodes state legitimacy and excludes the poorest sectors of society,

Conference papers, journal articles, and books abound, critiquing Latin American Pentecostals for their neglect and lack of political involvement. The pleas from scholars, including myself in the past, to encourage Pentecostals to break out of their "substitute societies" and take an active public role by addressing directly the political sphere, are mostly theoretical and likely unreasonable. Too often forgotten or lost within the euphoria of the mere existence of the newly established democracies in Latin America is the appalling lack of the basic accouterments of civil society. It is no doubt a mistake to identify levels of participation within social networks as the successful variable for democratic vitality instead of recognizing the resiliency of institutional antecedents that still have the power to give life to civil entities or withhold it.[17]

Declarations given to Pentecostals of "must do," "should do," and "may do" are easy to draft, but virtually impossible to implement, at least now. While a popular social movement (Pentecostalism) has the ability to link itself horizontally, the institutional "rules of the game" are written and administered with little input coming from the popular members of civil society, and certainly not from Pentecostals! In these environments, is it reasonable to propose that there are popular social movements of any stripe powerful enough to insist on their rights at the table of inclusion? Clearly, it is essential to engage a moral imagination.

One option for these Pentecostal groups is to create their own alternative institutions or associations. These alternatives are plausible, practical, and rightful expressions of significant participation in civil society. While offering spiritual assistance to be sure, they also function as instruments of social empowerment. Active involvement in Pentecostal groups often presents participants an experience rich enough to render not only a critical sense of identity and personal empowerment, but also to produce "value" for civil society.

If these Pentecostal groups stay committed to being effective transforming agents in civil society, this institution-building predicated on the active involvement of followers and dependent on the development of its own leaders will continue to attract and hold a constituency large enough that government entities must sooner or later acknowledge.[18] Over the long run, this model of social movement may hold out more legitimate and evolving possibilities for Pentecostals to effect future change directly upon the power structures that currently impede any high-level participation.

17. Harry E. Vanden and Gary Prevost, *Politics of Latin America: The Power Game* (New York: Oxford University Press, 2002).

18. The beginning of this capacity can be seen in certain contexts. The fifteenth-anniversary celebration of Fundación PIEDAD in Nicaragua was held at the National Stadium in Managua on June 30, 2001. The president, Arnoldo Alemán, and numerous government officials attended. Three local television networks transmitted the event.

The Fruit of a Moral Imagination: Fundación PIEDAD

There are numerous cases demonstrating how institution-building on the community level has been utilized effectively by evangelicals/Pentecostals to bring about structural change. To cite a specific example, Fundación PIEDAD is representative of the creation of an expanding evangelical educational infrastructure designed to alter existing social structures in local communities. Following the widespread conviction of sociologists and political analysts that the positive condition of children — education, nutrition, medical care, and ethical formation — is essential for any kind of democratic expression, PIEDAD has established a unified network of 300 schools in 22 nations providing education for 100,000 children.[19] PIEDAD not only provides education and healthcare, but as a result of its local influence, the association has been instrumental in bringing basic amenities including electricity, water wells, and/or running water that impact the entire community.

For the leadership of PIEDAD — faculty and administration — institution-building and involvement in community associations, along with many other forms of civilian participation, can serve as initial entry points providing indispensable political experience on a small and familiar scale, enabling many within the leadership to develop a lucid political vocation at the local level, preparing them for future direct involvement in national political life.

PIEDAD is a prime example of local evangelical/Pentecostal groups, while not intrinsically politically oriented, creating institutional structures capable of performing various educational, community development, social service, or even local political functions. By developing self-esteem within the most marginalized — the children — and by providing hope and arming them with skills applicable to the larger social system, Pentecostal social action programs like PIEDAD enable both teachers and students to take part in the larger social struggles for a better life and a more secure future.

That Latin American Pentecostals have a role to play on the stage of civil society, in contrast to their collective social marginalization of but a

---

19. The North American version of Fundación PIEDAD is Latin America ChildCare (LACC). Doug Petersen Sr. served as International Coordinator and President of LACC from its founding in 1976 until December 2000.

few years past, is a stunning paradigm shift. Over time, and with much persistence, community-based evangelical/Pentecostal associations comprised of millions of grassroots participants can little by little chisel away the obstinate colonial institutional remnants. As a result of the creation of alternative institutions (social capital and social networks) that by their nature provide critical leadership and political skills, and work outward from there, that gargantuan transitional leap from citizenry associations to national political involvement may not be such a quixotic ideal after all.

A Moral Imagination: The Future Is Now

Clearly, Pentecostals find little difficulty reading their Bibles and interpreting the guidance of the Spirit in such a way that moves them to ask for a better life for themselves and for their community. They readily show concern for other people's material and spiritual needs. Having demonstrated theological reflective evaluation of their individual action as it relates to personal morality and holiness, Pentecostals must now recognize the need for a more imaginative ethic where the message of the biblical text and the compulsion of the Spirit will direct them to address creative responses to the context of the evil about them. It is possible that Pentecostals, committed to a God who breaks into human history and utterly dependent upon the Spirit for empowerment, can practice a moral imagination that envisions a future where their creative and innovative social action programs are the fruits of linking theological reflection, the authority of Scripture, and the reality of concrete human experience to make a difference in the lives of people, the community, and the Latin American continent.

PART II

"The Spirit Among Cultures":
Pentecostal Theology and Cultural Diversity

CHAPTER 5

One God, One Spirit, Two Memories: A Postcolonial Reading of the Encounter Between Western Pentecostalism and Native Pentecostalism in Kerala

Paulson Pulikottil

Introduction: A Postcolonial Approach to Pentecostal Historiography

During the 1920s in the southern state of India called Kerala, a Pentecostalism introduced by missionaries from the West had the opportunity to meet the native Pentecostalism. Native Pentecostalism is the Pentecostal movement that arose among Christians of India who trace their Christian history to the first century AD without the direct involvement of Pentecostal missionaries from outside India. This encounter has some significant lessons for Pentecostal studies, particularly in relation to native churches and organizations. This case study of the encounter between Western Pentecostalism and native Pentecostalism uses insights from postcolonial theory and historiography.[1]

A postcolonial approach to historiography is different from traditional approaches in both content and perspective. A postcolonial approach has a distaste for grand narratives but lays special emphasis on

---

1. Those who are new to postcolonial theory will find a useful introduction in Padmini Mongia, ed., *Contemporary Postcolonial Theory: A Reader* (London: Arnold, 1996). Mongia offers an introduction to the history, various aspects, and critique of postcolonial theory along with selections from the leading scholars.

Originally published as "'As East and West Met in God's Own Country': Encounter of Western Pentecostalism with Native Pentecostalism in Kerala," *Asian Journal of Pentecostal Studies* 5, no. 1 (2002): 5-22.

locality and historical particularity. The concern of postcolonial historiography in general is to construct more limited and specific accounts of particular events and incidents, stressing the fact that each episode has a local and particular color. This approach thus ensures a place for those who are not given their due place in history.[2]

A postcolonial approach to history is also different in its perspectives: a postcolonial approach to history is considered as "history from below" or "voices from the edges." It tries to reconstruct history from the perspective of those who are left out by traditional histories, those who were not given their due place in history. This is what qualifies the Subaltern Studies project as a postcolonial approach.[3] Another important dimension is that it provides categories for understanding relationships between dominant groups and the subalterns, those who have placed themselves at the center of history and those who are pushed to the periphery.

A postcolonial approach to history is useful to Pentecostal historiography in many ways. First of all, it helps us recover Pentecostal history, which has not found a place in the grand narratives. Pentecostalism is (still) the religion of the subalterns in most parts of the world; they are not the subjects of the mainstream histories. It remains an undisputed fact that in the grand narratives created by the historians belonging to the historical churches, Pentecostalism has not been given due recognition. In the elitist historiography presented by the groups that are dominant, either by their place in history or by political or economic advantage, Pentecostalism and especially Pentecostalism in the non-Western cultures did not get their due place.

Second, it promises a deeper appreciation of the work of the Holy

---

2. A postcolonial critique of traditional historiography approaches can be found in Ranajit Guha, "On Some Aspects of the Historiography of Colonial India," in *Selected Subaltern Studies,* ed. R. Guha and G. C. Spivak (New York: Oxford University Press, 1988), pp. 37-44.

3. The Subaltern Study Group, which began in the 1980s, attempts to rewrite the history of India by focusing on those who were on the fringes and by reconstructing specific, local, and particular accounts of history. See the ten volumes of *Subaltern Studies* (New Delhi: Oxford University Press, 1982-1999), edited by R. Guha (1: *Writings on South Asian History and Society* [1982]; 2 [1983]; 3 [1984]; 4 [1985]; 5 [1987]; 6 [1989]); P. Chatterjee and G. Pandey (7 [1992]); D. Arnold and D. Hardiman (8: *Essays in Honour of Ranajit Guha* [1994]); S. Amin and D. Chakrabarty (9 [1996]); G. Bhadra, G. Prakash and S. Tharu (10 [1999]); and also R. Guha and G. C. Spivak, eds., *Selected Subaltern Studies* (New York: Oxford University Press, 1988); R. Guha, ed., *Subaltern Reader: 1986-1995* (Minneapolis: University of Minnesota Press, 1997).

Spirit, irrespective of the limits of time and space. The work of the Holy Spirit is universal and not limited to any place or time. Postcolonial historiography helps us look at particular historical events from the perspectives of the natives. Traditional Pentecostal histories describe Pentecostal history beginning with the Topeka revivals and gaining momentum at Azusa Street and spreading all over the world. The following quote illustrates this Eurocentric approach. While introducing the article on how Pentecostalism came to the city of Calcutta in India, L. Grant McClung comments: "Pentecostal church history has revealed that a common thread runs from Azusa Street through contemporary pentecostal [sic] denominations and their missionary expansion."[4] However, a postcolonial approach to history, which focuses on locality and particularity, is more open in its approach. Such an approach helps us explore the possibilities of the work of the Holy Spirit outside the West and the ways in which people in various parts of the world responded to its manifestation.

Third, it helps us explore voices from the contact zones of West and East or the intersection of their spaces. Pentecostalism in its present forms made its appearance either in the last phase of European colonialism or at the dawn of the emergence of new nation-states. In other words, Pentecostal missionaries entered the territories that had been colonial contact zones for centuries. How did the natives respond? What sort of resistance and acceptance did the missionaries receive from these natives who had already been through political, economic, and sometimes even ecclesiastical domination? This would help us to draw some useful lessons for enriching relationships between East and West. "As far as the East is from the West . . . ," the psalmist says, but on Pentecost, East and West were made to meet each other through the confession "One God, One Baptism, and One Spirit." However, did the confession and experience of the third person of the Trinity erase their historical memories? What happens when East and West — so far from each other politically, economically, socially, and ecclesiastically — actually meet? This is the question for us to explore.

4. L. G. McClung, *Azusa Street and Beyond* (South Plainfield, NJ: Bridge Publishing, 1986), p. 26. However, two decades later the same author revised his position where he seems to see the connection not between Azusa Street and world Pentecostalism but with Jerusalem. In 2006 he wrote: "Ask any Pentecostal about his or her spiritual heritage, and the answer you get will focus not on the 1906 Azusa Street revival in Los Angeles but on Jerusalem." See Grant McClung, "'Waiting on the Gift': An Insider Looks Back on One Hundred Years of Pentecostal Witness," *International Bulletin of Missionary Research* 30, no. 2 (2006): 64.

Pentecostal Origins in India

A Brief History of Native Pentecostalism

There were Holy Spirit revivals in India before the arrival of Pentecostal missionaries from the West. These revivals, influenced by the Holiness revivals in the U.S. and U.K., did not result in the formation of Pentecostal denominations in India. However, Pentecostalism as a movement that culminated in the formation of churches among the natives and led by the natives in India first emerged from the Syrian Christian community in the state of Kerala (ancient Malabar is included in the state of Kerala). Kerala has been a contact zone for ancient Christianity, Islam, Greeks, Chinese, and the European colonial powers beginning with the Portuguese.

Christianity in Kerala claims its origin in AD 52 when the Apostle Thomas arrived and preached the gospel to Jews and the native high-caste Brahmins.[5] In addition, there is evidence of migrations of Christians from Syria in the fourth century and the eighth century to Kerala.[6] Whether these theories can be proved or not, there was an ancient Christian community in Kerala, which shared ecclesiastical and liturgical traditions with Syrian Orthodox tradition before the arrival of the Portuguese in India in the fifteenth century. Travelers had described the presence of this community in Kerala long before the arrival of the Europeans.

The three stalwarts of native Pentecostalism in Kerala, and a host of their leaders and laypersons, came from this community. Pastor K. E. Abraham, co-founder and president of the Indian Pentecostal Church till 1974, was raised to become a Syrian Orthodox priest; another co-founder, Pastor P. M. Samuel, and the first president of the Indian Pentecostal Church of God, received training to become a priest in the Syrian Ortho-

---

5. Acts of Thomas, written in Syriac and dated in the fourth century AD, mentions that Saint Thomas, one of the twelve apostles, went to India to preach the gospel. For an English translation of this work, see A. F. J. Klijn, ed., *Acts of St. Thomas* (Leiden: E. J. Brill, 1962). Also see A. E. Medlycott, *India and the Apostle St. Thomas* (London: David Nutt, 1905). Though the work is described as apocryphal, scholars see in it a second-century tradition about the Apostle Thomas.

6. For a detailed discussion on the various sources regarding the origin of Christianity in Kerala, see A. M. Mundadan, *History of Christianity in India: From the Beginning up to the Middle of the Sixteenth Century (up to 1542)* (Bangalore: Theological Publications in India, 1984), pp. 21-66.

dox seminary; and another founder, Pastor K. C. Cherian, was a teacher in the church-run school and active in church activities.

The Syrian Christian community had recorded instances of revivals since the second half of the nineteenth century. Edwin Orr describes how as a result of these revivals new groups professing evangelical faith emerged from among the Syrian Christian community.[7] The first was the reformed Syrian church called the Mar Thoma Church and then a movement called Viyojitha Prasthanam (literally translated as the Separatist Movement) but better understood as the Holiness Movement. One stream of the Holiness Movement under the leadership of noted Malayalam poet K. V. Simon ended up in the Christian Brethren, and later the other led by K. E. Abraham ended up in Pentecostalism.

K. E. Abraham, a Holiness Movement leader in alliance with the Church of God (Anderson), was baptized in the Holy Spirit on April 20, 1923, in a meeting held by some native believers who believed in the baptism of the Holy Spirit and tarried for it. This was a turning point in the history of Syrian Christians in Kerala. The following years saw a great number of prominent Syrian Christian leaders embracing Pentecostal faith. K. C. Cherian, another schoolteacher and a former colleague of K. E. Abraham, joined the folds of Pentecostals in November 1924. P. T. Chacko became a Pentecostal believer in 1925 while he was a college student.

Pastor K. E. Abraham led a denomination called the Independent Separatist (Holiness) Church beginning in 1918 but was deserted by most of his followers for his doctrinal position on the Holy Spirit. He founded the South India Pentecostal Church of God along with the "faithful remnant" of his group who stood with him. In 1924 the Syrian Christian leaders who had been working independently of each other formed what was known as the South India Pentecostal Church of God (SIPCG). This can be considered the first indigenous Pentecostal denomination in India, now known as the Indian Pentecostal Church of God.

Arrival of Western Pentecostalism

Pentecostalism from the West arrived in Kerala in 1909 through the visit of George Berg. This American missionary of German descent arrived in

7. J. E. Orr, *Evangelical Awakenings in Southern Asia* (Minneapolis: Bethany Fellowship, 1975), pp. 134-39.

Bangalore in 1909 and preached in a Brethren convention in Kerala. Berg visited Kerala again in 1910 but had to confront tremendous opposition from the Brethren missionaries, forcing him to organize meetings on his own. Berg's third visit to Kerala was in 1911, in the company of an Indian missionary named Charles Cummins and Brethren expatriate missionaries Aldwinkle, Bouncil, and others, who received baptism in the Holy Spirit in the meetings of Thomas Barett. However, the first Pentecostal congregation was formed through the efforts of Berg in Kerala only in 1911. This was among first-generation Christians. Berg was the first missionary to reach out to the natives who did not speak English. Otherwise (foreign) Pentecostal mission was limited to people of foreign origin and those who spoke English.[8]

The next key player was Robert F. Cook, who came to India in 1912 following in the footsteps of Berg. Some of the congregations that Berg had founded joined the mission of R. F. Cook. At this stage, the former colleagues of Berg who were expatriate missionaries assisted Cook. Cook was able to establish many churches, particularly among the low-caste Hindus and Christians in Kerala. During his early days of mission work in India, Cook was an independent, but he later became a missionary affiliated with the Assemblies of God in the United States. Until 1926 Cook led a new Pentecostal denomination, the South India Full Gospel Church (SIFGC).[9]

Next in line to get involved in Kerala was Mary Chapman, who came to India as a missionary of the Assemblies of God in the United States in 1915. However, she was not involved in Kerala actively until 1921, since she stayed in Madras and only did itinerant work in South Kerala.[10]

The work of Western missionaries was mainly evangelism. They reached out to non-Christians (mainly low-caste Hindus) and to Christians who were the products of Western missionary efforts during the colonial period. However, their impact on Syrian Orthodox Christians was very low.

Western missionary influence on the spiritual formation of the leaders of the native movements was also minimal. Pastor K. E. Abraham, co-

8. G. E. Berg, "Feeding the Hungry in South India," *The Latter Rain Evangel,* April 1912, pp. 21-22.

9. R. F. Cook, *Half a Century of Divine Leadings and Thirty-Seven Years of Apostolic Ministry in South India* (Cleveland: Church of God, Foreign Missions Department, 1955).

10. Mary Chapman, "To Visit Travancore, South India," *The Pentecostal Evangel,* December 9, 1922, p. 13.

founder of Indian Pentecostal Church, claimed that he met the two leading figures of Western Pentecostalism, namely Chapman and Cook, only after he received his Pentecostal experience.[11]

The Clash Between Native and Foreign Pentecostalisms

With the arrival of the missionaries from the West in a land that already had a long Christian tradition and a burgeoning Pentecostal movement, Kerala turned out to be a contact zone for two streams of Pentecostalism that were one in their confession, experience, and rituals. Recorded history from both sides shows that they recognized the oneness of their faith and experience of the Holy Spirit and tried to travel together.

By 1923, there were three important Pentecostal movements in Kerala: the native movement by the name South India Pentecostal Church of God, the Assemblies of God under the leadership of Mary Chapman, and the South India Full Gospel Church under the leadership of R. F. Cook. In 1926, the South India Pentecostal Church of God and the South India Full Gospel Church merged to form the Malankara Pentecostal Church, with R. F. Cook as president and K. E. Abraham as vice-president. However, this did not last long. On January 30, 1930, the two movements that had merged to form Malankara Pentecostal Church of God parted ways to form SIPCG and SIFGC again.

This split was a rebellion of sorts and an adventure on the part of the native leaders. At that time, the native leaders were very much dependent on the financial support extended by Western missionaries. Financial and spiritual support from Western missionaries was very crucial because as the locals embraced Pentecostal faith, they were ostracized by their own community and also had to relinquish their ancestral property. Though penniless, and socially and economically vulnerable, the native leaders made the decision to part ways with the Western missions.

The native leaders also collaborated with the Assemblies of God missionaries, but this relationship also broke down after a few years. As Mary

11. He mentions that it was two months after he received baptism in the Holy Spirit that he met Pastor Cook, and that too was at the initiative of Cook. It was after three months that he met Ms. Chapman. He has devoted a section on how he met the "Western missionaries"; see K. E. Abraham, *Humble Servant of Jesus Christ (Yesukristhuvinte Eliya Dasan)* (Kumbanad: Pentecostal Young Peoples Association, 1965), pp. 86-87.

Chapman, the Assemblies of God missionary, moved to Kerala, the native leaders worked in collaboration with her colleagues. However, this cooperation came to a halt as the native leaders took a firm stand regarding financial dependence. Mary Chapman insisted (in line with the policy of her organization at the time) that she could fund church building projects only if the property was legally owned by the General Secretary of the Assemblies of God in the United States, while the native leaders insisted that the legal owners of the property be the local congregations. The native leaders considered this a violation of the freedom of the native churches and a covert attempt to bring the native movement under "western hegemony."[12] This led to the end of cooperation between the Assemblies of God and the Indian Pentecostal church in 1924, a breach that remains to be healed.

The native leaders' version of the conflict is reflected in various articles, leaflets, and the autobiography of Pastor K. E. Abraham. The native leaders described their experience of the Western missionaries using imagery of slavery: "being under the yoke of slavery" and "surrendering the freedom." The language had overtones of sarcasm when they described the ministry of the Western missionaries as "building for the sake of money" in the manner of "those who are employed by the government." Their refusal of financial support from the Western missionary organization was described as refusing to drink "the milk of the white cow." In defining the relationship with the Western missionaries they used terms like "autonomy," "independence," and so on.

The relationship and attitude of the native Pentecostal leaders towards the Western Pentecostal missionaries is reflected in three important sources. The first is a presidential speech made by Pastor K. E. Abraham in 1938 to a meeting of the representatives of IPC congregations. The second is the short history of Pentecostalism titled "Early Years of I.P.C.," and the third is the autobiography written by K. E. Abraham.

"Early Years of I.P.C." was written by K. E. Abraham in 1955. Whether he realized it or not, it was published on the twenty-fifth anniversary of the native Pentecostal leaders' parting of ways with the missionaries from Azusa Street! The purpose of this narrative is clearly stated in the introduction:

> The purpose of the publication of this book is that, those who have come to the Pentecostal fellowship recently and those youngsters who

12. Abraham, *Humble Servant*, pp. 142-43.

belong to the second generation of Pentecost must know about the details of early days Pentecostal ministry.[13]

K. E. Abraham, the co-founder of the Indian Pentecostal Church of God, was the first to write an autobiography as well. Published in 1965 and titled *Humble Servant of Jesus Christ,* it gives useful insights into how the native perceives himself and the alien. Though it is an autobiography of Abraham, he claims that it is the history of the denomination he headed: "My history, it is also the history of India Pentecostal Church of God."[14]

The Consciousness of "Syrianness" Among Native Pentecostal Leaders

Resistance to Subordination

In his studies on peasant insurgencies in India, Ranajit Guha has analyzed the reasons for such responses. Guha has pointed out that the reasons for rebellion should not be sought in external factors but in the consciousness of the native.[15] According to Guha, there are six elementary aspects of this consciousness: negation, ambiguity, modality, solidarity, transmission, and territoriality. The fourth of these, namely solidarity, which I would like to pay special attention to, is explained by P. Chatterjee:

> the self-definition of the insurgent peasant, his awareness of belonging to a collectivity that was separate from and opposed to his enemies, lay in the aspect of solidarity. . . . Often it was expressed in terms of ethnicity or kinship or some such affinal category. Sometimes one can read in it the awareness of a class.[16]

Chatterjee also suggests that this consciousness must have a history, which he goes on to describe:

13. K. E. Abraham, *The Early Years of I.P.C. (Malayalam),* 2nd ed. (Kumbanad, Kerala: Abraham Foundation Printers, 1986), p. i.

14. Abraham, *Humble Servant,* p. ii.

15. Ranajit Guha, *Elementary Aspects of Peasant Insurgency in Colonial India* (Delhi: Oxford University Press, 1983).

16. P. Chatterjee, "The Nation and Its Peasants," in *Mapping Subaltern Studies and the Postcolonial,* ed. V. Chaturvedi (London: Verso, 2000), p. 12.

Their experience of varying forms of subordination, and of resistance, their attempts to cope with changing forms of material and ideological life both in their everyday existence and in those flashes of open rebellion, must leave their imprint on consciousness as a process of learning and development.[17]

It is thus important to explore the consciousness and the history of this consciousness of the native leaders in order to understand their relationship and consequent dissociation with the Pentecostal missionaries from the West.

The Historical Roots of the "Syrianness"

One important aspect of this consciousness of the native is the fact that they are Syrian Christians. This "Syrianness" is evident in various autoethnographic remarks found in these narratives, especially in the autobiography of Pastor K. E. Abraham. He asserts his Syrian Christian identity through the description of his birth, his education, his brother's marriage, and of his own. In all these the leaders of native Pentecostalism affirm that they are Syrian Christians. The Syrian historical consciousness was dominant even after they became Pentecostals, renouncing their Syrian Christian ecclesiastical, theological, and ritual traditions. This is evident where, commenting on this issue, he uses the analogy of the relationship between the Roman Catholic Church and the Syrian Orthodox Church to explain the relationship with Pastor Robert Cook:

> Everybody knows that the Syrian community in Malankara was absorbed in the Roman Church for about fifty years in the seventeenth century and it came to its former state through the Coonen Cross Resolution by rejecting the relationship to the Roman Church. This does not mean that the Malankara church was founded after the resolution of Coonen Cross. Similarly, Indian Pentecostal Church of God had allied with the movement led by pastor Cook for a period of three years.[18]

17. Chatterjee, "The Nation and Its Peasants," p. 21.
18. Abraham, *Early Years of I.P.C.*, p. ii.

This Syrian Christian native consciousness influenced their imaging of the missionary, a fact that the missionaries from the West were totally uninformed of.

The Syrian churches were open to missionaries from overseas in the early years of Western missionary activity in Kerala. However, they did not allow the missionaries from overseas to invade their cultural, social, and ecclesiastical space. The Syrian metropolitans did encourage the missionaries to preach in their churches as long as they did not intervene with their own traditions and liturgical practices. However, the metropolitans did control the missionaries' activities. The cooperation with Western missionaries (mainly Anglican) went on in the area of Bible translation, production of literature, and allowing missionaries to hold evangelistic and revival meetings after the regular *Korbana* (liturgical service) in the church. Metropolitan Mar Dionysius sought the help of Claudius Buchanan to get the Bible printed in Syriac. In 1806 Buchanan got one hundred copies of the Syriac Bible printed. These were the first printed copies in Syriac that this community had ever had. During this time Mar Dionysius also got the Syriac version translated into the local language, Malayalam, and got it printed by the help of Buchanan.[19] Another metropolitan, Matthews Mar Athanasius, encouraged Western missionaries to visit and preach in the churches. However, this did not last long since the revival took on dimensions the Syrian church could not tolerate. In 1830, the Syrian Metropolitan Chepad Mar Dionysius (1827-1856) prohibited the work of the Western missionaries through an encyclical.[20] This had repercussions in the Syrian Christian community, as a number of enlightened Syrian Christians left the church and joined the Church Missionary Society. The major break came about half a century later by the formation of the Mar Thoma Church, a reformed Syrian church, in 1876.[21] The effect of this desertion and split is that the Syrian Christian community distanced themselves from the Western missionaries. It was more important for the

19. Claudius Buchanan's account of the translation and printing work is found in his book, *Christian Researches in Asia: With Notices of the Translation of the Scriptures into Oriental Languages* (London: T. Cadell & W. Davies, 1814), reprinted in Kuriakose Corepiscopa Moolayil, *Four Historical Documents* (Changanacherry: Mor Adai Study Centre, 2002), pp. 40-42.

20. For details, see C. P. Mathew and M. M. Thomas, *The Indian Christians of Saint Thomas* (New Delhi: ISPCK, 2005), pp. 48-80.

21. For details, see Mathew and Thomas, *Indian Christians*, pp. 81-95.

Syrian Christians to protect their cultural and ecclesiastical space from invasion than to see spiritual revival. Spiritual revival at the cost of ethnic and ecclesiastical identity was not negotiable.

Another significant instance is the alienation of the native leaders from the Western missionaries in the evangelical domain. The Christian Brethren movement gathered momentum in Kerala from 1897. It also commanded a good following, and the founding leaders were a German missionary by the name of Nagel (originally from the Basel Mission) and an Anglican missionary by the name of Grayson. Sometime in the early 1920s the Christian Brethren also faced a split. One of the native leaders, P. E. Mammen, advocated that the native churches should not be controlled by the foreign missionaries and began a movement for the freedom of native churches. Abraham mentions that he published a number of leaflets to promote his view that Western missionaries should not have control over the native churches. However, this led to a split in the Christian Brethren; the native leaders named their group "Syrian Brethren"![22]

The two incidents above suffice to illustrate how the consciousness of being a Syrian Christian superseded all other concerns.

The Formation of the Syrian Consciousness Among the Leaders

There are two key factors in the formation of this particular Syrian consciousness and a third historical factor that conditioned their imaging of the West. The first is the autonomy they enjoyed while being Christians in the Syrian Orthodox tradition; the second is the high social status they enjoyed under the Hindu rulers. The third is the effect European colonialism had on the Syrian Christian community.

The Syrian Christian community in Kerala belongs to the Syrian Orthodox tradition, and they still maintain a lively contact with their counterparts in the Middle East, particularly with the Syrian Patriarchate of Damascus. From time immemorial, the Syrian Orthodox See in Antioch has been the spiritual head of the church, while administration was in the hands of the local metropolitans. The relationship with the Middle East gave them an identity and determined their historical consciousness. This contact with the parent church had a setback due to the advance of Islam

---

22. Abraham, *Humble Servant*, p. 30.

into the Christian countries of the Middle East beginning in the seventh century, but contact was revived in the modern period.

Historically, the Syrian Christian community in Kerala enjoyed high social status as well. Around the seventh century, the local rulers of Kerala *(rajas)* recognized Christians as a higher caste and awarded them certain privileges and rights. This in fact helped Syrian Christians in Kerala to develop a sense of dignity and worth. The breakup of communication with the parent church in Syria helped in developing a sense of independence as well, which was upheld by the local Hindu rulers.[23] In the caste-ridden Indian society, this social status was crucial and had a great impact on their collective sense of dignity. Mundadan comments:

> Thus at the arrival of the Portuguese in India towards the close of the 16th century the Christians of St. Thomas were leading a life full of reminiscences of their past, and enjoying a privileged position in society and an amount of social and ecclesiastical autonomy. They had been leading a life at the core of which was an identity consciousness which, if not expressed in clear-cut formulas, was implicit in their attitude towards their traditions, their social, socio-religious and religious customs and practices, and their theological outlook.[24]

Syrian Christians Under European Colonialism

This situation was changed by the arrival of Vasco da Gama in Kerala on May 21, 1498. With the arrival of the Portuguese, the Syrian Christians of Kerala found themselves slipping slowly under the control of the Pope. The climax was reached in the year 1595, when Alexis de Menezes, the newly appointed Archbishop of Goa, landed in Kerala in order to submit

23. An anthropological study of the Syrian Christians is found in S. Visvanathan, *The Christians of Kerala: History, Belief and Ritual Among the Yakoba* (Delhi: Oxford University Press, 1999). In this study Visvanathan brings out the unique features of the Kerala Syrian Christian life, ritual, and beliefs and the relation of the Syrian culture to Hindu culture. For a very brief account of the integration of the Syrian Christians with the dominant Hindu culture, see Robert Eric Frykenberg, "Christians and Religious Traditions in the Indian Empire," in *The Cambridge History of Christianity: World Christianities, c. 1815-c. 1914*, ed. Sheridan Gilley and Brian Stanley (Cambridge: Cambridge University Press, 2006), vol. 8, p. 476.

24. A. M. Mundadan, *Indian Christians: Search for Identity and Struggle for Autonomy*, vol. 4 (Bangalore: Dharmaram Publishers, 1984), p. 28.

the church in Kerala to the control of the Roman Catholic Church.[25] In a letter Menezes wrote to Rome in 1597, he said his mission in Kerala was

> to purify all the churches from the heresy and errors which they hold, giving them the pure doctrine of the Catholic faith, taking from them all the heretical books that they possess. . . . I humbly suggest that [the Metropolitan] be instructed to extinguish little by little the Syrian language, which is not natural. His priests should learn the Latin language, because the Syriac language is a channel through which all that heresy flows. A good administrator ought to replace Syriac by Latin.[26]

The Synod of Diamper, which Menezes convened in 1599, was successful in forcing the Syrian Christians of Kerala to accept Portuguese domination.[27] C. B. Firth points out that after the synod, Menezes even burnt a large collection of books and documents belonging to the Syrian church wherever he could.[28] This was something that the Syrian Christians, who had been enjoying freedom and autonomy for more than fifteen centuries, could not stand. Revolt against foreign religious domination had already begun in 1595. This led to a large-scale revolt in January 1653, in which a huge gathering of Syrian Christians took an oath to fight for freedom. In the "Coonen Cross Resolution," as it was known, they declared themselves independent of the Roman Catholic Church.[29] In the revolt that ensued many Jesuit priests were targeted.

The freedom and social status they enjoyed for nearly two millennia gave the Christians a self-identity of dignity and independence. The Syrian Christian community's imaging of the Western missionary was conditioned

---

25. For the struggles of the Syrian Christians under Portuguese domination, see Mathew and Thomas, *Indian Christians,* pp. 29-43.

26. A. A. King, *The Rites of Eastern Christendom,* vol. 2 ([Rome: Catholic Book Agency] London: Burns & Oates, 1947), pp. 449-50.

27. A modern edition of the documents relating to the Synod of Diamper (also known as Udayamperur in Indian authors) is found in Scaria Zacharia, ed., *The Acts and Decrees of the Synod of Diamper 1599* (Edamata: Institute of Christian Studies, 1994).

28. C. B. Firth, *An Introduction to Indian Church History* (Madras: Christian Literature Society, 1968), p. 96.

29. The Malayalam adjective *coonen* means "bent" or "slanted." The tradition has it that those who took the solemn oath to leave the Roman Catholic Church and fight for the independence of the Syrian Christians tied a rope to a stone cross and took the pledge by holding the rope, since all of them could not touch the cross. The cross bent owing to the force of people trying to hold it, and thus this incident is known as the "Coonen Cross Pledge/Resolution."

by their experience of ecclesiastical domination under the Portuguese rulers and the Catholic Church. Their history was one of ecclesiastical and theological domination from which they had delivered themselves. While the Portuguese were still the political rulers, they made their church ecclesiastically independent of the Portuguese! They imaged themselves as people who had been invaded and who had freed themselves from the colonial powers.

The historical consciousness of the native Pentecostal leaders was Syrian at its core, shaped by the collective memories of their experience of the Portuguese rulers and the Roman Catholic Church as well as the European missionaries who invaded their space and from whom they consciously freed themselves.

The Theological and Ecclesiological Response of Indian Pentecostalism

Refusal to Reinvent the Holy Spirit

Operating within the framework of this historical consciousness, the native Pentecostal leaders' response has three important dimensions. The first is their refusal to let the Western missionaries reinvent the Holy Spirit in their contexts. The native Pentecostal in these narratives makes successful attempts to snatch history from the Western historians by guarding against any move to reinvent the Holy Spirit in Kerala. This he does by stressing that Pentecostal revivals regularly occurred in Kerala before Western Pentecostal missionaries arrived.

Abraham begins his history of Pentecostalism in Kerala by insisting that the revivals that took place in Kerala in 1873, 1895, and 1908 have to be taken as Pentecostal revivals.

> There were three powerful revivals that happened in the Malayalam speaking land during M.E. 1048, 1070, 1083 [A.D. 1873, 1895, 1908].[30] In all these three revivals people were filled with the Holy Spirit and spoke in other tongues. However, those who had these experiences in those days did not realise that they were speaking in tongues as they were endowed

30. M.E. stands for Malayalam Era, the calendar used in Kerala. AD 2001 is M.E. 1176-1177.

with the Holy Spirit; they did not have sufficient knowledge of scripture in this matter.[31]

Abraham snatches history from the West again by emphasizing that Pentecostal revival had reached Kerala before the first Pentecostal missionary arrived from the West. This he does indirectly by referring to his own personal experience of revivals before the advent of "Pentecostalism" in Kerala. He writes,

> I too was a participant in the spiritual revival that took place among the Christians of Kerala in 1908. I was only nine then. . . . I witnessed the power of God being poured out on many people and as a result of this their bodies being shaken, and they speaking with stammering lips. But I did not know what it was. However, only after I obtained the Pentecostal blessing I came to know what it really was.[32]

We noted earlier that he had attempted to exclude the Western missionary from his own personal experience of the Holy Spirit by claiming that it was after his Pentecostal experience that he met the two Pentecostal missionaries from America.

Western historians generally disregarded the pre-Pentecostal Holy Spirit revivals in India or failed to see any continuity between these and the Pentecostal churches. For example, Edwin Orr, noted historian of Christian revivals, concludes that until 1896 there had been no "Pentecostal outpourings where individuals exhibited a profound conviction of sin."[33] However, there is now a wider recognition of a fact that the native Pentecostals had been affirming in their discourses earlier: There are reports of the manifestation of the Holy Spirit in the second half of the nineteenth century (1872 onwards). The revival movement led by Justus Joseph (his English Christian name), a Brahmin convert to Christianity, was one of that sort. The non-Pentecostal native historian K. V. Simon has noted that in the services of this Christian movement there were revelations, dancing in the Spirit, etc., though he was critical of it.[34]

---

31. Abraham, *Early Years of I.P.C.*, pp. 5-6.
32. Abraham, *Humble Servant*.
33. Orr, *Evangelical Awakenings in Southern Asia*, p. 109.
34. K. V. Simon, *History of Holiness Churches in Malankara (Malankarayile Verpadu Sabhakalude Charithram)* (Idayaranmula, Kerala: n.p., 1938), p. 99.

Objection to Eurocentrism

The second aspect of their response is objection to the Eurocentric approach to Pentecostal history in India. Reaction against the Eurocentric presentation of Pentecostal history can be dated as early as 1955 in the narratives of native Pentecostal leaders. Twenty years after the foundation of the Indian Pentecostal Church, Pastor K. E. Abraham asserted that his denomination existed before the Pentecostal missionaries from the West established Pentecostal churches in India. In describing the purpose of the book in its introduction he says:

> Many people think that Indian Pentecostal Church of God is formed after the break with Pastor Cook. This is because of their ignorance of the early history of this movement. Readers of this book will realise that this movement (Indian Pentecostal Church) has been in existence under the name "South India Pentecostal Church" and for over three years worked in co-operation with the movement that was under the leadership of Pastor Cook and since the beginning of 1930 has been de-affiliated from this alliance.[35]

Earlier in his presidential address to the meeting of the representatives of IPC congregations in 1938 (eight years after the split) he asserted that

> Those who joined this fellowship recently may be surprised to know that it has been fifteen years since this movement started. Many think that this movement began after we left the relationship with Pastor Cook. It is not so! This movement was founded fifteen years ago by those ministers and congregations who accepted Pentecostal truth and decided to minister independently in central Travancore.[36]

And he went on to assert that

> Since Mr. Cook had convinced us that he is willing to work within the framework of independence of native congregations, we associated our movement then called "South India Pentecostal Church of God" with his movement along with the local congregations and ministers.[37]

35. Abraham, *The Early Years of I.P.C.*, p. i.
36. T. S. Abraham, ed., *The Sermons of Pastor K. E. Abraham* (Kumbanad, Kerala: K. E. Abraham Foundation, 1985), p. 1.
37. Abraham, *Sermons of Pastor K. E. Abraham*, p. 2.

He listed the number of congregations of the South India Pentecostal Church of God that they brought to this alliance and went on to conclude:

> From this it may be clear now that those who allege that Abraham and others ran away with Mr. Cook's people have not understood the reality of the matter. It may be now clear that it has been fifteen years since Indian Pentecostal Church began and has worked in association with the ministry of Cook for three and a half years.[38]

This illustrates that the natives who already had experienced contact with the West insist on being subjects of their own history. This important aspect of the native is something that needs to be taken seriously in considering relationships between the West and the East.

Rejection of Colonial Mimicry

The third aspect of this response I would call rejection of colonial mimicry. Postcolonial scholars have shown that colonialism has produced a class of interpreters between the colonizer and the colonized. This is a class of people who are natives by birth and physical features but in taste, in opinions, in morals, and in intellect are the colonizer. Frantz Fanon uses the phrase "black skin/white masks," to describe them, and V. S. Naipaul calls them "mimic men."[39] Homi Bhabha and others have developed this concept, calling it "colonial mimicry." In colonial mimicry the colonized pretend to have become one with those who have colonized them. V. S. Naipaul has described it thus:

> We pretend to be real, to be learning, to be preparing ourselves for life, we mimic men of the New World, one unknown corner of it, with all its reminders of the corruption that came so quickly to the new.[40]

On the part of the colonizers, they want to produce men who will resemble them in their tastes and morals, while on the part of the natives there is an

38. Abraham, *Sermons of Pastor K. E. Abraham*, p. 4.

39. See Frantz Fanon, *Black Skin, White Masks* (New York: Grove, 1967), English translation of *Peau noire, masques blancs* (Paris: Editions de Seuil, 1952).

40. V. S. Naipaul, *The Mimic Men* (London: Penguin, 1967), p. 146; cited by H. K. Bhabha, *The Location of Culture* (London & New York: Routledge, 1994), p. 88.

attempt to wear the colonial mask, to be one with the colonizers. Whatever direction this process takes in producing mimic men, the colonizer is constant and the change is towards that constant center.

Menezes had tried to produce such mimic men in the Syrian Christian community in Kerala, men who would speak Latin instead of Syriac and would become Roman Catholic in every way. The Coonen Cross Resolution has to be understood as a refusal by a certain section of the Syrian community to become such mimic men. In the line of those who refused to do colonial mimicry stand the Syrian metropolitans and the leaders of the Syrian Brethren movement, later to be joined by the native Pentecostal leaders.

Conclusion

In conclusion I should add that Pentecostal scholars from the non-Western countries need to explore ways in which they write the natives back into history and give them a due place in history. I must also say that even in the West, where historiography is mainly the venture of historians belonging to historical churches, Pentecostal historians need to engage in reconstructing the history of the Christian church from the edges.

In the light of the present study I submit that in such historiographical ventures, there is a great need to understand the historical consciousness of the natives. We need to ask what sort of historical memories they carry and what constitutes their consciousness of themselves and the Other.

Pentecostal historians also need to understand the language of domination and control in the contact zones of Pentecostalism. There is already rhetoric and discourse in place in almost all countries, which are developed as a result of their experience of colonialism. In trying to communicate the gospel it is important to understand how the native looks at the Other.

This approach to history also helps us clear up misconceptions about Christianity in general and Pentecostalism in particular in the colonized territories. In India at least, Christianity and colonialism are considered synonymous by those who advocate the Hindutva ideology. Hindutva reasons that Christianity was brought to India by the colonial powers, beginning with Roman Catholic missionaries following the Portuguese, and finally by the Anglican missionaries during the British Raj in India. They allege that the message and method of missionary work of the native Indian church is in continuity with that of the colonial missionaries. For them, the native missionaries are mimic men of colonialism.[41] However, postcolonial historiography helps give us snapshots of the natives' responses to Western missionaries and their historical consciousness, which is closer to that of their fellow natives than to the missionary from the West.

41. See A. Shourie, *Missionaries in India: Continuities, Changes, Dilemmas* (New Delhi: ASA Publications, 1995).

CHAPTER 6

Pentecostalism from Below: *Minjung* Liberation and Asian Pentecostal Theology

Koo Dong Yun

Traditionally, the birthplace of the twentieth-century Pentecostal movement is considered to be either the 1906 Azusa Revival or the 1901 Topeka Revival in the United States. Hence, many Pentecostals try to trace their lineage to these two revivals in order to appreciate and emphasize their roots. In other words, the perceived origin of Pentecostalism is America, and most American Pentecostals have imported this brand of Pentecostalism into overseas countries.[1]

Recently, however, some Pentecostal scholars have begun to challenge this assertion by maintaining that there is a multicultural component to the beginnings of Pentecostalism in the twentieth century. They for the most part tend to focus on black slave or African folk roots.[2] However, one also needs to add Asian origins in view of global Pentecostalism. Homegrown Asian Pentecostal movements, though still somewhat assisted by Western missionaries, were already blossoming before the arrival of American classical Pentecostal missionaries connected with the Azusa Revival.

1. See Stanley M. Burgess, ed., *The New International Dictionary of Pentecostal and Charismatic Movements* (Grand Rapids: Zondervan, 2002), p. xviii. This Western understanding is still prevalent in the introduction of this international dictionary. For another example, see Maynard Ketcham and Wayne Warner, "When the Pentecostal Fire Fell in Calcutta," in *Azusa Street and Beyond*, ed. L. Grant McClung Jr. (South Plainfield, NJ: Bridge Publishing, 1986), p. 26.

2. Byron Klaus, "The Holy Spirit and Mission in Eschatological Perspective: A Pentecostal Viewpoint," *Pneuma: The Journal of the Society for Pentecostal Studies* 27, no. 2 (2005): 328.

For example, K. E. Abraham, who was one of the founders of the Indian Pentecostal Church, averred that his Pentecostal denomination existed before the arrival of the missionaries of the Azusa-related churches. The traditional, Eurocentric or "Americentric" historiography of Pentecostalism more or less represents a "colonial," "imperialistic," and anachronistic construal, which was wrought by Western Christian scholars.[3]

Of course, Pentecostalism in Asia and Pentecostalism in North America share many common features; at the same, many differences exist between the two. For example, the early Pentecostal movements in India and Korea did not underscore the importance of speaking in tongues and the doctrine of the initial physical evidence as it was pushed by classical Pentecostals in the United States. Another difference is that classical Pentecostals carried a "separatist" proclivity, whereas early Pyongyang Pentecostals in 1907 exemplified an "ecumenical" or "unity" movement insofar as it united a variety of Christians from different denominations by the power of the Holy Spirit. Moreover, whereas most early classical Pentecostals in the United States chose to depart from the mainline denominations, the first Korean Pentecostals of 1907 stayed within the mainstream denominations such as Presbyterian and Methodist.

It is about time that Asian Pentecostals begin to explore "Pentecostalism from below." Instead of looking at it with the dominant Western colonizers' eyes, one needs to reinterpret it with a more native, non-Western, postcolonial viewpoint.[4] Pentecostalism is not exclusively owned by Americans and other Westerners. The historiography of the Pentecostal movement must be redirected and rewritten by native subjects, not exclusively by "colonizers," in order to bring forth more accurate and holistic pictures.

---

3. Paulson Pulikottil, chapter 5 of this volume, "One God, One Spirit, Two Memories: A Postcolonial Reading of the Encounter Between Western Pentecostalism and Native Pentecostalism in Kerala"; previously published as "As East and West Met in God's Own Country: Encounter of Western Pentecostalism with Native Pentecostalism in Kerala," *Asian Journal of Pentecostal Studies* 5, no. 1 (2002): 5-22. For a deeper understanding of post-colonialism, see Edward W. Said, *Orientalism* (New York: Vintage, 1979); Pui-lan Kwok, *Postcolonial Imagination & Feminist Theology* (Louisville: Westminster John Knox, 2005).

4. See Veli-Matti Kärkkäinen, "A Mapping of Asian Liberative Theology in Quest for the Mystery of God Amidst the Minjung Reality and World Religions," in *Asian Contextual Theology for the Third Millennium: Theology of Minjung in Fourth-Eye Formation*, ed. Paul Chung, Veli-Matti Kärkkäinen, and Kyoung-jae Kim (Eugene, OR: Pickwick, 2007), pp. 105-7. These postcolonial, indigenous attempts to rewrite and reinterpret Asian theology devoid of a long hegemonic Western influence are taking place in most Asian countries today.

In chapter 5, "One God, One Spirit, Two Memories," Paulson Pulikottil avers that Indian native "Pentecostalism" had been there long before the arrival of American Pentecostalism. To this, I want to add that Korean "Pentecostal" Christianity was already established prior to the arrival of classical Pentecostal missionaries influenced and disposed by the Azusa or Topeka revivals. "Pentecostalism" is broader and much more diverse and global even at its roots; however, many Western scholars have inculcated the notion that America is the only birthplace of the twentieth-century Pentecostal and charismatic movements. I want to refute this kind of narrow, colonial, egotistical, Western definition of Pentecostalism and try to reinterpret Pentecostalism from an Asian minjung perspective.[5]

This paper argues for three related theses: First, Asian Pentecostalism in its origins exemplifies more or less *a minjung movement* of the colonized, oppressed, and poor. Second, from the very beginning, modern (or twentieth-century) Pentecostalism has been multicultural and global, so it is imperative to add Asian origins in exploring the Pentecostal movements. Third, Asian Pentecostal theology in general typifies a holistic, "living" spirituality.

Minjung as the Subjects of Pentecostalism

Some people presume that *minjung* is a Korean word and only applicable to the particular Korean Christians who experienced political oppression in the 1970s. In this article, however, I argue that minjung in a broad sense existed long before the emergence of the minjung theology of the 1970s. Theologically, *minjung* means oppressed, alienated, exploited, and despised "people of God."[6] Thus, any group of people, even non-Koreans, can become a minjung vis-à-vis unjust and contemptuous treatment.

At the beginning of the twentieth century, most Asian countries remained colonies of the Western countries. From a Korean minjung view-

---

5. No single theological approach can exhaust the total reality or vitality of God and the world. Stories of minjung are not "metanarratives." A minjung approach, like any other human approach, comes with limitation and bias. See Michael Welker, *God the Spirit,* trans. John Hoffmeyer (Minneapolis: Fortress, 1994), p. 47.

6. The word *minjung* is a collective noun. Throughout this chapter, I use the word as singular when the word underscores the group as a unit, and I also regard it as plural when it highlights individual members of the group.

point, most peoples of Asia during this time represented "minjung" who suffered from the political oppression, social alienation, and economic exploitation of the Western and other imperialistic nations. For example, India was colonized by Britain, and Korea was colonized by Japan. In the face of this colonization, at least two kinds of minjung arose: (1) social-political and (2) Pentecostal. The social-political minjung has worked on social and political justice, whereas the Pentecostal minjung primarily has worked on spiritual, physical, and affective healing.

One can easily classify Pentecostalism as a "minjung" movement. In the United States, the Azusa Street revival exemplifies a minjung movement of the black people who have been racially discriminated against and economically exploited. In Korean Pentecostalism, it was the 1907 Pyongyang minjung, who had lost their national sovereignty to Japan and were alienated by many Japanese people. Indians at the beginning of the twentieth century also underwent political oppression and mistreatment by the imperialists of the British Empire.

At its roots, the twentieth-century Pentecostal movement was not primarily a white middle-class movement in which the participants were looking for exotic, supernatural, supervenient feelings, like an emotional high from a rock concert. At the center lay desperate and dejected people (minjung) who tried to survive each day. In other words, "subjects" and "biographies" of the primordial Pentecostals had to do with the "minjung" who had been alienated by the dominant class. By and large, the early Pentecostals in America and Asia could not afford to go to hospitals, so they went to local churches and prayed for their healing.[7] They also possessed *han* and anger toward colonizers and oppressors, but they were not allowed to express these negative emotions. Hence, they went to their churches and vented their frustration. Jesus Christ was there to listen to the testimonies and heartaches of these minjung! Pentecostalism at the outset was a religious movement of neither the bourgeoisie nor aristocrats, although some of the major Pentecostal denominations in the United States such as the Assemblies of God and the Church of God (Cleveland, TN) today have become more and more predominantly white middle-class denominations.

7. See Allan Anderson, "The Contextual Pentecostal Theology of David Yonggi Cho," in *David Yonggi Cho: A Close Look at His Theology & Ministry,* ed. Wonsuk Ma, William Menzies, and Hyeon-sung Bae (Baguio, Philippines: APTS Press, 2004), p. 159.

Revolutionary Aspects in the Lukan Writings

Although Pentecostals often have been accused of being overly "Lukan," I insist that Pentecostalism today is not Lukan enough. Most scholars agree that both Luke and Acts in the New Testament share the same author. More than any other Gospel, Luke shows a special interest in the poor.[8] Only in Luke's Beatitudes does it remark, "Blessed are *you poor,* for yours is the kingdom of God" (Luke 6:20). Unlike Matthew's version, it drops the phrase "poor *in spirit*" (Matthew 5:3).[9] In another case, Matthew 5:6a states, "Blessed are those who *hunger and thirst for righteousness.*" By contrast, Luke 6:21a says, "Blessed are you that *hunger now.*" Once again, Luke eliminated the words "for righteousness." Again, only Luke's Beatitudes have this sentence: "Blessed are you that weep now, for you shall laugh" (6:21b). Luke speaks of special blessings given to the poor, hungry, thirsty, and weeping, while woe is given to the rich (6:24).

In Luke's Gospel, a salient aspect of salvation deals with "liberating the poor and oppressed." In Luke 4:18-19, Jesus Christ reads a passage from Isaiah 61:1-2: "The Spirit of the Lord is upon me, because he has anointed me to preach good news to *the poor.* He has sent me to proclaim release to the captives and recovering of sight to the blind, to set at *liberty* those who are *oppressed,* to proclaim the acceptable year of the Lord."[10] According to Jesus, this passage not only refers to the futuristic eschaton, but the Day of the Lord or the year of Jubilee has also arrived. In Luke 6:21, Jesus claims to the Jewish people in the synagogue, "Today this scripture is fulfilled in your hearing."

Additionally, this passage alludes to the year of Jubilee (once every fifty years), when debts are remitted, slaves are liberated, and sins are forgiven. Moreover, Isaiah 61:1-2 also speaks of the liberation of Israel from the nation of Babylonia. One can infer from this passage that the good news involves not only one's individual personal salvation but also sociopolitical liberation. Salvation covers a revolutionary aspect, even though it calls for a nonviolent one.[11]

---

8. Marinus de Jonge, *Christology in Context: The Earliest Christian Response to Jesus* (Philadelphia: Westminster Press, 1988), p. 103.

9. In this paragraph, I am using the Revised Standard Version, 2nd ed.

10. Italics added.

11. Mark A. Powell, *What Are They Saying About Luke?* (New York: Paulist Press, 1989), pp. 86-89.

93

Acts 2 also reveals the "revolutionary" aspect of the last days between Pentecost and the Second Coming of Christ.[12] Not only will God pour out the Holy Spirit on Israelite kings, priests, and prophets, but God will also pour out the Spirit on *slaves* and *women* (Acts 2:18), who were more or less subjugated during the first century. Furthermore, they will also prophesy (Acts 2:18c).[13] The people (minjung) who have been oppressed and subjugated will receive the same or even more of the Spirit's blessings in these last days. With the outpouring on the day of Pentecost, the oppressed minjung with charismata were enabled to become the *center* and *subjects* of God's salvation history.

In terms of this revolutionary Lukan aspect, Pentecostals have not been Lukan enough. On the whole, the Pentecostal movement in the past has tended to underscore individual, spiritual, affective aspects of salvation, while it was not diligent in retrieving these liberationist aspects of the socio-political gospel.

From a minjung perspective, Pentecostalism remains foremost a Christian movement in which the powerless, weak, and oppressed become the powerful, strong, and liberated by the outpouring of the Holy Spirit.

Understanding Minjung in a Narrow Sense

Who are *minjung*? *Minjung* is a Korean word that derives etymologically from two Chinese characters. *Min* means "people," and *jung* signifies "the mass." Hence, *minjung* literally means "the mass of people."[14] But this understanding of minjung is grounded on Chinese etymology. Suk-hun Ham has sought to find an original Korean equivalent before the infiltration and domination of the Chinese language into the Korean culture. He comes up with the native Korean word *tsi-al,* literally meaning "seed."[15]

12. See French Arrington, *The Acts of the Apostles* (Peabody, MA: Hendrickson, 1988), p. 27.

13. In this passage Luke quotes from Joel 2:28-32.

14. The Commission on Theological Concerns of the Christian Conference of Asia (CTC-CCA), *Minjung Theology: People as the Subject of History*, ed. Yong Bock Kim (Maryknoll, NY: Orbis Books, 1981), p. 16; Boo-woong Yoo, *Korean Pentecostalism: Its History and Theology* (New York: Peter Lang, 1988), pp. 197-98. See also Paul S. Chung, *Martin Luther and Buddhism: Aesthetics of Suffering* (Eugene, OR: Wipf & Stock, 2002), pp. 109-10.

15. Suk-hun Ham, "Tsi-al-ui Cham-theut" [The True Meaning of Seed], in *Min-jung-*

Figuratively speaking, *minjung,* as the seed of the Korean soil, signifies the propagative source of living things such as humans, animals, plants, and so forth.

A theological translation of *minjung* refers to *the people of God* who do not possess political power, economic wealth, social status, and advanced education in contrast to the wealthy and dominant class.[16] This word, however, does not remain static; rather, it is dynamic and multifaceted. Thus, one cannot pin down this word with a precise definition, because various facets of minjung are rectified from time to time.

Byung-mu Ahn, a prominent minjung theologian from South Korea, finds a prototype *(ochlos)* of minjung in the Gospel of Mark. First, he introduces the two Markan words used to designate "the people" who followed Jesus in the first century: (1) *ochlos* (ὄχλος), and (2) *laos* (λαός). In the Gospel of Mark, the word *ochlos* was consistently employed in order to describe the people who gathered around Jesus. In contrast, Mark does not use the term *laos* except for the two instances in 7:6 (quoting directly from the Old Testament) and 14:2 (referring to the chief priests and lawyers). Furthermore, Paul in his epistles never employs this word *ochlos.*[17]

According to Ahn, Mark was the first one to start using the term *ochlos* in the New Testament, and it referred to the people who were labeled "sinners" and "tax collectors." These *ochlos* were alienated and persecuted by the ruling class. Jesus Christ expressed a special compassion toward them because they were like sheep without a shepherd (Mark 6:34). Jesus called the *ochlos* "his mother and his brothers" (Mark 3:34-35). These *ochlos* in Mark represented the "minjung" of Galilee.[18] In Mark, Jesus stood and befriended the *ochlos,* the minjung, and promised the future of God to them.[19]

Many people understand the word *minjung* with a narrow definition that only refers to the oppressed South Koreans who participated in the

kwa Han-kuk-sin-hak [Minjung and Korean Theology], ed. Committee of Theological Study of KNCC (Seoul: Korea Theological Study Institute, 1982), pp. 9-13. This book is written in Korean.

16. Yong-hak Hyun, "Minjung Sok-e Sung-yuk-sin-hae-ya" [To Be Incarnated Among Minjung], in *Minjung and Korean Theology,* p. 15.

17. Byung-mu Ahn, "Jesus and the Minjung in the Gospel of Mark," in Kim, ed., *Minjung Theology,* pp. 138-40.

18. Ahn, "Jesus and the Minjung," p. 141.

19. Ahn, "Jesus and the Minjung," p. 151.

socio-political Christian movement during the 1970s. Furthermore, minjung theology is delimited to a Korean theology that arose from the Christian experiences of being politically oppressed by Jung-hee Park's regime.[20] Also, minjung theology carries exclusively Korean stories of oppression and persecution. Although minjung theology remains a branch of "Korean theology," minjung as "the people of God" have existed long before the emergence of minjung theology in the 1970s and even go beyond the Korean national boundaries. Furthermore, minjung exemplifies a universal term that applies to a community of people who undergo alienation, oppression, discrimination, or exploitation.

Globalization of Minjung in a Broader Sense

The word *minjung* does not designate a fixed concept but a relational and fluid notion.[21] Minjung does not merely consist of a group of Koreans; in the truest sense, minjung transcends ethnic, racial, and national boundaries.[22] Boo-woong Yoo posits that *minjung emerge when common people undergo socio-cultural alienation, economic exploitation, or political oppression.*[23] For instance, a group of women become a minjung when they are dominated by men or a socio-cultural structure. An ethnic minority group becomes a minjung when they face political and economic discrimination by a dominant ethnic group. A particular racial group becomes a minjung when they experience discrimination by a race that is ruling.[24] Factory workers and farmers become a minjung as they are exploited by evil and selfish employers.

20. Kwang-sun David Suh, "A Biographical Sketch of an Asian Theological Consultation," in Kim, ed., *Minjung Theology*, p. 16.

21. Ahn, "Jesus and the Minjung," p. 150.

22. See Chung, *Martin Luther and Buddhism*, pp. 170-72. Chung elaborates on many forms of minjung in the Old Testament and New Testament times, such as the Jews in the Exodus, another group of Jews after the destruction of Jerusalem in A.D. 70, and later oppressed groups of Christians and Gentiles.

23. Yoo, *Korean Pentecostalism*, p. 205.

24. Cf. Jürgen Moltmann, "Minjung Theology for the Ruling Classes," in Chung, Kärkkäinen, and Kim, eds., *Asian Contextual Theology for the Third Millennium*, p. 71. Moltmann writes, "It [minjung theology] is a contextual theology of the suffering people in Korea, and is therefore open for people all over the world, the people of God's kingdom whom Jesus called blessed." Here he speaks of a global application of minjung theology.

Some of the Korean Christian minjung who had been marginalized and oppressed by the ruling class in the 1970s later became an upper-middle class or members of the ruling political party of South Korea in the 1980s and 1990s. These people who used to be the minjung in the 1970s were being accused by others of being "oppressors" as they became organized and acquired socio-political power. In other words, once being a minjung does not mean that they will remain always a minjung; some members of the minjung in the 1970s can become oppressors of other minjung in a later period, especially when a social or political revolution becomes successful.

The Black Pentecostal Minjung in America

Twentieth-century American Pentecostalism finds its real beginning in the Azusa Street revival in 1906, which was led by the black preacher William Seymour. From a Korean minjung perspective, the Azusa Revival can be considered a *black minjung movement.* These African Americans at the beginning of the twentieth century exemplified a minjung, who underwent racial discrimination and economic exploitation by the ruling classes. The Azusa Revival started in the poorer quarters of Los Angeles with the black people who were marginalized and oppressed.[25]

In January 1906, William Seymour, an African American student of Charles Parham, arrived in Los Angeles with a burning desire to preach the gospel. After some initial hardships, Seymour experienced one of the most vigorous revivals in church history. Soon, the Azusa Street revival caught the media's attention. As a result, thousands of people came to visit the Azusa Street Mission, and they went back to their home churches to report the excitement of what they had witnessed.[26]

About fifty years later, another mighty wind, *ruah,* of the Holy Spirit started to blow within mainline churches in the United States. Later, this wind came to be known as the "charismatic" or "neo-Pentecostal" movement. First, this "charismatic" movement occurred within mainline

25. Robert Owens, *Speak to the Rock: The Azusa Street Revival* (Lanham, MD: University Press of America, 1998), p. 64.

26. Koo Dong Yun, *Baptism in the Holy Spirit: An Ecumenical Theology of Spirit Baptism* (Lanham, MD: University Press of America, 2003), pp. 13-16. See Edith Blumhofer, *Restoring the Faith* (Chicago: University of Illinois Press, 1993), pp. 55-62.

Protestant churches (i.e., Presbyterian, Lutheran, and Anglican) and in
1967 spread to Roman Catholic churches.

The great Azusa Street revival in 1906, the benchmark of twentieth-
century Pentecostalism in America, represents a black minjung movement.[27] In actuality, the revival was spawned in the house of Richard and
Ruth Asberry located on 214 North Bonnie Brae Street, where "Negro
washwomen" constituted the primary audience.[28] The crowds became bigger and bigger than could be handled in a single house, so they had to meet
in the abandoned building at 312 Azusa Street.[29] Undoubtedly, in the beginning, the revival began with lower-working-class blacks, later joined by
other ethnic groups. According to Harvey Cox, the main constituencies of
the early stage of the Pentecostal movement were the poor, outcast, and despised people.[30]

The African American participants of the Azusa Revival typified a
minjung in America who possessed a suppressed *han,* a salient word of
minjung theology which denotes a deep feeling of grudge or despair.[31] The
Azusa Street Mission provided a setting in which the frustrated African
Americans were able to eject the suppressed emotions, such as fear, anger,
and shame by means of shouting-out and ejaculatory prayers.[32] This re-
leasing of the negative emotion was categorized as *han-pul-yi* by minjung
theologians.[33]

27. For more information on the black origins of Pentecostalism, see Walter
Hollenweger, "A Black Pentecostal Concept: A Forgotten Chapter of Black History: The
Black Pentecostals," *Concept* 30 (June 1970); Ithiel Clemmons, "True Koinonia: Pentecostal
Hopes and Historical Studies," *Pneuma: The Journal of the Society for Pentecostal Studies* 4
(Spring 1982); Walter Hollenweger, *Pentecost Between Black and White* (Belfast: Christian
Journals Limited, 1972).

28. Robert Anderson, *Vision of the Disinherited: The Making of American Pentecostalism*
(New York: Oxford University Press, 1979), p. 65.

29. Blumhofer, *Restoring the Faith,* p. 56.

30. Harvey Cox, *Fire from Heaven: The Rise of Pentecostal Spirituality and the Reshaping
of Religion in the Twenty-first Century* (Reading, MA: Addison-Wesley, 1995), p. 67.

31. Kwang-sun Suh, "The Korean Pentecostal Movement and Its Theological Understanding," in *A Study on the Pentecostal Movement in Korea* (Seoul: Korean Christian Academy, 1982), pp. 47-65.

32. Owens, *Speak to the Rock,* p. 74.

33. See Donald Gelpi, *The Conversion Experience* (New York: Paulist Press, 1998), pp. 34-
37. *Han-pul-yi* can be understood as part of affective conversion in Gelpi's categories.

The Indian Pentecostal Minjung in South Asia

Many Christians and scholars still attest that the Apostle Thomas was martyred and buried in South India.[34] In addition, many Syrian Christians migrated into Kerala (the southwestern state of India) in the fourth and eighth centuries, and some Christian churches in this state still have their allegiance to the Syrian Orthodox patriarch.[35] In this regard, the Indian church boasts a long tradition before the arrival of Western missionaries.

According to Gary McGee and Stanley Burgess, the Pentecostal and Pentecostal-like movements in India emerged at least forty years before the North American and European Pentecostal movements. Two major revivals in the southern states in India took place before the twentieth century. The first major one occurred in Tirunelveli (in Tamil Nadu state today) in 1860-61. This revival broke out after exposure to the revivals in the United States, England, and Ulster in 1857-1859. John Christian Aroolappen was the main leader of the revival, which manifested many charismatic gifts such as glossolalia, glossographia, interpretation of tongues, prophecy, dreams, visions, and other miracles. The next major revival took place in Travancore (in Kerala state today) in 1874-75. Two of the main leaders of this were Kudarapallil Thommen and Justus Joseph.[36]

Some of the noted characteristics of the revivals in Tirunelveli and Travancore were indigenous leadership and negation of caste. Participants of these revivals called for a liberation of people oppressed by the caste system and the composition of Christian music by Indian believers.[37] Hence, one can easily detect the liberation aspects from these early "Pentecostals" of India.

In accordance with Ivan Satyavrata, the origin of the twentieth-century Pentecostal movement in India is found at the Mukti Mission in Pune, India, in June 1905.[38] While Pandita Ramabai was teaching on John 8, her au-

---

34. Ivan M. Satyavrata, "Contextual Perspectives on Pentecostalism as a Global Culture: A South Asian View," in *The Globalization of Pentecostalism: A Religion Made to Travel*, ed. Murray Dempster, Byron Klaus, and Douglas Petersen (Oxford: Regnum, 1999), p. 204.

35. See Pulikottil, chapter 5, "One God, One Spirit, Two Memories," pp. 72-73 above.

36. Gary McGee and Stanley Burgess, "India," in *The New International Dictionary of Pentecostal and Charismatic Movements*, pp. 118-19. Hereafter, this dictionary is cited as *NIDPCM*.

37. McGee and Burgess, "India," p. 119.

38. Satyavrata, "Contextual Perspectives on Pentecostalism," p. 204.

dience started praying out loud, feeling a sensation of burning and conviction of sin, speaking in various tongues, crying aloud, and manifesting
other charisms. This Mukti Revival eventually spread to many other areas.[39]

The main leader of the Mukti Revival was Pandita (Sarasvati Mary)
Ramabai, who was known as a Christian saint in India. She wore many
hats, as a social reformer, scholar, visionary educator, and Pentecostal pioneer. In 1882, she became a widow mainly due to her Christian faith. In
1889, she opened her first home (the Sharada Sadan) for widows in Bom-
bay (Mumbai), which thereafter moved to Pune in 1895.[40]

Due to the bubonic plague and famines, this home had to move to
Kedgaon in 1900, where she created the Mukti Sadan. The Mukti Sadan
was a self-sufficient ashram with its own farm and services.[41] In this
home for dispossessed widows and deserted orphans, people experienced
the baptism in the Holy Spirit and "fire" — a burning sensation, and it
became known as a center for the twentieth-century Pentecostal movement in India.

From a minjung perspective, I can readily say that the early Indian
Pentecostal movements found in Tirunelveli, Travancore, and Kedgaon
represent minjung liberation movements. One needs to remember that India during this time period was a colony of the British Empire. These Pentecostal revivals were led by native, colonized Indians, and some of the
participants attempted to abolish the oppressive caste system. At Mukti,
one of the most influential Christian revivals in South Indian history
broke out among these deserted women and children led by the
marginalized widow Ramabai. To these colonized, oppressed, deserted
minjung in India, God chose to pour out the Holy Spirit, and this revival
epitomized a true origin of Asian Pentecostalism.

---

39. J. Edwin Orr, *Evangelical Awakenings in India* (New Delhi: Masihi Sahitya Sanstha,
1970), pp. 110-11.

40. R. V. Burgess, "Ramabai, Sarasvati Mary (Pandita)," in *NIDPCM*, p. 1017.

41. Karl Sabiers, *Little Biographies of Great Missionaries* (Los Angeles: Robertson Publishing, 1944), p. 59.

The 1907 Pyongyang Pentecostal Minjung in Korea

The Historical Context of the 1907 Pyongyang Revival

Beginning in 1903, several local revivals preceded the 1907 great Pyong-yang revival. Hence, Christians in Korea already sensed a great revival coming to their land.[42] Robert A. Hardie, a Methodist missionary, led many revivals on the northeast coast of Korea. As a result, it was esti-mated that ten thousand Koreans turned to Christ during 1904.[43] The re-vival on the east coast continued and grew bigger and bigger in 1906. Hence, many Presbyterian and Methodist missionaries were quite satis-fied with the results of 1906 and did not expect anything bigger than what they had seen in 1906.

In September 1906, however, Korean Christians were exposed to the Kassia Hills revival in India (1905-06) through the sermons of Howard Agnew Johnston. He reported that 8,200 converts had been baptized in the Kassia Hills during the two years. These statistics about the Kassia Hills challenged the missionaries in Pyongyang, so they gathered and prayed ev-ery day for a great revival in Pyongyang.[44]

The annual Bible training class met at the Central Presbyterian Church of Pyongyang from January 2 to 15, 1907. There were more than 1,500 Christians, mainly consisting of Presbyterians and Methodists. Dur-ing the daytime, they focused on Bible study; during the night, evangelistic worship took place. At one of these evening worship services, the great Pyongyang revival broke out.[45]

The great Pyongyang revival began during the Monday-night service at the Central Church of Pyongyang *(Jang Dae Hyun),* which occurred on January 14, 1907.[46] During the noon prayer meeting on Monday, people were praying earnestly for a revival. When people entered the church building that night, the presence of the Holy Spirit seemed to overtake

---

42. Young-hoon Lee, "Korea Pentecost: The Great Revival of 1907," *Asian Journal of Pentecostal Studies* 4, no. 1 (2001): 73-74.

43. Jonathan Goforth, *When the Spirit's Fire Swept Korea* (Cavite, Philippines: Presbyte-rian Theological Seminary, 1956), p. 8.

44. Goforth, *When the Spirit's Fire Swept Korea,* pp. 8-10.

45. Yoo, *Korean Pentecostalism,* p. 79.

46. C. Hope Flinchbaugh, "A Century After North Korean Revival: Dreams of an En-core," *Christianity Today,* January 31, 2007.

them. Graham Lee and William Blair were the only two foreign missionaries present at the beginning of the revival.[47] Following a short sermon, Mr. Graham Lee, who was an American Presbyterian missionary, called for prayers. He said, "If you want to pray like that, all pray."[48] So the whole congregation started to pray out loud together. (For Koreans, this shout-out prayer is known as *Tong-sung-ki-do*.) Regarding the effect of shout-out prayer that night, William Blair writes, "The effect was indescribable — not confusion, but a vast harmony of sound and spirit, a mingling together of souls moved by an irresistible impulse of prayer."[49]

There were other noticeable phenomena occurring that Monday night besides *Tong-sung-ki-do*. People in the church confessed their sins publicly with little hesitation. Some with contrite hearts confessed their hatred against the Japanese. Others in tears confessed their bitterness against foreign missionaries. One person confessed his hatred toward the Reverend Blair.[50] Another great noticeable phenomenon was a great sound of weeping. Almost everyone in the building wept. *Chul-ya-ki-do* (all-night prayer vigil) was also an eye-grabbing event. Lord William Cecil, an English eyewitness of the revival, stated, "From eight in the evening till five in the morning did this same go on."[51] Others were also beating the floor with either fists or heads. Some of the congregation also raised their arms outstretched toward heaven. Indubitably, the whole place was filled with emotion.[52]

The Participants of the 1907 Pyongyang Revival as a Minjung

The Korean people in 1907 were a minjung who had been oppressed, exploited, and discriminated against by the Japanese. In the 1890s, Korea became the battleground between China and Japan and between Russia and Japan. As a result, Koreans suffered greatly from these wars, and soon were under the control of all these nations at once. Thus, Korea was losing its

47. William Blair and Bruce Hunt, *The Korean Pentecost and the Sufferings Which Followed* (Carlisle, PA: The Banner of Truth Trust, 1977), p. 8.

48. Blair and Hunt, *The Korean Pentecost*, p. 71.

49. Blair and Hunt, *The Korean Pentecost*, p. 71.

50. Blair and Hunt, *The Korean Pentecost*, p. 73.

51. Yoo, *Korean Pentecostalism*, p. 80.

52. Blair and Hunt, *The Korean Pentecost*, pp. 72-73.

autonomy. The Japanese protectorate of Korea began in 1905, and finally Japan annexed Korea into their empire in 1910. Hence, when the Pyongyang revival broke out in 1907, Korea had already lost her political independence. Koreans of this time were politically oppressed and economically exploited. Losing their national independence to Japan, many Koreans lived with shame, guilt, and *han* (deep grudge). Even in the midst of Japanese oppression though, Koreans seemed to have some religious freedom.

The Pyongyang revival was by no means a spiritual movement led by the ruling *yangban* class in Seoul. By and large, most participants and leaders of this movement came from the northern parts of Korea, not from the greater Seoul area where most people of the ruling class resided. The leaders of the revival more or less did not stem from the ruling Confucian *yangban;* rather, they came from the predominantly lower and middle classes. The main leader of the revival, Seon-ju Kil, who had been a devout Daoist herbalist before he converted to Christianity, grew up in a deprived family.[53] He later became an ordained Presbyterian minister and turned out to be the leading and most conspicuous Korean leader of the 1907 revival.[54] Even in looking at the revival from a traditional Korean perspective, the Pyongyang revival exemplified a minjung movement for minjung people at the turn of the twentieth century.

Even though there was not much socio-political freedom given to Koreans during the second half of that decade, some religious freedom was allowed by the Japanese. As a result, many Christian churches afforded healthy and safe settings where wounded Koreans gathered and shared their frustration and negative feelings. Through various Bible study groups and evangelistic worship services, many Koreans in Pyongyang eventually experienced religious conversion by encountering Jesus Christ.

During the revival, it is evident that *affective conversion* also took place. These Koreans suppressed negative emotions, such as guilt, shame, fear, and anger under the rule of Japan, and they needed to be released in order to be emotionally healthy; otherwise, dysfunctional personalities

---

53. See Sung-deuk Oak, *"Pyongyang Dae-bu-heung-un-dong-kwa Kil-sun-ju Yung-sung-eui Do-kyu-jeok Yung-hyang"* [Spiritual Seismic Shifts Among the Daoist-Christians in Pyongyang: Kil Sun-ju's Daoist-Evangelical Spirituality During the Great Revival Movement], *Han-kuk-ki-dok-kyo-oa Yuk-sa* 25 (September 2006): 57-96.

54. For more information on Kil, see Jae-hyun Kim, "Indolence" [*On Haeta*], *KIATS Theological Journal* 1, no. 1 (2005): 86-95.

would develop. The churches during this time were able to provide many opportunities for Koreans to vent their suppressed emotions. The records indicated that some people at the revival meeting cried out loud and prayed out loud (a form of catharsis). Others were beating the floor with fists or their heads and screaming in agony *(han-pul-yi)*.[55] Many of these oppressed Koreans were able to release their *han*. As a result, many of them during worship services were able to retrieve positive emotions such as sympathy, affection, friendship, love, and forgiveness. Some Korean Christians even confessed their hatred toward the Japanese and asked for God's love in order that they could forgive the Japanese.

The Pyongyang Revival as a Pentecostal Movement

In order to construe the 1907 Pyongyang revival as a paradigmatic Pentecostal movement, one first has to define the essence or distinctiveness of Pentecostalism. The author contends in *Baptism in the Holy Spirit* that three salient features of the American Pentecostal movements are (1) the Lukan orientation, (2) the vitality of experience, and (3) the verifiability of the Spirit.[56] And these features are easily found in that revival. An American eyewitness of the revival, William Blair, compared this revival with the Pentecost event in Acts 2.[57] Moreover, many participants not only experienced the living Christ but also affective conversion by being liberated from guilt, shame, fear, and anger. Furthermore, James Gale, a Presbyterian missionary, reported the occurrence of glossolalia during the revival.[58] Therefore, even when one analyzes the 1907 Pyongyang revival with an American Pentecostal lens, it will be hard to deny that the Pyongyang revival was a "Pentecostal" movement. I have argued, however, that it is better to interpret the twentieth-century Pentecostal movements as multicultural, global phenomena even from the outset.

---

55. Blair and Hunt, *The Korean Pentecost*, p. 72.
56. Yun, *Baptism in the Holy Spirit*, pp. 131-45.
57. Blair and Hunt, *The Korean Pentecost*, pp. 71-72.
58. James Gale, *Korea in Transition* (New York: Eaton & Mains, 1909), p. 216.

The Socio-Political Minjung

In *Korean Pentecostalism: Its History and Theology,* Boo-woong Yoo introduces two kinds of minjung: (1) socio-political and (2) Pentecostal.[59] The socio-political minjung primarily fought for social and political justice, whereas the Pentecostal minjung mostly worked on spiritual healing of the nation. Indubitably, both kinds of minjung were needed in order to liberate the Korean nation. In the face of the political oppression and economic deprivation in the 1970s, the socio-political minjung in South Korea arose in order to bring political liberation and appropriate distribution of revenues to companies. The participants of this minjung movement often had to undergo house-arrests, torture in prison cells, and even loss of life.[60]

Minjung theology in Korea emerged in the context of the political oppression of the dictator Jung-hee Park and the economic deprivation of city workers and rural peasants. During the 1970s, the fall of South Vietnam into the hands of the Vietnamese communists, and North Korean threats of invading South Korea helped Park increase his dictatorial measures. With the excuse of maintaining the national security of South Korea, he often manipulated the crowds and eliminated his political opposition.[61]

Modern industrialization in South Korea truly took off in the 1970s through modernization and urbanization. At that time, South Korea did not possess the natural resources, capital, and technology that were essential for economic growth, but it had a relatively well-educated, industrious workforce.[62]

Park's regime borrowed capital from wealthy foreign countries and distributed it arbitrarily by choosing the entrepreneurs who would support his dictatorship. Park's regime solely focused on economic growth and at the same time severely undermined the welfare of workers. This eventually engendered protest movements in South Korea.[63] Under these circumstances a group of theologians and Christian ministers issued "The Declaration of Korean Christians 1972," which urged people to fight for the poor and suffering minjung.

During the second half of the 1970s, many theologians endeavored to

59. Yoo, *Korean Pentecostalism,* p. 220.
60. Suh, "A Biographical Sketch," p. 16.
61. Yoo, *Korean Pentecostalism,* p. 191.
62. Yoo, *Korean Pentecostalism,* p. 191.
63. Yoo, *Korean Pentecostalism,* p. 192.

delineate minjung theology. Several articles were published in a variety of journals, and soon minjung theology grabbed the attention of many Koreans as well as Christians outside Korea.[64] The Commission on Theological Concerns of the Christian Conference of Asia and the Korean National Council of Churches sponsored the Asian Theological Consultation, held in October 1979.[65] This setting afforded international, interdenominational, and interdisciplinary dialogues among its participants, and as a result minjung theology became known globally.

Without a doubt, most socio-political minjung belonged to the powerless, oppressed, uneducated, and underprivileged groups, but many point out that minjung *theologians* did not. A frequent criticism of these minjung theologians is that they were not "subjects" of the minjung movement; rather, they remained the "objective observers" who wrote and sold the minjung biographies for their own benefit and credit. It is evident that some minjung theologians reflected the elite class who were highly educated. On the contrary, the real subjects of the political minjung did not receive any credit, and often died without social and medical help. One may still argue that "minjung theology" does not represent the authentic socio-political minjung; rather, it is an aristocratic, objective reflection on the suffering of the minjung.

The Pentecostal Minjung Experiencing Affective and Physical Conversion

The author endorses six forms or elements of conversion. In *The Conversion Experience,* Donald Gelpi expatiates upon five forms of conversion. In addition to Bernard Lonergan's three kinds of conversion (namely, intellectual, moral, and religious), Gelpi supplements two more kinds: affective and socio-political conversions. Hereto, the author adds "physical" conversion. The six kinds or forms of conversion remain distinct and interrelated, but they are not separable. The six forms resemble one another in two ways: (1) Each form engages "a turning from" and "a turning to." (2) Each converts from the irresponsible living to the responsible life. Out

64. Kwang-sun David Suh, "Korean Theological Development in the 1970s," in Kim, ed., *Minjung Theology,* p. 41.
65. Suh, "Korean Theological Development," p. 41.

of the six forms of conversion, five — all except for religious conversion — can transpire in secular and natural settings. A human can initiate these five kinds of conversion, but religious conversion only God can initiate.[66]

The first conversion that Gelpi addresses is *moral conversion*. In the realm of morality, there are two subcategories: (1) personal moral and (2) socio-political. Out of the two, Gelpi experienced a *personal moral conversion* first. Reared in the Deep South, Louisiana, Gelpi grew up with racial prejudice. He believed at the time that African Americans were essentially inferior to white people. This racial bias represented the conventional morality in the Deep South, and Gelpi bought in to this attitude. An initial moral conversion took place while attending a high school where Jesuits incessantly condemned racism. Eventually, he conceded and renounced it in his heart. Gelpi points out that in many cases, one needs to break away from "traditional" and "conventional" morality, which comes with both virtue and vice. Hence, a mature adult conscience must go beyond conventional morality into "autonomous" morality, constituted by examined, self-critical beliefs. Simply having a noetic admission is not good enough; one should act upon it responsibly.[67]

The second form of conversion refers to *socio-political conversion*, which deals with larger, social institutions such as government, the economy, class structure, and ecclesiastical structure. Whereas personal moral conversion mainly focuses on personal rights and duties, socio-political conversion pays attention to the universal, common good. Several years after renouncing racial bigotry, Gelpi became actively involved with the political and social fight against racism — this could have been counted as his initial socio-political conversion. Fighting against world hunger, nuclear disarmament, and environmental preservation exemplify acts of socio-political conversion.[68]

The third form of conversion is *intellectual conversion*. When one takes personal responsibility for the truth or falsity of one's beliefs and for the adequacy or inadequacy of the frames of reference, an intellectual conversion occurs. Many modern scientific studies have been presented with in-

---

66. Donald Gelpi, *The Conversion Experience: A Reflective Process for RCIA Participants and Others* (New York: Paulist Press, 1998), pp. 24-25.

67. Gelpi, *The Conversion Experience*, pp. 29-30.

68. Gelpi, *The Conversion Experience*, p. 31.

adequate frames of reference. These reductionistic frames of reference allow neither the asking nor answering of necessary questions. For instance, Newtonian physics does not possess a frame of reference to aptly explain genuine human free will.[69]

Truth can be grasped rationally and imaginatively. Rational truth is derived by logical and inferential thinking, whereas imaginative truth is available through art, poetry, and literature. By unduly focusing on rational truth, modern sciences tend to undermine the realm of imaginative truth. Hence, intellectual conversion also takes place when one realizes one's inadequate frame of reference.[70]

When human beings are young, we usually follow the teachings of our parents or pastors, and do so without serious critical reflection because we simply trust them. In other words, we follow their conventional wisdom. Many young people neither have the courage nor maturity to go beyond conventional beliefs. A person converts intellectually when one descries some aspects of prejudice or error in his or her conventional belief system. Every communal horizon has some truths and some unverifiable prejudices. Intellectual conversion signifies that a person cannot simply accept everything taught by reliable people even including parents and pastors. Although we should respect their mature wisdom and opinion, they too are fallible beings, and even they are not exempt from error or falsity. Acquiring truth involves more than mere memorization and confessing of creeds; it requires an active mind and critical analysis.[71]

The fourth kind of conversion is described as *affective conversion*, which promotes personal emotional health. Empirical and clinical studies of human emotion reveal that suppressed negative emotions tend to bring forth psychological problems. Negative emotions include shame, fear, anger, and guilt, whereas positive emotions embrace sympathy, affection, friendship, love, and forgiveness. Nonetheless, the systemic suppression of negative emotions engenders a variety of personality dysfunctions. Nervousness exemplifies the first level of dysfunction. Emotional rigidity, antisocial behavior, self-hatred, and suicide are examples of the severe suppression of negative emotions.[72]

---

69. Gelpi, *The Conversion Experience*, p. 33.
70. Gelpi, *The Conversion Experience*, p. 34.
71. Gelpi, *The Conversion Experience*, p. 34.
72. Gelpi, *The Conversion Experience*, pp. 34-35.

Physical conversion stands as the fifth form of conversion. Salvation is much more than a personal, individual conversion. Salvation involves the conversion of the entire creation with *ji* (cognition), *jung* (emotion), *eui* (action and physicality). All of God's creation *(ktisis)* is longing for salvation (Rom. 8:20-22). The earth needs to be liberated from various kinds of pollution and abuse by modern industrialization. Our human bodies too need to undergo a physical conversion from a deviated, diluted, and sick body to a well, functional, glorious body (Rom. 6:23).

Religious conversion exemplifies the sixth form of conversion. In contrast to the other five kinds of conversion, God alone initiates this religious conversion, to which humans respond. Religious conversion transpires in the realm of faith. Religious conversion assumes an authentic encounter with God or a transcendental reality. The reality of God has been revealed through the incarnation of the Son and the action of the Holy Spirit.[73]

In Gelpi's terminology, the Pentecostal minjung for the most part worked on affective and physical conversion. The solid labors of the working class were exploited systematically by owners and employers, so that many hard-working people were struggling to pay for their basic necessities such as rent and groceries. In addition, people could not express their feelings of political repression by Park's dictatorship. These conditions of the working class created a great frustration among various minjung. The negative feelings of frustration were vented in many Pentecostal/charismatic churches. As a result, minjung experienced *affective conversion*. In addition, through many hours of labor with toil and moil, the bodies of minjung became ill and ailing, but they could not afford to seek medical treatments. Therefore, they went to God on their knees and prayed all night long for a divine healing *(physical conversion)* so that they could bring their ragged bodies to work in order to earn enough money for one more day of survival.

The Korean Pentecostal Minjung in the 1970s

The groundbreaking book of minjung theology entitled *Minjungkwa Hankuksinhak (Minjung and Korean Theology)* was first published in 1982.

---

73. Gelpi, *The Conversion Experience,* pp. 37-39.

In this Korean book, David Kwang-sun Suh endeavored to find minjung as well as a particular theology done by real minjung. Surprisingly, he found other minjung in the Pentecostal/charismatic movement.[74] "Recently," he wrote, "I visited various places of the 'Spirit Movement' [Pentecostal/charismatic movement], which was also creating some controversy among Korean Christians, and I saw an incredible growth of these churches with healing and glossolalia [speaking in tongues] of the Holy Spirit. In this movement, I found and met *minjung*."[75] Suh detected the other side of minjung in nondenominational and Pentecostal/charismatic churches. Numerous members of the Korean minjung found encouragement, consolation, and spiritual healing from the Pentecostal fellowship of the Yoido Full Gospel Church in Seoul, the largest Christian church in the world in terms of numbers. Boo-woong Yoo labeled these Korean participants the "Pentecostal minjung."[76]

Suh argues further that these Pentecostal minjung rediscovered the importance of pneumatology and gifts of the Holy Spirit such as healing and mystical experiences. They have been allured by the Spirit's power and hypnotized by propaganda and powerful manifestations in their Pentecostal/charismatic churches. Suh more or less construes the Korean Spirit/ Pentecostal movement as a rebellion against the traditional Confucian hegemony. The major problems in this movement, however, arose when it became more and more shamanistic and material-success oriented instead of participating actively in the suffering of the oppressed, alienated minjung.[77]

Unlike the Pentecostal movement in America, whose adherents left the mainline denominational churches and created their own churches and denominations, most participants of the Spirit/Pentecostal movement in

---

74. The Korean phrase translated by the author as the "Pentecostal-Charismatic movement" literally means "Spirit Movement." This movement remained interdenominational and ecumenical insofar as many Presbyterian, Methodist, Holiness, and Baptist churches participated in it.

75. Kwang-sun Suh, "Minjungkwa Sunglyung" [Minjung and Holy Spirit], in *Minjung and Korean Theology* (Seoul: Korea Theological Study Institute, 1985), p. 303, author's translation.

76. Yoo, *Korean Pentecostalism*, pp. 205-6.

77. Suh, "Minjungkwa Sunglyung" [Minjung and Holy Spirit], pp. 310-16. Harvey Cox also notices the success- and quantity-oriented tendency of Korean Pentecostalism (see Cox, *Fire from Heaven*, p. 234).

Korea stayed in their traditional denominational congregations and worked on revival and renewal of their churches. As a matter of fact, many Korean mainstream denominations — including Presbyterian and Methodist — carry "Pentecostal" elements in their spirituality. Therefore, in order to comprehend the reality of the Pentecostal minjung, one should include not only Pentecostal-denomination churches (e.g., the Korean Assemblies of God) but also the mainstream Christians who robustly engaged in the Spirit/Pentecostal movement in Korea.

During the 1970s in South Korea, political oppression, economic exploitation, and dehumanization elicited numerous negative emotions among the Korean minjung. These negative emotions needed to be released in various forms of catharsis. The systemic suppression of negative emotions gradually brought forth *han*. Many public demonstrations took place in the 1970s — such as marching in the streets and throwing pieces of rock and Molotov cocktails in their fight against puppets of the dictator Park — which helped the Korean socio-political minjung release their negative emotions. This was a method of *han-pul-yi* (catharsis) by the socio-political minjung.

The Pentecostal minjung in the 1970s, in contrast, sought for a different cathartic means, such as revival meetings and Pentecostal/charismatic worship services. In August 1974, a national, ecumenical revival crusade, titled "EXPLO '74," was held in Seoul. This crusade was led by the Pentecostals Yonggi Cho and Joon-gon Kim. On the first night, more than a million people attended the meeting. The author, having attended the crusade, detected emotional release of people's frustration by means of *Tong-sung-ki-do* (shouting-out, ejaculatory prayer), clapping, crying, and speaking in tongues. This crusade not only provided a setting for religious conversion (personal evangelism), but it also brought forth affective conversion (emotional healing). The Korean minjung underwent emotional, affective healing by venting their *han*.

During the 1970s, the Yoido Full Gospel Church in Seoul remained a home for many Pentecostal minjung who possessed neither economic wealth nor social status. Some of these Pentecostal minjung lived in poverty-stricken slums (known as *pan-ja-chon*) and could not attend worship services of the mainline churches in Seoul inasmuch as they could not even afford to dress up on Sunday. To these minjung belonging to the lowest of the low, David Yonggi Cho preached *sam-bak-ja-ku-won* (three-beat salvation) and *o-jung-bok-eum* (the fivefold gospel) so that these Pentecostal minjung could procure hope and "will to live."[78] Cho was especially well known for his three-beat salvation on the basis of 3 John 1:2, which spoke of three key elements in one's salvation: (1) spirit, (2) body, (3) environment.[79] Cho asserted that redemption or salvation of Christ was much broader, deeper, and wider than merely "spiritual."[80] To put it another way, Cho was teaching a (w)holistic, "living" Asian soteriology in contrast to a noetic, speculative, Euro-American soteriology.[81] To the dying and suffering minjung without a chance to receive medical treatments, Cho suitably introduced the Full Gospel of hope by preaching healing in the atonement as well as physical and financial blessings available via the ransom of Christ on the cross. Consequently, many Pentecostal minjung underwent miraculous divine healing and regained hope and the will to live.

In the past, many mainline Christians in South Korea (e.g., Roman Catholics, Presbyterians, Methodists) accused the Pentecostal minjung of not participating in the socio-political aspect of the gospel. This criticism finds some warrant, but the Pentecostal minjung still engaged in various forms of socio-political conversion, albeit in a more subtle way. They endeavored to implement the teaching of Matthew 6:3, "But when you give to the needy, do not let your left hand know what your right hand is doing." So their activities were not as visible as those of the socio-political minjung, who were marching on the streets against Jung-hee Park's regime and creating labor unions. As a result, these socio-political minjung received the attention of the media, both domestically and internationally. In contrast, the Pentecostal minjung engaged in social action quietly by providing essential items such as rice for starving families (known as *ku-je-sa-up*). They prayed for political progress in Korea and encouraged people to vote. Surely, they did not endorse revolutionary theology, but promoted the principles of democracy. But more importantly, charismatic/Pentecostal churches provided the places where these wounded and oppressed minjung could find rest and emotional healing. At the same time, the

78. See Veli-Matti Kärkkäinen, "March Forward to Hope: Yonggi Cho's Pentecostal Theology of Hope," *Pneuma* 28, no. 2 (2006): 253-63.

79. Yonggi Cho, *Seong-kong-ae Yi-leu-neun Ji-he* [Wisdom That Produces Success] (Seoul: Yong-san, 1976), p. 44.

80. Cho, *Seong-kong-ae Yi-leu-neun Ji-he* [Wisdom That Produces Success], p. 17.

81. See Hyeon-sung Bae, "Theology of David Yonggi Cho as a New Theological Paradigm of Korean Theology for the New Century," in Ma, Menzies, and Bae, eds., *David Yonggi Cho*, pp. 163-64.

socio-political minjung too did not forget to bestow practical items of need on the poor. In that sense, God utilized the whole Korean minjung, both the socio-political and Pentecostal, in order to liberate Koreans from the bondage of sin.

The Indigenous/Shamanic Aspect of the Korean Pentecostal Minjung

In 1995, Harvard theologian Harvey Cox published a pivotal book on Pentecostalism titled *Fire from Heaven*. In chapter seven, Cox delineates two essential elements of fast-growing religions in today's world. First, they are able to include and transform many aspects of preexisting religions. Second, they are able to equip their congregants to live in societies that undergo rapid changes. The fast growth of Korean Pentecostalism became possible because it afforded these two elements.[82] The Korean Pentecostal churches absorbed and transformed pre-Christian religious practices, namely, those of shamanism, Buddhism, and Confucianism. In accordance with Cox, Yoido Full Gospel Church of Seoul incorporated some shamanistic practices into its worship. The Korean Pentecostal churches produced a setting where thousands of people, who might have been too embarrassed to exercise the rituals of the old-time shamanistic rituals, could do it in a more generous situation with the label of Christianity.[83] Furthermore, Cox does not have a problem with interpreting the Apostle Paul as a Jewish shaman.

I have been deeply impressed by Professor Cox's acute and poignant analyses of Korean Pentecostalism as well as other Asian Pentecostal groups. I also believe that Cox is correct that many Asian Pentecostals integrated certain rituals of their indigenous religions, but I insist they did it most likely without a clear intention. I am certain that Cox does not employ the term *shaman* in a negative and derogatory sense, but most Christians in South Korea do. Here, Cox, being an "outsider," tends to overlook derogatory connotations of the Korean word *moodang* (shaman). Historically and traditionally, many Koreans use the word in order to disparage their political opponents and persecute lower-class people. The word has such a pejo-

---

82. Cox, *Fire from Heaven*, p. 219.
83. Cox, *Fire from Heaven*, pp. 225-26.

rative meaning that most Koreans reject any type of association. As Cox tells in his book, most Korean Pentecostals vehemently refute the shamanistic elements in their rituals. In fact, when Korean Pentecostal Christianity was expanding like wildfire, some of the mainline Protestant Christians used the term in order to damage the legitimacy and orthodoxy of the Pentecostal churches, calling them "heretics."[84] As a result, Korean Pentecostals had to fight vigorously against that idea by distancing themselves from shamanistic practices. Therefore, most Korean Pentecostals insist that key elements of Pentecostalism such as healing, exorcism, and glossolalia unequivocally stem from the biblical writings, not from shamanism.

Conclusion

In the process of probing Pentecostalism from a minjung perspective, two characteristics stand out: First, Asian Pentecostalism in its origin represents a minjung movement of the colonized, oppressed, and poor. With the outpourings of the Holy Spirit, these powerless and hopeless Asians found hope and healing. Second, twentieth-century Pentecostalism even in its origin was already multicultural and global. It was not just a North American phenomenon; rather, at the beginning of the twentieth century, God poured out the Spirit on "all people" and all continents, including the colonized, subjugated Koreans and Indians.

Nonetheless, many Pentecostals in the Two-Thirds World as yet live with colonial, imperialistic, Euro-American understandings of their Christian traditions. They simply assume that Pentecostalism was created by white Americans or Europeans. It is vital to remember and promulgate the fact that people (minjung) who have been discriminated against, oppressed, and colonized were the subjects and leaders of Pentecostalism in its origins, both in Asia and America. Even at the present time, the Mighty Wind (Spirit) still blows more robustly among the poor and the subaltern around the globe.

---

84. See Ig-Jin Kim, *History and Theology of Korean Pentecostalism: Sunbogeum (Pure Gospel) Pentecostalism* (Zoetermeer, The Netherlands: Uitgeverij Boekencentrum, 2003). This book contains the official report of the *Tonghap* Presbyterian denomination on David Yonggi Cho's "Pseudo-Christianity" (1994) that impugned the credibility of Cho and the Yoido Full Gospel Church.

CHAPTER 7

Sanctified Saints — Impure Prophetesses: A Cross-Cultural Study of Gender and Power in Two Afro-Christian Spirit-Privileging Churches

Deidre Helen Crumbley

For emphasis, it is repeated here that female members during menstruation are not allowed to come within the precincts of the Church until after their sanctification after seven clear days (Lev. 15:19; Matt. 5:17-19). . . . They are not allowed to perform any spiritual functions connected with conducting of services in the Church other than saying the prayers when asked and reading portions of the Bible quoted by the preacher. . . . [U]nder no circumstances shall women say the grace during devotional services or lead men in prayers . . . in accordance with St. Paul's injunction (1 Cor. 14:34-35; Genesis 3-16).[1]

There is neither Jew nor Greek, there is neither bond nor free, there is neither male nor female: for ye are all one in Christ Jesus. (Gal. 3:28 KJV)

Introduction

Methodological Concerns

This paper opens with two quotations. The first is from the constitution of an African Instituted Church (AIC), which selectively weds Christian and

---

1. Celestial Church of Christ Constitution 1980, published by the Board of Trustees for the Pastor-in-Council of the Celestial Church of Christ (Nigeria Diocese), p. 50. Hereafter, this document will be cited parenthetically in the text as CCCC, followed by page number.

African religious traditions. The second is regularly quoted from the pulpit of an inner-city African American Sanctified Church. In the first, women may not speak in church and are excluded from both ritual space and high office; in the other, women have held both ritual and political power as doctrinal arbiter and sole ultimate authority. Despite virtually antithetical gender practices, in both churches the Spirit shapes worship and doctrine, biblical literalism grounds theological reflection, and religious adepts serve as human conduits of divine revelation. How might socio-cultural legacy, the gender of the founder, and institutional complexity inform the extremes of gender practices in these two churches, and what strategies might this suggest for addressing women's leadership in the global Pentecostal and charismatic movement?

To answer this two-part question, this investigation, using a case study ethnographic approach,[2] delineates the socio-cultural legacies, gendered leadership, and organizational processes of each church, and then explores how differences in these areas might explain their differing gender practices. What follows, then, is an intellectual exercise of sifting through rich ethnographic material for interpretive clues to address what the invitation calls "a major issue" for twenty-first-century Pentecostal/charismatic churches — namely, "the role of women in church ministry and leadership," opportunities for which "have gradually eroded."

The case study churches are the Celestial Church of Christ (CCC), an Aladura ("ala" = owners of "duura" = prayer) church, founded among the Yoruba of West Africa, and the Church of Prayer Seventh Day (COPSD),[3] an African American inner-city storefront Sanctified Church founded in the northeastern United States. The Celestial data was collected during four consecutive years of field work in Nigeria, expanded upon by ongoing communications with the Celestial Church in America, where a half million Africans immigrated between 1992 and 2002; of these, 75,000 are Nigerians,

2. The ethnographic endeavor is one of delving deeply into the particular. In the study of religion, it immerses a researcher in the minutiae of faith as a lived experience and entails thickly describing the ritual and symbols of a specific faith. As enriching as such in-depth research is, at certain points, one longs for an intellectual opportunity, such as the one provided by writing this article, to step back from phenomena and to engage, not so much in rigorous comparative analysis, as to reflect on wide-ranging data in the same intellectual moment.

3. The author, at the request of the church members, has used pseudonyms for the church and its leader.

who have helped establish Aladura Christianity within the American religious landscape.[4] Data about COPSD follows from a larger book project about the author's home church. Complicating the distinctions between emic and etic, between "the researcher" and "the researched," this approach reflects a perspective in the anthropology of religion, which considers the beliefs of the researcher to be integral to the ethnographic endeavor.[5]

The members of the two case study churches may not refer to their faiths as "Pentecostal" or "charismatic," yet they share with these a practice of privileging Spirit in ways that directly, and often dramatically, inform worship, doctrine, and authority structures. In this study, then, Spirit-privileging churches, such as those found in the Pentecostal, charismatic, and Holiness movements are characterized by (1) the experienced immanent Spirit often embodied within and expressed through believers, e.g., by glossolalia, religious dance, prophesying, or healing; (2) biblical literalism that shapes church doctrine, discipline, and theological reflection; and (3) divine will as revealed through human conduits whose spiritual adeptness lends them charismatic authority.

Female Ordination in Pentecostal and Holiness Churches

The extremes of gender practices represented by the case study churches mirror that of the Pentecostal, charismatic, and Holiness movements, in that some churches prohibit female ordination, others have ordained women from their emergence, and still others ordain women but only to certain levels. For example, the Church of God (CHOG, Anderson, Indiana), a Holiness denomination, has "ordained" women in various ministries from early in its history, with Sarah Smith answering her call in 1882

---

4. See U.S. Department of Homeland Security, 2003, "Immigrants," http://www.dhs .gov/xlibrary/assets/statistics/yearbook/2002/IMM2002text.pdf, pp. 12-14, 17-18; cf. especially the essays by Jacob K. Olupona, Elias Bomba, Akinade Akintunde, Regina Gemignani, and Deidre Crumbley in Jacob Olupona and Regina Gemignani, eds., *African Immigrant Religion in America* (New York: New York University Press, 2007).

5. Walter Randolph Adams, "An Introduction to Explorations in Anthropology and Theology," in *Explorations in Anthropology and Theology*, ed. Frank Salamone and Walter R. Adams (Lanham, MD: University Press of America, 1997), pp. xi-xii, 1-3; and Bennetta Jules-Rosette, *African Apostles: Ritual and Conversion in the Church of John Maranke* (Ithaca, NY: Cornell University Press, 1975), pp. 15, 22, 207.

and Jane Williams bringing her entire African American congregation in Charleston, South Carolina, into the CHOG fold in 1886. However, while "in 1925 women served as pastors of one third of all CHOG congregations," they comprised "only 2% of its senior pastors" in 2002, due to the fact that "pulpit committees refuse to consider women as pastoral candidates and . . . their ordinations [were] delayed despite a valid call to ministry."[6]

The Assemblies of God (AG) has ordained women since its inception in 1914, and women may aspire to the office of General Superintendent as there is no injunction against a woman holding this highest church office. Still, women are outnumbered at the highest levels of the AG organization.[7]

In the history of the Church of God (Cleveland, Tennessee), founded in 1886, Etta Lamb and Lillian Trasher (who later joined the Assemblies of God), pioneered churches at home and abroad, but in 1909 the church banned women's ordination. Today, the church website is clear about its commitment to developing the leadership of men and women. Now women are ordained like men — as "exhorters" and "ministers," but not on the third level, as bishops.[8] The two churches in this study, then, are

6. Jeannette Flynn, *Go! Preach My Word* (Anderson, IN: Warner Press/Church of God Ministries Inc., 2004), pp. 5, 10-11. The Church of God (Anderson) website states that "since its inception, women have been a vital part of the Church of God movement. . . . God has used women and men alike to accomplish his work" (http://www.chog.org/Ministriesand Programs/WomeninMinistry/tabid/413/Default.aspx; accessed 17 May 2007). Paula Walford, administrative assistant to Rev. Jeannette Flynn, explains Rev. Flynn's office as being one of CHOG's three team directors; the only position above this level is that of the general director, currently held by Dr. Ronald V. Duncan (telephone interview with Paula Walford, 21 May 2007).

7. Rev. Arlene Allen, National Director of Women's Ministry Department, in her analysis of the status of women in the church, explained that Assemblies of God (AG) church policies provide access to leadership to women across the board, up to and including the highest levels of church governance (telephone interview with Arlene Allen, 17 May 2007). In her 17 May 2007 email, Joy Wootton, Administrative Coordinator to the National Director, dates the origin of ordained women's ministry as 1914, adding that men and women hold the same kinds of ministry positions. She also directed me to the Assemblies of God Women in Ministry website, www.WomenInMinistry.ag.org (accessed 17 May 2007), which, among other things, describes strategies to help credentialed women be successful on "dual-gender teams."

8. "*We commit ourselves to identifying and developing individuals whom God has called and . . . will demonstrate our commitment by:* Creating an environment in which men and women with ministry gifts are developed to serve as servant-leaders" (http://www.churchofgod.cc/about/mission_vision.cfm; accessed 17 May 2007).

mined as sources of ethnographic clues to the extreme range of gender practices in these and other Spirit-privileging churches.

The case study churches are also described as "Afro-Christian," a concept that is explored at greater length elsewhere.[9] Drawing on Hood's transcontinental and transnational conceptualization of "Black Religion" and "Afro-cultures,"[10] Afro-Christianity, in this study, refers to the way people of Africa and its Diaspora rework symbolic content and institutional forms of Christianity, often within situations of inequitable cultural contact, by wedding, to varying degrees, African and non-African symbolic and ritual content, in ways that reflect an internal logic of intersecting cultural legacy and social adaptation.

The remainder of this paper falls into three parts: The first is an introduction to the case-study churches — their institutional origins, beliefs, and practices. The next section explores how differences in their cultural, historical, and institutional dynamics might inform differences in their gender practices. The paper concludes with a discussion of findings and their implications for addressing women's leadership in Spirit-privileging churches.

The Case-Study Churches: Origins, Beliefs, Practices

The Celestial Church of Christ

Origin Narrative: The Bush, the Call, and the French. Abandoned and lost, Samuel Oshoffa found himself wandering in "the bush," which he had entered to pursue his trade in ebony wood. When he emerged three months later, he did so as an empowered West African prophet-healer. His visions and miracles attracted loyal followers, and when he returned to Porto Novo, capital of the Republic of Dahomey, now Republic of Benin, members of established mission churches, the Aladura, and Muslims congregated around him — some skeptical, some convinced (CCCC, 2-12). In 1947, Dahomey was governed by French colonial rulers who were uncom-

9. See Deidre Helen Crumbley, "On Both Sides of the Atlantic: A Transatlantic Assessment of Afro-Christian Independent Church Movements" (forthcoming).

10. See Robert E. Hood, *Must God Remain Greek? Afro Cultures and God-Talk* (Minneapolis: Fortress, 1990), pp. 10, 35-41, 76, 210, 204-5, 208-10.

fortable with the potentially destabilizing affect of proliferating indigenous churches. Additionally, established churches tended to be hostile toward Oshoffa, who eventually fled his homeland in 1951, resettling in Nigeria, the native land of his mother, and a country where Aladura churches had been proliferating since 1918.[11]

The Celestial Church of Christ (CCC) that Papa Oshoffa introduced into the Nigerian religious landscape was revealed to him on September 29, 1947, in a visionary call to establish a church for "nominal" African Christians who, during crises, abandon Christianity for "pagan" traditional African religions. The gift of "miraculous works of Holy divine healing" and revelation were bestowed on Oshoffa to bring these lost Africans back to Christ (CCCC, 2). With its skilled and readily available prophets and prophetesses, along with formalized and personalized rituals of purification, healing, and protection, CCC displaced traditional diviners and healers in the lives of Celestial believers. It has since spread from West Africa into Britain and throughout both Europe and North America, including the cities of Los Angeles, New York, Dallas, and the Research Triangle of central North Carolina.

Central Beliefs and Practices: Revealed Knowledge, Protecting Power. Celestial doctrine embraces the Christian Trinity of Father, Son, and Holy Ghost, in which Jesus Christ is the redeemer of souls and worker of miracles. God is Creator, who intervenes, through the Holy Ghost, in the daily life of believers. All aspects of the Celestial Church, including its tenets, are "revealed through the Holy Spirit as promised by our Lord Jesus Christ" (CCCC, 29; see John 14:25). Each parish has its own local prophets and prophetesses, who undergo varying degrees of training and testing before qualifying for this office. The paramount prophet, however, was the pastor-founder Oshoffa, premier conduit of divine knowledge. Therefore, not to comply with Celestial "tenets" as revealed to the founder represents noncompliance with divine revelation, and those who presumed to question or advise the founder were readily asked, "Were you in the bush with me?" — i.e., Did God call you or me to found this church?

Evil is neither denied among Celestial Christians nor ignored. Evil is identified and aggressively resisted through prayer and ritual. The sacred text is literally interpreted, Old and New Testament alike. The menstrual

---

11. A. U. Adogame, *Celestial Church of Christ* (Frankfurt: Peter Lang, 1999), p. 26; cf. CCCC, pp. 4, 13.

rite in the opening quotation is supported by referencing Old Testament levitical purity rites and the New Testament gospel. Similarly, New Testament wonders performed by Jesus and his disciples are cited to legitimate the miracles of the pastor-founder Oshoffa (CCCC, 31-33).

Celestial members are readily identifiable by their "white garments" or "sutana," and by not wearing shoes once they don these gowns. Celestial worship is highly formal when compared to the liturgy of other major Aladura churches, such as the Church of the Lord Aladura (CLA) or Christ Apostolic Church (CAC). Still, the Spirit is embodied, for while clapping is forbidden, the Spirit "shakes" members who may speak in unknown tongues. The Spirit also works through the bodies of prophets and prophetesses to reveal future or hidden events in the life of believers. The Celestial compound is a place of holiness, protection, and power, where special prayers are made — for example, by women seeking deliverance from barrenness, and where the vulnerable, such as pregnant women, may repair for "abo" or protection.

Gender Practices: Proclaiming the Gospel — Excluded from the Pulpit. Celestial "tenets" consist of twelve "rules and regulations."[12] Three of the twelve directly address gender. They prohibit men sitting next to women in the church, women from the compound when menstruating, and women from the altar area, behind which ordained males sit, at all times (CCCC, 29-30). Still, Celestial women are not excluded from all aspects of church life and governance.

Women sit on the parochial committees of their local parish, and the diocesan "General Committee" includes appointed lay members, "one male and one female" (CCCC, 38-46). Women's organizations and committees also have emerged, and at least one woman has earned the high status and epithet of "right arm" to the pastor, her opinion informing national and international discourse on succession and church unification.[13]

12. The first eleven tenets are prohibitions against (1) traditional African religious practices, (2) the use of tobacco products, (3) alcoholic beverages, (4) pork, (5) red and black clothing, (6) wearing shoes within church premises, (7) men sitting next to women within church premises, (8) menstruating women within church premises, (9) women approaching the altar area and leading worship, (10) all colored candles except white, and (11) fornication and adultery. The twelfth is a general exhortation for all members "to be clean in body and in soul" (CCCC, pp. 29-30).

13. Material related to Mrs. Sodeinde was accessed 14 March 2007: http://www.cccipc.org/IPC/pastor-in-council/nov03/pic_nov_03_page3.htm. Also see www.celestialchurch.com/

Furthermore, while women may not preach within the church, they may do so "outside the sanctuary" and to a congregation of women. Thus, Celestial women members have been at the forefront of pioneering parishes in Africa and abroad.[14]

Furthermore, women may hold church offices or "anointments" and can ascend lay or prophetic hierarchies, rising from the level of "sister" to "superior senior" levels. Similarly, male members rise through either lay or prophetic hierarchies to superior senior levels. At this level, however, the power structures change radically, for there are no anointments above this level for female members. To rise above this level to that of "evangelist" requires ordination. Since ordination is prohibited to women, only men can become ordained "evangelists" and aspire to the highest office of "pastor" who heads the Celestial Church.

The Church of Prayer Seventh Day

Origins: The Stable, the Call, and the Great Migration. World War I was raging in Europe, as Mother Brown sat alone in the upper room praying for direction in the inner city of Philadelphia. She knew that she had been called to preach as a young woman in Virginia, even though members of her Baptist church told her, "God never called a woman to preach." Indomitable, she continued in prayer, alone, in the "little upper room" she had rented above a horse stable in North Philadelphia. One day, she had a vision in which she saw wild goats on the top of a mountain. When they suddenly ran down the mountain and lay at her feet, she knew what this vision meant: God would send her a church.

Shortly thereafter, people began to "come into the church" that grew along matrifocal extended-family lines. Mother Brown would be central to the life of the church and the lives of founding members, for more than a teacher, preacher, and healer, she was the mouthpiece of God. As her teachings drew upon the Bible, and the Bible is considered the literal word of

---

news/newsroom/ccc_meets_in_ny.htm (accessed 8 April 2004); see also Deidre Helen Crumbley, "Patriarchs, Prophets, and Procreation: Sources of Gender Practices in Three African Churches," *Africa* 73, no. 4 (2003): 584-605, esp. 584; and O. Obafemi, *Life and Times of Papa Oshoffa*, vol. 1 (Nigeria: n.p., 1985), p. 6.

14. Deidre Helen Crumbley, "Impurity and Power: Women in Aladura Churches," *Africa* 62, no. 4 (1992): 505-22, esp. 509.

God, the authority of Scripture was conflated with her personal charisma, so that, on the rare occasion she was opposed, she did not hesitate to quote the injunction: "Touch not mine anointed, and do my prophets no harm" (1 Chron. 16:22).

Recently arrived from the rural South, the vast majority of "saints," or members, were part of the Great Migration, which would relocate about five million southern blacks in industrialized cities like Philadelphia throughout America between 1915 and 1960.[15] With the Great Migration came the spread of the Sanctified Church, an institutionalized legacy of African-derived slave religion valorized by the American Holiness movement.[16] Most of the "saints" or members had been Baptists in the South, but were attracted to Mother Brown's upper room because she "taught the Word" and she laid hands on saints to "heal their conditions." The membership of the church has stabilized at about a hundred adults and children; it remains an unaffiliated institution and has survived the death of the pastor founder who lived to be 105 years old.

Central Beliefs and Practices: The Holy Ghost, the Law, and the Millennium. The Holy Ghost is experienced-spirit that "fills" the saints and is manifested bodily through shouting — the holy dance of the saints — healing, and tongues. The Old and New Testament are literally interpreted; Jesus is redeemer of a sinful world that is fast approaching the end of time and the coming of the millennium. God, as creator and intervening judge, bestows blessings on commandment-keepers, for although Jesus' self-sacrifice is redemptive, "faith without works is dead" (James 2:20 KJV).

Worship consists of "pressing through" to receive the Holy Ghost, shouting, and glossolalia. In addition, serious attention is given to communal reading and studying "the Word." Ritual observances include the

15. Alferdteen Harrison, *Black Exodus: The Great Migration from the American South* (Jackson: University Press of Mississippi, 1991), p. vii.

16. For details, see Albert J. Raboteau, *Slave Religion: The Invisible Institution in the Ante-bellum South* (New York: Oxford University Press, 1978), p. 149; Raboteau, introduction to *God Struck Me Dead: Voices of Ex-Slaves*, ed. Clifton Johnson (Cleveland: Pilgrim Press, 1993), p. xxiii; Cheryl Sanders, *Saints in Exile: The Holiness-Pentecostal Experience in African American Religion and Culture* (New York: Oxford University Press, 1996), pp. 3-5; Zora Neale Hurston, *The Sanctified Church* (Berkeley: Turtle Island, 1981), pp. 101-5; and Cheryl Townsend Gilkes, "Together and in Harness: Women's Tradition in the Sanctified Church," in *Black Women in America: Social Science Perspectives*, ed. Micheline R. Malson et al. (Chicago: University of Chicago Press, 1990), pp. 223-44, esp. 228.

Deidre Helen Crumbley

weekly twenty-four-hour Sabbath, annual Passover/Communion, with foot washing. Traditionally, women and girls wear white dresses with white mantles on their heads, while men and boys wear black suits.

Women at the Helm. Female leadership is both normative and divinely sanctioned in the COPSD. Biblical passages sanctioning women's subordination, e.g., 1 Corinthians 14:34-35, are not avoided, but the passage in Galatians cited above is regularly quoted. While gender is rarely addressed directly, the author grew up conversant with biblical narratives about Deborah the judge of ancient Israel and New Testament references to Lydia, Priscilla, Eunice, and Lois.

While Mother Brown was advised by female "head saints," and male deacons handled financial matters, she had the final word in all matters. Prior to her death, she also put an organizational structure in place, which replaced the pastorate with a "biblically based" dual-governance structure consisting of an all-male "deacon" board responsible for "business" matters and a body of male and female "Elders," responsible for spiritual direction:

> Then the twelve called the multitude of the disciples unto them and said, "It is not reason that we should leave the word of God, and serve tables. Wherefore, brethren, look out among you seven men of honest report full of the Holy Ghost and wisdom, which we may appoint over this business. But we will give ourselves to prayer, and to the ministry of the word." (Act 6:2-4 KJV)

Literalism is applied selectively, here, for while the all-male deacon board complies with the "seven men of honest report," the "twelve" apostles, who are male in the biblical text, become a body of male and female "Elders" (who in most cases were spouses and founding church members). The outcome is a male-female power-sharing arrangement, nuanced by seniority. Today, the Elders, who range from their seventies to their nineties, consist of more females than males, males having died earlier than their female spouses. Elders are the object of greater deference and status than are deacons. Furthermore, while they "lead" the church "spiritually," Elders also have informal veto power over the deacons' proposals. Thus, they directly affect administrative discourse and decision-making.[17]

17. Deidre Helen Crumbley, "Miraculous Mothers, Empowered Sons, and Dutiful Daughters: Gender, Race, and Power in an African American Sanctified Church," *Journal of Anthropology and Humanism* 32, no. 1 (2007): 30-51.

Gender Legacies and Female Leadership in the Matrix of Socio-Cultural and Theological Factors

Gender Legacies in the African Independent Church

In addition to their gender practices, the two churches differ in socio-cultural legacies, gender of the founder, and institutional scale. One is African, male founded, and global; the other is African American, female founded, and has remained an unaffiliated congregational church. How might these differences inform their differing gender practices?

For Westerners unfamiliar with African gender practices and inundated by persistent images of Africa as dark, dangerous, and backwards, it would be easy to assume that the ritual and administrative constraints on Celestial churchwomen follow naturally from African gender practices. However, the gender practices of the Yoruba people, among whom Aladura churches emerged, have traditionally included women in leadership roles in social, political, and religious spheres. Yoruba women were traditionally free to initiate divorce and to remarry.[18] Domestic and public arenas of mother-wife and entrepreneur overlap, and women's control of the marketplace fostered financial autonomy.[19] Furthermore, while Yoruba society is virilocal and patrilineal, there is also a tendency among some Yoruba toward bilateral kinship, allowing children to inherit land through the mother.[20]

The term *oba*, previously mistranslated "king," is the un-gendered Yoruba word for ruler, some of whom have been female in major Yoruba

18. Judith Hoch-Smith, "Radical Yoruba Female Sexuality: The Witch and the Prostitute," in *Women in Ritual and Symbolic Roles*, ed. Judith Hoch-Smith et al. (New York: Plenum Press, 1978), pp. 265-66, 295.

19. See Dorothy Remy, "Underdevelopment and the Experience of Women: A Nigerian Case Study," in *Toward an Anthropology of Women*, ed. Rayna R. Reiter (New York: Monthly Review Press, 1975), pp. 358-71, esp. 370-71; Niara Sudarkasa, "The 'Status of Women' in Indigenous Africa Societies," in *Women in Africa and the African Diaspora*, ed. Rosalyn Terborg-Penn, Sharon Harley, and Andrea Benton Rushing (Washington, DC: Howard University Press, 1987), pp. 25-39; and Sudarkasa, "Female Employment and Family Organization in West Africa," in *The Black Woman Cross-Culturally*, ed. Filomina Chioma Steady (Cambridge, MA: Schenkman Publishing, 1981), pp. 49-63, esp. 49-55.

20. J. S. Eades, *The Yoruba Today* (Cambridge: Cambridge University Press, 1980), pp. 37-38 and 49-50, and J. D. Y. Peel, *Ijeshas and Nigerians: Incorporation of a Yoruba Kingdom 1890s-1970s* (Cambridge: Cambridge University Press, 1983), pp. 51-52.

kingdoms. It should be noted, however, that Yoruba names are largely un-gendered, i.e., Bola can be the name of a male or female, which compli-cates the process of determining the gender of recorded *oba*. As *Iyalode*, women have headed the female-dominated marketplace, while directly af-fecting palace politics.[21] In the religious sphere, the Supreme Being *Oludumare* is genderless, despite earlier mistranslations of *Oludumare* as Father-God.[22] The *orisa*, or divinities, however, can be male or female, and they possess both men and women devotees.[23] Not only have Yoruba women been *orisa* priestesses but also *babalawo*, the priest who serves the paramount Yoruba oracle, *Ifa*.[24]

Such gender practices in West African societies have been described as a "dual-sex" system in which women operate within power arenas that are separate from, but not subordinated to, men's arenas.[25] Traditional Yoruba society, like most, but not all human societies,[26] is not without constraints on women's roles and bodies. Most pre-colonial *obas* appear to have been male, and female *babalawo* seem the exception to the rule.[27]

21. On this point, see Oyèrónké Oyewùmí, *The Invention of Women* (Minneapolis: Uni-versity of Minnesota Press, 1997), pp. 84-91 and 107-12; Eades, *The Yoruba Today*, p. 99; and LaRay Denzer, "Yoruba Women: A Historiographical Study," *The International Journal of Af-rican Historical Studies* 27, no. 1 (1994): 1-39, esp. 10.

22. Oyewùmí, *The Invention of Women*, pp. 136-42; Ifi Amadiume, *Male Daughters, Fe-male Husbands: Gender and Sex in an African Society* (London; Atlantic Highlands, NJ: Zed Books, 1987), p. 123; Mercy Amba Oduyoye, *Daughters of Anowa: African Women and Patri-archy* (Maryknoll, NY: Orbis Books, 1995), pp. 173-80; J. D. Y. Peel, *Religious Encounter and the Making of the Yoruba* (Bloomington: Indiana University Press, 2000), p. 119; and H. Turner, *History of an African Independent Church: The Church of the Lord (Aladura),* 2 vols. (London: Oxford University Press, 1967), vol. 2, p. 42.

23. Diedre Badejo, *Osun Seegesi: The Elegant Deity of Wealth, Power, and Femininity* (Trenton, NJ: Africa World Press, 1996), pp. 175-77, and M. T. Drewal, *Yoruba Ritual: Per-formers, Play, and Agency* (Bloomington: Indiana University Press, 1992), pp. 172-77, 180-86, 190.

24. Karin Barber, *I Could Speak Until Tomorrow: Oriki, Women, and the Past in a Yoruba Town* (Washington, DC: Smithsonian Institution Press, 1991), pp. 103, 288-89.

25. Nkiru Nzegwu, "Gender Equality in a Dual Sex System: The Case of Onitsha," *Ca-nadian Journal of Law and Jurisprudence* 7 (1994): 73-95, esp. 84-95.

26. Shan Shan Du, "'Husband and Wife Do It Together': Sex/Gender Allocation of La-bor Among the Qhawqhat Lahu of Lancang, Southwestern China," *American Anthropologist* 102, no. 3 (2000): 520-37, and Du, *"Chopsticks Only Work in Pairs": Gender Unity and Gender Equality Among the Lahu of Southwest China* (New York: Columbia University Press, 2002), pp. 1-12, 107-35, 185-96.

27. Crumbley, "Patriarchs, Prophets, and Procreation," pp. 591-94.

Moreover, traditional menstrual rites required women to avoid holy places and objects when menstruating. Such menstrual rites also have been associated with female subordination and the reassertion of male domination.[28] However, what is significant in the Yoruba case is that the state of "ritual impurity" for women is temporary. Thus, having a female body, with its natural reproductive processes, traditionally did not permanently disqualify Yoruba women from social, political, economic, or religious leadership. In contrast, in the Celestial Church, women are prohibited both from ordination and from the altar area, behind which ordained men are seated. The gender patterns of the Celestial Church, then, diverge sharply from Yoruba tradition rather than simply follow from them.

Gender Legacies in the African American Church

The gender dynamics inherited by the saints of COPSD reflect what Gilkes describes as a "dual-sex" West African cultural legacy of normative female leadership, buttressed by the leveling effect of North American racial practices.[29] Chattel slavery in America shifted the control of black bodies, male and female alike, along with their labor and offspring, to slave owners, thereby undermining black male and female relationships and requiring black women to assume leadership roles to maintain their offspring. In the South, after emancipation, the threat and actual rape of black women reasserted white male dominance, and being female did not exempt them from the racial violence of lynching.[30] Black women entered the labor market to supplement their husbands' salaries, which were diminished by racially biased hiring and compensation practices. Often working as domestics,

28. Mary Douglas, *Purity and Danger: An Analysis of the Concepts of Pollution and Taboo* (London: Routledge & Kegan Paul, 1966), pp. 3-4, 35, 113.

29. Gilkes, "Together and in Harness," and Gilkes, "The Politics of Silence: Dual-Sex Political Systems and Women's Traditions of Conflict in African-American Religion," in *African-American Christianity*, ed. Paul E. Johnson (Berkeley: University of California Press, 1994), pp. 80-109.

30. Fifty of 2,522 black people lynched between 1889 and 1918 were women. Pregnancy did not preclude lynching. See Donna L. Franklin, *What's Love Got to Do with It? Understanding and Healing the Rift Between Black Men and Women* (New York: Touchstone Books, Simon & Schuster, 2000), pp. 124-25 and 152-53; and Jewel L. Prestage, "Political Behavior of American Black Women: An Overview," in *The Black Woman*, ed. La Frances Rodgers-Rose (Beverly Hills, CA: Sage, 1980), p. 239.

black women dealt with sexual harassment by white men and labor exploitation by white women. Because they were less likely to be fired than their husbands, their steady but low wages were crucial to the economic stability of their families.[31]

Black women's leadership in the economic arena extended to the religious sphere as well. Sanctified churches, in particular, tended to provide greater opportunities for female leadership than older Black Independent Churches, some of which resisted female ordination until the mid-twentieth century.[32] By the First World War, Sanctified churchwomen like Ida B. Robinson and Bishop Mary Magdalena Lewis Tate were answering the "call" to preach the gospel by starting their own churches.[33] Mother Brown stands in this tradition, leaving her Baptist home church to start the COPSD.

Still, not all Sanctified churches have welcomed women into their ordained ministry, for the Church of God in Christ (COGIC), the largest and oldest institutionalized Sanctified church, has yet to ordain women. Thus,

31. Patricia Hill Collins, *Black Feminist Thought: Knowledge, Consciousness, and the Politics of Empowerment* (New York: Routledge, 1991), pp. 49-54; Prestage, "Political Behavior of American Black Women," p. 238; Judith Rollins, *Between Women: Domestics and Their Employers* (Philadelphia: Temple University Press, 1985), pp. 67-79, 131-55, 162, 186-88, 212-13; and Franklin, *What's Love Got to Do with It?* pp. 152-56.

32. The African Methodist Episcopal Zion (AMEZ) began formally ordaining women as early as 1884, while the African Methodist Episcopal (AME) church did not do so until the 1940s, and the National Baptist Convention, not until 1953. See Jacquelyn Grant, "Black Women and the Church," in *All American Women: Lines That Divide, Ties That Bind*, ed. Johnnetta B. Cole (New York: Free Press, 1986), pp. 359-69, esp. 362 and 368; Delores Carpenter, "Black Women in Religious Institutions: A Historical Summary from Slavery to the 1960s," *The Journal of Religious Thought* 46 (1989-1990): 7-27, esp. 12 and 18; and William J. Walls, *The African Methodist Episcopal Zion Church: Reality of the Black Church* (Charlotte, NC: AME Zion Publishing House, 1974), p. 48.

33. See Estrelda Alexander, "Gender and Leadership in the Theology and Practice of Three Pentecostal Women Pioneers (Mary Magdalena Lewis Tate, Aimee Semple McPherson, Ida Robinson)" (Ph.D. diss., Catholic University of America, 2003), pp. 78-126; 176-224; Felton Best, "Breaking the Gender Barrier: African-American Women and Leadership in Black Holiness-Pentecostal Churches 1890-Present," in *Flames of Fire: Black Religious Leadership from the Slave Community to the Million-Man March*, ed. Felton O. Best (Lewiston, NY: Edwin Mellen, 1998), pp. 153-68, esp. 158-65, 168; and Cheryl Townsend Gilkes, "Some Mother's Son and Some Father's Daughter: Gender and Biblical Language in Afro-Christian Worship Tradition," in *Shaping New Vision: Gender and Values in American Culture*, ed. Clarissa W. Atkinson, Constance H. Buchanan, and Margaret R. Miles (Ann Arbor, MI: UMI Research Press, 1987), pp. 73-95, esp. 81.

while Mother Brown's leadership follows logically from West African gender legacies reinforced by American racial practices, this does not appear to have happened across the board among black churches, given the historical resistance to female ordination in black church history even into the twenty-first century.

Gendered Leadership in the African Independent Church

The Celestial Church was founded by a Yoruba man, raised in a Yoruba area where women were especially successful in an active market region.[34] Female autonomy and a dual-sex gender system would have been normative for him, so why did the gender practices of the church he founded depart so dramatically from them? One explanation is that it reflects the impact of inequitable culture contact. Oshoffa came of age during French colonial rule. The Catholic Church was a strong missionary presence, and at the age of seven he was sent to a Methodist mission for several years (CCCC, 5). Neither of these churches had embraced the ordination of women, and colonial educational and hiring practices tended to limit the social latitude of African women, leaving them more dependent on their husbands and outside the pulpit.[35]

Another explanation is that Celestial's gender practices are a conse-

---

34. Crumbley, "Impurity and Power," pp. 515, 518.

35. See Karen Armstrong, *Shifting Ground and Cultured Bodies: Postcolonial Gender Relations in Africa and India* (Lanham, MD: University Press of America, 1999), p. 9; Oyewùmí, *The Invention of Women*, 124-28, 130-35, 150-56; LaRay Denzer, "Domestic Science Training in Colonial Yorubaland, Nigeria," in *African Encounters with Domesticity*, ed. Karen Tranberg Hansen (New Brunswick, NJ: Rutgers University Press, 1992), pp. 117-39, esp. 116-17 and 121, and Denzer, "Yoruba Women," pp. 19-20 and 25-28; A. Mama, *Women's Studies and Studies of Women in Africa During the 1990s* (Senegal: Codesria, 1996), pp. 4, 28, 37, 61-66; Amadiume, *Male Daughters, Female Husbands*, 134-35; R. I. J. Hackett, "Sacred Paradoxes: Women and Religious Plurality in Nigeria," in *Women, Religion and Social Change*, ed. Y. Y. Haddad and E. B. Findley (New York: State University of New York Press, 1985), pp. 248-71, esp. 254-55, 260-63, and 268; Oduyoye, *Daughters of Anowa*, pp. 104, 172; Karen Sacks, "An Overview of Women and Power in Africa," in *Perspectives on Power and Women in Africa, Asia and Latin America*, ed. J. F. O'Barr (Durham, NC: Duke University, Center for International Studies, 1982), pp. 1-10, esp. 5-7; and L. N. Predelli, "Marriage in Norwegian Missionary Practice and Discourse in Norway and Madagascar, 1880-1910," *Journal of Religion in Africa* 31, no. 1 (2001): 36-37.

quence of an "unholy alliance" between African and European gender asymmetries intersecting and reinforcing each other.[36] But whether imposed or willingly adopted, constrained female leadership and the gender asymmetry do not necessarily follow from male leadership. For example, Josiah O. Ositelu founded the Church of the Lord-Aladura (CLA), self-described as "Pentecostal in Power," in 1930.[37] From its inception, women functioned in leadership roles, and by 1959 the founder established the ordination of women as "a divine injunction." Additionally, for each male office there is a female office with the same duties and responsibilities.[38] As in the Celestial Church, CLA members comply with menstrual rites. Thus, an ordained female minister on her period does not enter the sanctuary of the parish she heads but manages church affairs through her representative; however, when her period is over, so is the restriction. Compliance with menstrual rites, then, does not necessarily indicate low female status, and a male founder does not necessarily predict male-dominated church hierarchies.[39]

Gendered Leadership in the African Independent Church

Common sense suggests that a female-founded church sets precedence for and fosters women's leadership. However, a female founder guarantees neither gender egalitarian structures nor a female successor. Ellen White is described as the co-founder of the Seventh Day Adventist (SDA) Church along with James White and Joseph Bates. Nevertheless, her prolific prophetic writings, not theirs, are readily cited during SDA sermons as biblical commentary. After her death in 1915, women's leadership dropped dramat-

36. E. Schmidt, "Patriarchy, Capitalism, and the Colonial State in Zimbabwe," *Signs: Journal of Women in Culture and Society* 16, no. 4 (1991): 733-56, esp. 734, 741, and 753-56.

37. Rufus Okikiolaolu Olubiyi Ositelu, *African Instituted Churches* (New Brunswick, NJ: Transaction Publishers, 2002), p. 201.

38. Turner, *History of an African Independent Church*, vol. 2, pp. 46, 48; E. S. Sorinmade, *Lecture Delivered to Mark the 10th Anniversary of the Death of Dr. J. O. Oshitelu* (Abeokuta, Nigeria: Ake, 1976), p. 12; and Church of the Lord (CLA) Constitution 2001 (Shagamu, Nigeria: Grace Enterprises, 2001), pp. 10-18 and 60-61.

39. Deidre Helen Crumbley, "Power in the Blood: Menstrual Taboos and Female Power in an African Instituted Church," in *Women and Religion in the African Diaspora*, ed. Marie Griffith and Barbara Savage (Baltimore, MD: Johns Hopkins University Press, 2006), pp. 81-97.

ically, and today, while both men and women complete four-year seminary training, women are "commissioned" while males are ordained, and only an "ordained" minister can aspire to be president of the worldwide SDA church.[40]

In the Sanctified tradition, Bishop Tate, mentioned above, founded a very successful Church of the Living God, Pillar and Ground of the Truth, which incorporated women into leadership on every level of the church along with men.[41] Several branches or "dominions" of her churches survived her demise, and the largest of these was pioneered by Archibald White, who disapproved of women bishops, the number of which has decreased dramatically over time.[42] While women are still at the helm in the COPSD, the power structure that Mother Brown put in place before her death ended the centralization of power in a sole female leader. Without a formal constitution delineating the process of Elder formation as part of a permanent organizational structure, might another power structure emerge that goes the way of many new religious movements as they become more stable institutions?

Scale, Complexity, and Structuration

Often, as new religious movements become more established, egalitarian tendencies, such as gender equity, are displaced by "structuration" — a re-

---

40. See Bert Haloviak, "A Place at the Table: Women and the Early Years" (2007), http://www.sdanet.org/atissue/wo/haloviakchapter.htm; and Kit Watts, "Moving Away from the Table: A Survey of Historical Factors Affecting Women Leaders," http://www.sdanet.org/atissue/wo/welcome2.htm (both accessed 8 March 2007). Heidi Ford, who directs the Women's Resource Center at La Sierra University, a Seventh Day Adventist (SDA) institution, noted that the subject of women's ordination has been raised at the worldwide meeting of church "divisions" from around the world, held every five years. In 1995, the North American Division proposed that female ordination be decided on the division level. It is noteworthy that this was voted down, in large part, because those supporting the proposal were outnumbered by delegates from the developing world, where SDA, like many Christian denominations, is growing exponentially and which tends to be socially and theologically conservative (telephone interview, 8 March 2007, with Heidi Ford, Director of the Women's Resource Center, La Sierra University; also see http://www.adventistwomenscenter.org/, accessed 11 May 2007).

41. Alexander, "Gender and Leadership," pp. 106-13.

42. Alexander, "Gender and Leadership," pp. 80, 98, 114-15; and Best, "Breaking the Gender Barrier," pp. 164-65.

turn to institutionalized hierarchy.[43] The Celestial Church, within the lifetime of the founder, spread abroad into developed nations. As one church leader observed, such rapid growth made it necessary to "get organized." A written constitution was published in 1980, formalizing the exclusion of women from high office and sacred spaces. However, women are recalled, from its emergence, as falling primarily into two categories — devoted believers and adepts or ritually careless practitioners digressing from protocols of purity and propriety.[44]

Although these representations eventually became institutionalized roles as the church became more organized, it is important to note that structuration is not inevitable. In the Church of the Lord-Aladura (CLA), women's leadership roles actually expanded with organizational formalization — menstrual rites notwithstanding. Resurgent hierarchy, then, is not inescapable. Regardless of dominant ideologies, social constraints, and cultural legacies, people can and do make choices that favor gender equity. Another example of this is the creative dual governing structure that Mother Brown put in place before her death, in which men and women share power, and age is venerated.

Conclusion: Interpretation and Implications

This essay poses a two-part question: How might socio-cultural legacy, leadership, and institutional complexity inform the antithetical gender practices of the case study churches, and what strategies might this suggest for addressing women's leadership in other Spirit-privileging churches? First, it is clear that socio-cultural legacies, leadership style, and organizational scale inform gender practices, but in very complicated and sometimes surprising ways. A cultural legacy of women-inclusive leadership, whether integral to traditional culture as in the case of the Yoruba, or but-

---

43. Victor Turner, *The Ritual Process: Structure and Anti-Structure* (Chicago: Aldine Publishing, 1969), pp. 133-35, 139, 153.

44. For example, his elder sister Elizabeth Ekundayo became one of his earliest followers after he raised her son from the dead, and his wife Yaman not only accompanied Oshoffa on his evangelical outreach, but received a divine visitation. However, in contrast to these images of devotion, there are narratives of women castigated for being on their periods in the sanctuary and for not donning the white sutana (see Crumbley, "Impurity and Power," p. 505; and CCCC, pp. 2, 7, 14, 18, 22).

tressed by structural racism in the United States, fails to predict or preclude female leadership. Secondly, a female founder guarantees neither gender equity nor female succession, and a male founder does not predict male-dominated structures. Finally, while structuration may tend toward re-engendered hierarchies, these can be preempted by the imponderables of human agency. These findings preclude simplistic conclusions and make a strong case for careful ethnographic attention to detail, especially of unfamiliar gender practices, such as those that certainly will inform the twenty-first-century Pentecostal and charismatic movement as it rapidly expands among developing people of the Global South and among those living as minoritized groups within developed nations.

In addition to providing a heuristic for assessing gender practices in a globalizing church, and beyond a caveat against overgeneralizations, the ethnographic clues provided above also point to a thematic relationship that has consequences for policy formation. This relationship derives, not from an exploration of differences between the churches, but rather of what they have in common. I refer, here, to the tendency of Spirit-privileging churches toward biblical literalism and the valuing of divine revelation. Both Mother Brown and Papa Oshoffa were highly venerated for their charismatic gifts. To their church members, they were divine mouthpieces, speaking for God through literally interpreted Holy Scripture revealed to them through the Holy Spirit.

Thus, their gender practices, though extremely different, are legitimated by the authority of their charismatic leaders' holy pronouncements from the same literally interpreted Bible. Biblical literalism, however, is selective, if only because biblical content reflects over two millennia of Judeo-Christian sacred text production and translation, filtered through diverse cultural lenses. In Spirit-privileging churches, selective literalism has the potential to liberate or constrain women's leadership — or both, depending on the exercise of human imagination and agency. When the tongues have quieted and the shouting has died down, when the heady days of revival give way to church-building, the saints are faced with the same challenges that face all human beings — namely, how to regularize relationships, divide work, and apportion resources in day-to-day life. There is a tendency for new movements to reintroduce hierarchy as they become more formalized, but institutionalized inequity is not inevitable.

Spirit-privileging churches offer at least two gifts to world Christianity. One is the democratization of mysticism, which transforms all believ-

ers into "saints" and makes intense experiences of divine intimacy normative rather than the exception to the rule. Another is the pre-eminence of
ongoing divine revelation over fixed canons, church disciplines, and by-
laws. The element of revitalization, usually limited to the early stages of a
religious movement, is incorporated into the core of Pentecostalism by its
Spirit-driven critique of mere religiosity. While formal structures are essential to institutional sustainability, in churches where the Spirit is the ultimate authority, rules — including gender rules — are subject to inspired
reformulation.

To embrace intimate experience of the Spirit is to claim the power to
challenge dominant ideologies. This is what Holiness and Pentecostal
Christians did when they first broke with established churches in late
nineteenth-century America. In the intervening century, that counter-
culture vitality has waned, but it need not disappear — and with it the
brightest and the best churchwomen. The challenge to Spirit-privileging
churches in the twenty-first century is to reclaim the Spirit of resistance to
social injustice. As Jeannette Flynn, one of the three directors of the
Church of God (Anderson) writes:

> If the wind of the Spirit blew the church to commitment and practices
> that disregarded the cultural norms of society that was fine with those
> early pioneers. Conformity to the dominant culture was no match for
> conformity to Christ and his leadership of a church that indeed imag-
> ined a new way of being the people of God. . . . Will we have the imagi-
> nation, courage and grace to follow where they led?[45]

---

45. Flynn, *Go! Preach my Word*, p. 12.

CHAPTER 8

Sankofa: Pentecostalism and African Cultural Heritage

Ogbu U. Kalu

Introducing the Cultural Discourse

The explosion of Pentecostalism in Africa needs an explanation. Recent scholarship on African Pentecostalism tends to start from the contemporary and urban experiences to explore the impact of external cultural forces and show how Africans respond to the forces of externality and globalization. Pentecostalism is imaged as the religious vanguard. From here, assertions are made that ignore in-depth ethnographical research and presume a higher degree of urban ethos than exists in Africa. This discourse does not recognize the force of cultural villagization of the modern public space; that most of the inhabitants of the towns carry medicine made in the villages to empower their successful foraying in the towns. As Ellis and ter Haar observed, "many Africans today who continue to hold beliefs derived from the traditional cosmologies apply these to everyday life even when they live in cities and work in the civil service or business sector. Religious worldviews do not necessarily diminish with formal education."[1]

It matters where an analysis starts or is located because many studies of African Pentecostalism that are placed in the contemporary period and in the context of urbanity and urban culture miss the force of the movement's fit into the indigenous worldviews and the Pentecostal practices in the rural contexts.

---

1. Stephen Ellis and Gerrie ter Haar, *Worlds of Power: Religious Thought and Political Practice in Africa* (New York: Oxford University Press, 2004), p. 51.

The burden of this chapter is a cultural discourse that reconstructs the movement's response to the system of meanings embodied in the symbols and worldviews of indigenous African religions and cultures. It starts from a different location to explore the *cultural* discourse that argues that Pentecostalism has grown because of its cultural fit into indigenous worldviews and its response to the questions that are raised within the interior of the worldviews. It asserts that the indigenous worldview still dominates contemporary African experience and shapes the character of African Pentecostalism. Therefore, African Pentecostalism is the "setting to work" of the pneumatic seed of the gospel in Africa, at once showing how Africans appropriated the gospel message, how they responded to the presence of the kingdom in their midst, and how its power transformed their worldviews. Exercising a measure of agency, African Christians absorbed new resources generated internally and externally in reshaping their histories. The face of Christianity acquired a different character in the encounter because it was now expressed in the idiom of the African world. This means that the conversation partners in shaping Pentecostal ideology and praxis are the indigenous religions and cultures, the experiences of individuals and communities of contemporary cultures, and competing religious forms in urban and rural contexts, biblical resources, and a certain ecclesiastical tradition or the pneumatically driven Pentecostal image of the church. These are not discrete categories but shape the *being, saying, and doing* of the Pentecostal movement. They are useful sources for revisiting the debate on Pentecostal response to African cultural heritage.

It is argued that when Pentecostal discourse is rooted in both the African past, an area that has received inadequate attention, as well as the experiences in contemporary cultural terrains, its full character will be illuminated. But the task here is to fill the lacuna in Pentecostal scholarship by focusing on the specific contextuality, the Africanness of the phenomenon and its place within African maps of the universe. It argues that the contemporary experience in Africa does not start from globalizing cultural forces, though the implosion of these forces compels much readjustment. Rather, the force of traditional cultures in determining behavior and policy in the modern public space compels an in-depth study of its salience and resilience. Pentecostal cultural policy demonstrates an acute awareness of this powerful reality for the majority of Africans, in a continent where most people live in the rural areas and where the urban dwellers cultivate their roots in their villages. Urban migrants are often engaged in circular migration from the rural-to-urban and return.

Sankofa: Discourses on Pentecostalism and the African Past

The force of the past for the present is illustrated in the cultural policies of African governments. Many African countries have dug deeply into tradi-tional values for cultural symbols of unity. In the rainbow ideology of South Africa, the television features a stimulating jingle, *Simunye-e-e-e, we are one!* In Ghana, *Sankofa*, a Twi word, is one of the symbols used to pro-mote unity based on the recovery of Ghanaian cultural heritage. Each of the symbols affirms a salient value that should be cultivated. *Sankofa* is the bird that turns its head to look backwards in the direction from where it came because a person who is not conscious about where a journey started may not know where he or she is going. This symbol urges people to "go back and take it," or look back and reclaim the cultural heritage.

There are two contested images of African Pentecostal cultural policy. The first is that Pentecostals essay to destroy the past. In his *African Cathol-icism: A Voyage in Discovery,* Adrian Hastings complained that the Pente-costal attack against indigenous culture constitutes a regression from the achievements by the African Instituted Churches on the gospel-culture in-terface.[2] Apparently the matter is subtle. Birgit Meyer suggests that the Pentecostal attitude may be inherited from the missionary traditions; that the Ewe converts translated or appropriated the missionary message about the devil. Pentecostals have followed *en suite* to embed the missionary rhetoric about Satan in a wide range of the ingredients of African indige-nous cultures. But she added that "by emphasizing continuously that be-ing born again entails a complete break with the past, Pentecostals even celebrate the notion of rupture much more than nineteenth- and early twentieth-century Protestant missionaries."[3]

Other scholars argue that Pentecostalism merely valorized changes that indigenous religious movements had initiated; all parties are engaged

2. Adrian Hastings, *African Catholicism: A Voyage in Discovery* (London: SCM Press, 1989).

3. Birgit Meyer, "Make a Complete Break with the Past: Memory and Postcolonial Mo-dernity in Ghanaian Pentecostalist Discourse," *Journal of Religion in Africa* 28, no. 3 (1998): 316-49; see p. 318.

in worldview maintenance with competing narratives; this explains why cultural tradition often attacks this new religious form as an invasive virus. Still others emphasize how Pentecostalism engages the resources of African indigenous cultures in pursuit of its own agendas. They draw attention to large areas of resonance between Pentecostalism and African maps of the universe. David Maxwell, using data from Zimbabwe, illustrates the resonance between Pentecostalism and the spirit-possession cults and traditional witchcraft cleansing mechanisms. He argues that they share a common appeal, seek empowerment to combat evil, and share the egalitarian idiom.[4]

A second dimension of the contested perspectives images Pentecostal cultural policy as subtle: that while affirming the reality of the powers of indigenous gods and cultures, Pentecostals essay to transform these cultures by contesting patriarchal ideology and the control exercised by the elders and "big men" of the village and clan. The attraction for charismatic women and youth, he argues, comes from the fact that "the new churches are also the heirs of older witchcraft eradication movements."[5] The Pentecostals do not ignore but engage the primal contexts and renew the social system by critiquing and redefining possession: they brand all cults (central and peripheral) as satanic, exorcise all, and breed skepticism. But they do not stop there. They provide an alternative "white," clean possession by the Holy Spirit *(Mzimu Woyera)* that is safer and less expensive.

Through a transformational cultural response, Pentecostalism becomes a new form of possession replacing the old by deploying an identical mechanism. Among the Igbo of southeastern Nigeria, the *dibia afa* and *dibia ogwu* ("diviner" and "herbalist") recognized that this new religious form was a stronger competitor than the old missionary cultural policy because it was as much concerned with spiritual power as the indigenous religion. Birgit Meyer observed that

> the proponents of Pentecostalization stood much closer to traditional worship than they themselves were prepared to acknowledge. Exactly because they regarded local gods and spirits as really existing agents of Satan, they strove to exclude them with so much vigor, thereby placing themselves in a tradition of *'Africanization from below'* which was devel-

4. David Maxwell, "Witches, Prophets and Avenging Spirits," *Journal of Religion in Africa* 25, no. 3 (1995): 321-25.
5. Maxwell, "Witches, Prophets and Avenging Spirits," p. 316.

oped by the first Ewe converts and which had much in common with African cults propagating radical cleansing.[6]

This explains why Pentecostals would speak about *deliverance* rather than exorcism. They do not just expel the demonic force but refill the person with a healthier, clean spirit so that the person can become truly human and achieve the vaunted life goals of a community. It is a revaluation of culture to transform it into an instrument for building *ubuntu*. Thus, there are three models of relationship instead of one hostile posture in the conversation between Pentecostalism and indigenous culture: they inculturate its resources, prophetically contest it, and are often counterattacked by the guardians of the sacred groves.

Rijk van Dijk's study[7] of Chilomoni, a suburb of Blantyre, further illustrates the subtlety: he recognizes the Pentecostal interest and attention to the reality within traditional religions and cultures. But he argues that the movement's attitude highlights the element of parody and skepticism:

> While Pentecostalism in its deliverance ideology and praxis has never been skeptical about the powers that lie behind manifestations of social, political or even religious authority, the bearers of those powers tend to meet in Pentecostal praxis a lot of parody and ridicule: a form of indirect contestation.

From a certain perspective, Pentecostal studies benefit from the scholarship in the broader field of African church history. There, recent scholarship has emphasized the continuity of African primal religions in African Christianity, the exchange of symbols, images, and material things, the agency of decoders as well as encoders, the modes of appropriating the message of the gospel by the hearers, and the varieties of ways that African cultures have reshaped the music, dance, and liturgy of Christianity and raised new theological questions and grassroots reflexive theologies in response to contemporary experiences.

6. Meyer, "Make a Complete Break with the Past," p. 319.

7. R. van Dijk, "Witchcraft and Skepticism by Proxy: Pentecostalism and Laughter in Urban Malawi," in *Magical Interpretations, Material Realities*, ed. H. L. Moore and T. Sanders (London: Routledge, 2001), pp. 97-117; see p. 110.

Ogbu U. Kalu

Precarious Vision: Anatomy of the African Worldview

Some scholars have argued that each culture is a universe of signs comparable to language, a configuration of images, concepts, and interpretations. Through the process of enculturation, this grammar is acquired unconsciously by the individual members of the society. Charles H. Kraft concluded: "At the core of culture and, therefore, at the very heart of all human life, lies the structuring of the basic assumptions, values, and allegiances in terms of which people interpret and behave. These assumptions, values and allegiances we call worldview."[8] Worldview is a picture that points to the deep-level assumptions and values on the basis of which people generate surface-level behavior; it provides the motivation for behavior and gives meaning to the environment. Like the rest of culture, it is inherited unconsciously but deliberately transmitted. It could be encrusted in customs, myths, proverbs and folklore, music and dances. For instance, in many African indigenous cosmogonies, the human world began from an anthill sitting in a marsh. The Supreme Being sent a deity with bellows to dry the land. Differences in such myths of origin tend to reflect the ecology of the community or other ideological considerations. This indicates that worldviews are not static but could be reshaped by culture wars. Cultural change can often be detected as battering waves chipping away the crusts, initiating a process of separation, reconstruction, and reprioritization as a new way of viewing the world emerges.

Africans conceive time in a cyclical pattern. Life moves from birth to death and back to life by reincarnation. This movement of time is derived from the agricultural cycle among pre-industrial peoples. As their predominant economic activities move from planting to harvest and back to planting, as the sun and moon appear and disappear only to return in an endless cycle, life is conceived to follow a similar pattern. Reality is divided into two: the human world and the spirit world. But each is a replica of the other; thus if an achieved person or a chief dies, he will still live like one in the spirit world. This explains why some communities bury slaves to continue serving their master in the spirit world. Tied to this is an anthropology in

8. Charles H. Kraft, *Anthropology for Christian Witness* (Maryknoll, NY: Orbis Books, 1996), p. 10; Paul G. Hiebert, *Anthropological Insights for Missionaries* (Grand Rapids: Baker Books, 1985), p. 46; M. G. Kraft, *Understanding Spiritual Powers* (Maryknoll, NY: Orbis Books, 1995), p. 20.

which a creator deity delegated subalterns to mold human beings from clay while he himself breathed life-giving breath into them. The blood transmits the life into all the body system. At death, the personality-soul or life-breath continues a new life cycle in the spirit world, now as an ancestor who is still a member of his earthly family. This is the concept of the living-dead. Death is not an end but the beginning of a new vista of living.

This organic perception is underscored by the conception of space. The African perceives three dimensions of space: the sky, the earth (consisting of land and water), and the ancestral or spirit world. It is an alive universe as each space is peopled with some of the four components of spiritual powers: the *Supreme Being* as the creator and the major subaltern *divinities* inhabit the sky. Manifesting as the sun, lightning, thunder, moon, stars, they serve as oracles, arbiters in human affairs, and agents in ritual dynamics. The major force or divinity on the earth is the *Earth deity*, which is responsible for fertility and nurture of life of humans, animals, and plants. Land looms large in this cosmology. In many myths of origin, it is said that during creation the *Supreme Being* sent some deities to perch on anthills and dry the marshy earth; thus was the world formed. Some stayed back and inhabited rocks, trees, caves, streams, and rivers, and thus imbued physical nature with divine power. Beyond *nature spirits* are *patron spirits* for certain professions such as farming, hunting, fishing, blacksmithing, trading, and other economic pursuits. Thus, all the realms of life are sacralized; there is no distinction between the sacred and the profane. The eco-theology in this religious landscape is very important but cannot be pursued here.

There are *human spirits* on the land because each human being has a guardian spirit who determines his or her fate in the passage through life. In some cultures, the individual would make a wooden figure of the personal daemon and sacrifice to it daily for empowerment in the pursuits of life. In the gender construct, the marine spirits are imaged as daughters to the Earth deity. Marine spirits can be munificent and give riches to devotees. Barren women propitiate marine spirits for children; musicians consort with them for melodious songs; so do artists seeking for inspiration. The connection between commerce and the arts with marine spirits runs as deep as the depths of seas. But marine spirits could be wicked beings that cause those under their control to be morally unstable and wayward. Their flashy gifts do not last; marriages contrived by them do not succeed, and children from marine spirits are often plagued by inexplicable illness.

These elements of instability force the afflicted to diviners who will assist in extricating the individual from covenants made by parents or by the person with marine spirits.

Next to the deities and spirits, the third component consists of the *ancestral spirits* which inhabit the earth-beneath. Imbuing the whole of the world of the living are the fourth component, *spiritual forces* which individuals can acquire through rituals for enhancing life-force. They are nonpersonal beings such as they call *mana* in Oceania: mysterious, ubiquitous power that permeates all areas of life and can be used for good or in anti-social manners to harm or diminish the capability of another person's life-force, fortunes, and resources. The negative uses could be operated through words, thoughts, attitudes, and behavior in sorcery or witchcraft practices. Witchcraft is the use of human psychic powers to do evil, unlike sorcery that employs magical incantations, implements, objects, medicine, and other paraphernalia. With either method, curses could be put on individuals and families by envious or wicked people. Evil forces are without bodily forms, so they embody people, animals, and physical objects and manipulate these to harm people. The vision of existence is a precarious one as evil forces, which invest the human world as a siege, endeavor to ruin the capacity of individuals, families, and communities from living a prosperous life. Ruth Marshall has shown that this scenario holds equally well for the modern urban setting in Africa:

> With increasing economic hardship and zero-sum struggle for survival, great strain is put on the extended family as the basic domestic unit. Relatively successful family members often resent the pressure put on them by a variety of near and distant relatives. . . . Young people striving for upward mobility not only desire a relative freedom from such pressures, but also protection from resentment and jealousy in the form of witchcraft, most feared and dangerous in the hands of blood relatives.[9]

Affliction is a pivotal issue in the theology of the African primal world. It can be caused by a contravention of moral code. For instance, the Earth deity supervises the moral order on the land. Matters such as stealing, adultery, incest, other forms of wrongdoing, and breakdown in social relations are abominations to her. Failure to propitiate her is visited with afflictions

9. Ruth Marshall-Fratani, "Mediating the Global and Local in Nigerian Pentecostalism," *Journal of Religion in Africa* 28, no. 3 (1998): 278-315; see p. 283.

that take different forms such as illness or misfortune. The manifestation may be individual or communal. Political instability, economic disaster, upsurge in mortality rate, increase in robbery, and other unwholesome social facts are regarded as disease, requiring divinatory diagnosis and spiritual cure. Disease could, therefore, be caused by religious, social, and natural causes. To reestablish the security of the moral order and reconcile broken social relationships, medicine becomes important. A diviner diagnoses the problem and provides curative and protective spiritual powers — either through herbs or by covenanting the individual or community to protective spirits. Festivals, dances, masquerades, and commensality are employed to reenergize ancestral and other covenants and heal the community from untoward conditions. Finally, it has been shown through a survey of 615 spirits occupying the religious ardor of the Igbo of southeastern Nigeria, that different cultural theaters in Africa prioritize which deities are central for their needs. The challenges of the ecosystem are core determinants for prioritizing their choices.

This is a charismatic worldview. Going through life is like spiritual warfare, and religious ardor may appear very materialistic as people strive to preserve their material sustenance in the midst of the machinations of pervasive evil forces. Behind it is a strong sense of the moral and spiritual moorings of life. It is an organic worldview in which the three dimensions of space are bound together; the visible and the invisible worlds interweave. Nothing happens in the visible world that has not been predetermined in the invisible realm. The challenge for Christianity is how to witness to the gospel in a highly spiritualized environment where the recognition of the powers has not been banished in a Cartesian flight to objectivity and enlightenment. The power question is ultimate and suffuses the African primal worldview, demanding an answer from the new Christian change-agent. It points to the need for continuity in change. Earlier missionary efforts to sidestep with charitable institutions and a Western worldview failed, leaving the field open for re-evangelization. The born-again people have picked up the gauntlet. The argument here is that Pentecostalism in Africa derived its coloring from the texture of the African soil and from the interior of its idiom, nurture, and growth; its fruits serve more adequately the challenges and problems of the African ecosystem than the earlier missionary fruits.

Ogbu U. Kalu

Kindred Atmosphere and Resonance:
Pentecostal Reconstruction of the Primal Worldview

The major contribution of the Pentecostal movement is how it addresses the continued reality of the forces expressed in African cultural forms. They deploy four strategies: adopt a posture of spiritual warfare, use the covenant imagery to describe the relationship between human beings and the gods, explore swaths of resonance between the Bible and African indigenous worldviews, and reinvent a theology that reclaims God's rule over the whole inhabited earth. It resembles the old strategy of "spoiling the Egyptians."

Contrary to the early missionary attitude that urged rejection, Pentecostals take the African map of the universe seriously, acknowledging that culture is both a redemptive gift as well as capable of being hijacked. Pentecostals perceive a kindred atmosphere and resonance between the Bible and African indigenous religions. Pentecostals, therefore, explore the lines of congruence that go beyond destruction of the old to a new construction of reality.

African worldviews share an identical creation myth with the Genesis saga, earth created from a watery terrain. Among the Igbo, the Supreme Being, Chukwu, sent a smith as an agent with bellows to dry the land. Anthills appeared. At the structural level, there appears to be a major difference between the indigenous and the biblical worldviews. The New Testament worldview is constructed on a linear perception of time. Time moves as a continuum from the past through the present to the future. In the worldviews of most African communities, time is perceived as cyclical. But on a closer look, both worldviews are in the Bible and they share a three-dimensional perception of space. The Bible declares that, at the name of Jesus, "every knee shall bow" whether it exists in the heavens, earth (land and water) or in the earth-beneath (ancestral world).

Both traditional African culture and Pentecostalism affirm that "things which are seen are made of things which are not seen" (Heb. 11:3b) and that events in the manifest world are first decided in the spirit world; therefore, in salvatory conflict situations, "the weapons of our warfare are not carnal." The biblical worldview images the Christian life to be just as precarious as the traditional African imagines. The enemy is ranged in a military formation as principalities, powers, rulers of darkness, wickedness in high places, and demons. The Pentecostal goes through life as keenly aware of the pres-

144

ence of evil forces as the African does. Life is secured through a good relationship with the supernatural. The Bible, for instance, prescribes both obedience and active maintenance of the covenant with God; it therefore contains a diatribe against the competing covenants with other gods. These are imaged as snares; therefore, the need for testing of spirits. The promise of land was a key component of the covenant. Similarly, when there is a drought or famine or social distress, Africans look to the land and to their relationship with the earth deity because the earth deity sustains the economic and moral order. The Pentecostals do likewise: they bring to the problem the importance of the land among the Israelites. Brueggemann said that land referred to actual earthly turf and also symbolically to express the wholeness of joy and well-being characterized by social coherence and personal ease in prosperity, security, and freedom. Land as promise, holy, and a symbol of our covenant relationship with God has tremendous resonance in the attitude to land in African primal societies.[10] The "brethren" plumb the resonance and move to the impact of pollution caused by the actions of rulers and the ruled. Shrines, festivals to Baal and Ashteroths, witchcraft and corruption are all listed as sources of the woes. IMF and World Bank are evangelists of the Beast who is equally behind the European Union and the divinity of the market economy that is "SAPping" African countries with debt repayment. SAP is Structural Adjustment Program and comes with "conditionalities" that exacerbate poverty.

Pentecostals appreciate the tensile strength of the spiritual ecology in Africa and the clash of covenants in their efforts to displace the illegitimate spirits at the "doors" of individuals and "gates" of communities with a legitimate spiritual authority. Salvation is posed as a conflict scenario. The Garrick Braide missionaries reflected this in a simple chorus which declared that "Jesus has come and Satan has run away!" From this power and authority structure, there are human beings who are given false powers by evil forces to exercise control over individuals, families, and communities. Satan even promised Jesus some of these if he complied. Thus, Pentecostals perceive dictatorial and corrupt rulers as being "possessed" subalterns of higher spiritual forces. The Pentecostals imagine that these spirits exercise psychic powers over the individuals through witchcraft and sorcery that constitute soul-to-soul attack. This is built on the biblical anthropology. All of life is subjected to the authority of Christ and, while not deny-

---

10. Walter Brueggemann, *Land* (Philadelphia: Fortress, 1977), p. 2.

ing personal responsibility, it recognizes that individuals and circumstances could be driven by forces beyond their control.

Here, the Pentecostal explanation for witchcraft and sorcery by appeal to a biblical anthropology is fascinating. Arguing that God formed man and breathed himself into the body and man became *nephesh,* a living soul, the fall is imaged as a house that collapsed, burying the spiritual resources. The soul *(psyche),* consisting of the intellect, willpower, and emotions, constitutes the strongest part of the person, seeking to dominate both the person's spirit *(pneuma)* and the body *(soma).* Salvation comes by the spirit of God, taking over the *pneuma* and exuding the power into the *psyche,* redeeming the constituent parts and recovering the *soma,* which is driven by lusts of the flesh, the eye, and the pride of life. In this anthropology, witchcraft operates in the quest to tap the latent powers of the soul and use these to perform false miracles or hurt other people by a soul-to-soul attack. Sorcery worsens matters by using things that provide contact with the victim. It could be the hair, clothes, food, and the like.

Both worldviews, traditional African and Pentecostal, are attentive to the power of words and names. God spoke things into being. Jesus spoke and people were healed and situations changed. Similarly, in indigenous religions, covenants are spoken into binding relationships, libations are followed with spoken prayers, and incantations and curses are pronounced. In oral cultures, the words of parents are so powerful that they can affect the fate of their children. Modern psychologists explain this well. Christians are, therefore, admonished to also speak the reversal to curses by using the name of Jesus, the blood, and the resources of the Holy Spirit. They have been given power to speak changes into being. Human beings become co-creators with God. As Wink said, *onoma,* name, is a metonymy, the part representing the whole. Renaming of people and places was a part of signifying a new relationship with the divine. In African cultures names have meaning and importance. The Nuer name their favorite cattle after their best friends as a mark of love. The name of Jesus designates his office, dignity, and the power of God in him. The text often cited is 1 John 5:8 and many others recounting the powers of Jesus and his position in the Godhead. This explains why Pentecostals use command and the power of word and name in the deliverance process and avoid the use of instruments, limiting these to olive oil and anointed handkerchiefs and laying on of hands.

Finally, the Pentecostals completely took over the Pauline use of the word *kosmos,* which can refer to the material universe and the inhabitants of the world, but which Paul fastens on the third usage referring to worldly affairs — the worldly goods, endowments, riches, pleasures, and allurements *(kosmetikos)* which seduce from God. Thus, behind the classical idea of *kosmos* as an orderly arrangement is a mind behind the system, a world system established after the fall by a *kosmokrator,* a world ruler, the prince of this world, in rebellion. Friendship with him is enmity with God. It is a short step from here to perceive territorial spirits allocated to various spaces for ungodly activities. This idea was, after all, very prominent in Judaism and in the early church. There is a confluence of the spiritual and material worlds, denying the myth of materialism. Walter Wink has in his trilogy (1984-1992) explored the language of power in the New Testament and concluded that

> Principalities and powers are the inner and outer aspects of any given manifestation of power. As the inner aspect they are the spirituality of institutions, the 'within' of corporate structures and systems, the inner essence of outer organizations of power.[11]

Analyzing further, he argues that the language of power pervades the whole New Testament, and while it could be liquid, imprecise, interchangeable, and unsystematic, a clear pattern of usage emerges. "Powers" could be used to refer to heavenly, divine, spiritual, invisible forces as well as to earthly, human, political, and structural manifestations as long as we realize that the "world" of the ancients was not a physical planet spinning in an empty space in a rotation around a nuclear reactor, the sun; it was a single continuum of heaven and earth, in which spiritual beings were as much at home as humans.[12] Paul used *dynamis* to focus on the spiritual dimension of power in its capacity to determine terrestrial existence for weal or for woe. Later, this word assumed more the designation for God's enemies, engaged in a cosmic struggle to assert lordship over the earth.

Some have assumed that African Christians have manufactured demons and enlarged their provenance. But they abound in Jewish literature as defecting angels, sired giants who were drowned in the flood; their spirits live on as demons, evil spirits, or "powers of Mastema." Their leaders were variously called Azazel, Mastema, Satan, and Belial. Early Christians

---

11. Walter Wink, *Naming the Powers: The Language of Power in the New Testament* (Philadelphia: Fortress, 1984), p. 5.

12. Wink, *Naming the Powers,* p. 15.

devised elaborate instructions on how to discern them. The ministry of Jesus was very much a cosmic battle in which Jesus rescued humanity from evil powers. Therefore, African Pentecostals have equated principalities, powers, and demons with the various categories of spirits in the worldview and as enemies of man and God. They reinforce the causality pattern in the primal worldview before providing a solution beyond the purviews of indigenous cosmology. They rework the Pauline structure with native ingredients:

1. PRINCIPALITIES
    i. Apollyon (Rev. 9:11)
    ii. Abaddon
    iii. Belial
    iv. The Beast; symbol: the leopard
    v. Ariel

2. POWERS
    i. Ashteroth (agricultural deities)
    ii. Baal (shrines on the earth, worship of earth deity)
    iii. Magog (e.g., Ogun, the Yoruba powers for medicine related to cutlass, gun, iron)
    iv. Beelzebub (god of witchcraft, wizardry)
    v. Asmodee (goddess of sexual immorality)
    vi. Mammon (spirit that induces the allure of money)
    vii. aimon (celestial demons empowering occultists)
    viii. Aritan (magic, satanic justice)

3. RULERS OF DARKNESS
    i. Ogeaso (Bini), Ogbanje (Igbo) — spirits of children who come with a pact to return early into the spirit world
    ii. Jezebel, dark goddess of the loins, seductive spirit, harlotry
    iii. Molech, promoter of nudist fashion and pornography
    iv. Leviathan, a spirit that attracts people into unwholesome covenants
    v. Jephtha, patron of thieves and robbers

By turning the Bible into a canon of tribal history and weaving it into the indigenous worldviews, Pentecostals directly address the problems of evil forces: (1) They mine the interior of the worldviews to establish that the same covenantal structure exists in both; therefore the solution to the problem of affliction and defeat in life is to exchange the covenant with the wicked spirits for the covenant with Christ. (2) They produce large quantities of literature as discourses that expose these forces and show individuals and communities how to overcome their dangerous and destructive influences. (3) They enable individuals and groups to constitute historical agents, empowered to do battle with these principalities and powers. And (4) they incite public testimonies about the works and victory over the wicked forces. Former agents of the spirits describe in gory details their years of bondage serving the false spirits; they combine these accounts with a wide range of self-help discourses featuring exposures of spiritual machinations at ground-level, occult, and territorial spirit levels. Testimonies in public worship become ceremonies of degradation and bridge-burning.

They do not reject the past wholesale but engage with it, refashioning the history, and domesticating it. They use the Bible as a resource for explaining the past and critiquing the present. The Pentecostal approach to the African map of the universe comes out most clearly in the response to the current legitimacy crises and economic collapse. For instance, the corruption in the state is attributed to the operation of the hunter or Nimrod spirit among African rulers, descendants of Ham. The collapse of the African economy is due to the shedding of blood through internecine fratricide and civil wars. These bring curses reminiscent of the Cain-Abel saga in which the land withheld her increase because the land was polluted with blood. Emigration follows ineluctably as the earth spews out her people. After the spiritualized diagnosis of the malaise of the political economy, follows the task of raising an army that will rescue the land. This approach fits into the tradition of iconic prophets whose duty was to "forth-tell" the meaning behind events. The real question may not be the spiritualizing of events but whether such prognosis is based on adequate empirical data. Philip Jenkins has, therefore, brought together the seed of the arguments by John Mbiti and Kwame Bediako — that scholarship should pay attention to the centrality and uses of the Bible among Christians in various regions of the world.[13]

---

13. Philip Jenkins, *The New Faces of Christianity: Believing the Bible in the Global South* (New York: Oxford University Press, 2006); J. S. Mbiti, *Bible and Theology in African Christianity* (Nairobi: Oxford University Press, 1986).

The language of God in Pentecostal liturgy buttresses this fact. They explore the language communities use in addressing their sustaining divinities, ancestors, and the Supreme Being and use these to describe God and Christ, showing that they are superior to all the powers available in the people's map of their universe. The reconstructed world is brought home to individual lives and circumstances by applying a "bumper sticker" hermeneutics or "experiential literalism." Cheryl B. Johns said that Pentecostal hermeneutics is praxis-oriented, with experience and Scripture being maintained in a dialectical relationship. The Holy Spirit maintains the ongoing relationship. The truth must be fulfilled in life experiences. Lived faith is the result of the knowledge of the Scriptures.[14] The emphases are on the experiential, relational, emotional, oral faith, immediacy of the text, and a freedom to interpret and appropriate the multiple meanings of the biblical texts. By a pneumatic illumination, it recognizes a spiritual kinship between the authors and readers and ongoing continuity with the New Testament church. Personal and corporate experiences weave into the hermeneutical task.

The literature on this matter has burgeoned; suffice it to point to the emphasis on the power of the Word in spiritual formation, resisting forces that could lead one to backslide, reversing curses, deliverance, and commanding the things the Lord's hands have made. The "brethren" arrive for Bible studies and Sunday worship with notebooks to take down the message or "revelations" so as to apply these during the week for victory. Everyone is urged to be an overcomer and "demon destroyer." This is hermeneutics for conscientization, choreographed with a vigorous homiletic that mines the people's experiences, dramatizes these, props them with "real-life" testimonies, and brings the promises in the Bible to respond to the problems so that no one should leave bearing the burdens of yesterday. A pastor would tell the story of a woman who was carrying a heavy load. A car stopped and offered to assist the woman; she accepted the offer, got into the car but continued to carry the load on her head instead of setting it down. The congregation would indicate that it was a foolish thing to do. Often a sermon would be interrupted with choruses to bring home a point. Pentecostal homiletic is language crafted in a transformative manner and choreographed as a ritual of validation and commitment. As

14. Cheryl B. Johns, *Pentecostal Formation* (Sheffield: Sheffield Academic Press, 1993), p. 86.

Rambo argues,[15] the songs, dances, and the yells elicit audience participation and aid believers in performing religiously before rationalizing the process. Such rituals offer knowledge in a distinct form that enables the believer to understand, experience, and embody the new way of life.

Swallowing the Magicians' Serpents: A Conclusion

Generally, Western scholarship brands African Christianity as conservative and biblicist even though some of the literature on the end time prophecies from the Western world provides the armory for this application of the Bible to both contemporary events and the African primal map of the universe. Pentecostal leaders bring together materials from both internal and external sources in a manner that the unlettered could understand, because behind the macro-economics of the global market is the divine will. Pentecostals urge members to avoid judging by sight but by revelation as to which spirits are operating behind manifest events. Land deliverance is only one of the strategies employed. It is subtle and avoids overt iconoclasm: believers can "walk" around shrines as hostile, polluted ground and command the spirits to leave. Sometimes, during emotional crusades, those with authority over the land and affairs of the community will be asked to confess the iniquities of the fathers that are being visited upon their progenies and to hand over the land to the authority of Jesus. This symbolic action will ensure prosperity for all the people. In these ways, the born-again brethren in Africa bring a spiritual solution to the great issues of the day, taking the context, the worldview, and the ecology seriously but within the gospel mandate.

When Moses encountered the magicians in the house of Pharaoh, the narrative pointed to the undeniable fact that the magicians were able to produce serpents. They had and exercised powers. But the serpent produced by Moses swallowed the others to indicate that his rod of authority was more powerful. This informs the attitude of Pentecostals to African traditional cultures and religions. Unlike the enlightened missionary cultural policy, Pentecostals accept the power and reality in the symbols and rituals of communities and bring a "pneumatic knowing" to respond. Just as the primal societies wove covenants and encapsulating strategies to

15. L. Rambo, *Understanding Religious Conversion* (New Haven: Yale University Press, 1993), pp. 113-16.

maintain cosmic order, Pentecostals essay to reshape the covenants, world-view, social-control model, and individual life journeys and goals so that individuals and communities will have a better life. They reshape the community's sense of order. These strategies could be illustrated with cultural ingredients from domestic and social domains, arts and aesthetics, religious life and public space, and especially with communication — the use of symbols, speech, and media to construct a new reality. The vibrancy and efficacy of the combined force of these strategies have given the new movement a high profile.

The movement can best be understood within the strand in African church historiography that has urged attention on the weave between religious ecology and the forms of Christian allegiance. It is a response to the deep-level challenges of the eco-theater, applying the pneumatic resources of biblical theology which missionary theology and practice had muted. Working within African maps of the universe, they have shown how a creative use of biblical promises can transform the lives of many with tools of hope in the midst of the darkness that has hit Africa at noontide. They have exploited the elasticity in the African worldview, its capacity to make room within its inherited body of traditions for new realities, which though seemingly from outside, come in to fulfill aspirations within the tradition and, then, to offer quite significantly the basis of self-understanding within the tradition. Kwame Bediako says that this is what Paul did with Jewish traditions in the letter to the Hebrews.[16] Pentecostals have fleshed out their faith in the context of contending religious and social forces in Africa. The use of external cultural resources to create an emergent culture started with Western encounter with Africans. The genius of the movement lies in the degree of cultural creativity in appropriating, gestating, and reconstructing the extravenous with fresh imagination and energy. Culture and race were the contested set of signifiers in action in colonial Christianity, and African Christianity was stamped with values of anti-structure from the onset. Pentecostalism has produced a culture of continuity by mining the primal worldview, reproducing an identifiable character, and regaining a pneumatic and charismatic religiosity as existed in traditional society. In conclusion, the achievement of Pentecostals lies in their innovative responses to the challenges embedded in the African map of the universe.

16. Kwame Bediako, *Christianity in Africa: The Renewal of a Non-Western Religion* (Edinburgh: Edinburgh University Press; Maryknoll, NY: Orbis Books, 1995), p. 84.

PART III

"The Spirit Among Religions":
Pentecostal Theology and Religious Plurality

CHAPTER 9

Pentecostal Pneumatology of Religions: The Contribution of Pentecostalism to Our Understanding of the Work of God's Spirit in the World

Veli-Matti Kärkkäinen

Introduction: The Pneumatological Renaissance

Once called a stepchild of theology, in the shadow of the Father and Son, the Spirit has now been restored to her proper place; the "Cinderella of theology" has entered the divine ball.[1] In recent years, one of the most exciting developments in theology and religious studies has been an unprecedented interest in the Holy Spirit. The reverberations can be felt across a broad range, from the academic, ecclesiastical,[2] and religious worlds to new spiritual movements such as Green Pneumatology or Liberation Pneumatology. The resurgence of pneumatology has to do, among other things, with the better knowledge of the rich spiritual and pneumatological traditions of the Eastern Orthodox churches who have accused their Western counterparts of "forgetfulness of the Spirit," and with the dramatic spread of the Pentecostal and charismatic movements.[3] Many

---

1. Both Jürgen Moltmann, *Spirit of Life: A Universal Affirmation* (Minneapolis: Fortress, 1993), and Alister E. McGrath, *Christian Theology: An Introduction* (Oxford, UK, and Cambridge, MA: Blackwell, 1994), p. 240, use the analogy of Cinderella.

2. A case in point is the 1996 Annual Meeting of the Catholic Theological Society of America, which focused on pneumatology with the theme "Toward a Spirited Theology: Challenges of the Holy Spirit to Theological Disciplines." For conference papers, see *Proceedings of the Catholic Theological Society of America*, ed. E. Dryer (Chicago: CTSA, 1996), p. 51.

3. Until recently it was a commonplace to introduce pneumatological treatises with a lament over the Spirit's neglect. There were several reasons for this "oblivion of the Spirit":

developments beyond Christian theology such as new interest in spirituality in the postmodern world,[4] influences from Eastern religions and new
religiosities of the West, and the transition from an old "mechanistic"
worldview towards a dynamic *Weltanschauung* and scientific paradigm
have also contributed to the rise to prominence of pneumatology. According to the Roman Catholic Elizabeth Dryer,

> Renewed interest in the Holy Spirit is visible in at least three contexts:
> individual Christians who hunger for a deeper connection with God
> that is inclusive of all of life as well as the needs of the world; the church
> that seeks to renew itself through life-giving disciplines and a return to
> sources; and the formal inquiry of academic philosophy and theology.
> In effect, one can hear the petition, "Come Creator Spirit" on many lips
> these days.[5]

My aim in this presentation is to offer a reading of the state and contribution of Pentecostal spirituality and theology to our understanding of
the role of the Spirit in the world and in relation to religions. My presentation falls into three uneven portions. First, I will give a brief statement — a

the "depersonalized" approach to the Spirit stemming from St. Augustine's idea of the Spirit
as *vinculum amoris* (the bond of love between the Father and Son); the Western *filioque* view
(the Spirit proceeds both from the Father and Son, thus making the Spirit subordinate); the
biblical hint according to which the Spirit is "the Unknown Third" who never draws attention to himself; and the church's weariness over charismatic and prophetic movements that
have threatened order and hierarchy. See further, Veli-Matti Kärkkäinen, *Pneumatology: The
Holy Spirit in Ecumenical, International, and Contextual Perspective* (Grand Rapids: Baker
Academic, 2002), chap. 1; Kärkkäinen, "The Ecumenical Potential of Pneumatology," chap. 5
in *Toward a Pneumatological Theology: Pentecostal and Ecumenical Perspectives on Ecclesiology, Soteriology, and Theology of Mission*, ed. Amos Yong (Lanham, MD: University Press of
America, 2002).

4. According to John R. Sachs, there "is an incredible interest today in the Spirit and
spirituality. People are paying attention to the spiritual dimension of their lives and often
seem to be experiencing the Spirit in ways and places that often challenge traditional theologies and Church structures and sometimes have little connection with traditional religious
practice. The Spirit is present and active beyond the official structures and ordained ministries of the Church." John R. Sachs, "'Do Not Stifle the Spirit': Karl Rahner, the Legacy of
Vatican II, and Its Urgency for Theology Today," in *Catholic Theological Society Proceedings*,
p. 15.

5. E. Dryer, "Resources for a Renewed Life in the Spirit and Pneumatology: Medieval
Mystics and Saints," in *Advent of the Spirit: Orientations in Pneumatology, Conference Papers
from a Symposium at Marquette University, April 17-19, 1998* (photocopy), p. 1.

map, rather — of the current state of pneumatology, reflection on the Spirit, in contemporary theology. Second, I attempt to outline key features of a Pentecostal/charismatic take on pneumatology in general, and third, in the main part of my essay, I consider the relation of Pentecostal pneumatology to religions and the way Pentecostals understand the work of God in the world. In other words, my ultimate purpose for the presentation is to locate Pentecostal pneumatology in the wider theological framework of reflection on the Spirit. During the discussion I will further specify and focus my discussion.

What Is New and Novel in Contemporary Pneumatology?

The most noted contemporary Christian pneumatologist, Jürgen Moltmann, aptly sets the stage for considering the need for significant turns and developments in Christian theology of the Spirit that are emerging at the beginning of the third millennium:

> In both Protestant and Catholic theology and devotion, there is a tendency to view the Holy Spirit solely as the Spirit of redemption. Its place is in the church, and it gives men and women the assurance of the eternal blessedness of their souls. This redemptive Spirit is cut off both from bodily life and from the life of nature. It makes people turn away from "this world" and hope for a better world beyond. They then seek and experience in the Spirit of Christ a power that is different from the divine energy of life, which according to the Old Testament ideas interpenetrates all the living. The theological textbooks therefore talk about the Holy Spirit in connection with God, faith, the Christian life, the church and prayer, but seldom in connection with the body and nature.[6]

Indeed, in the past the doctrine of the Spirit was mainly and often exclusively connected with topics such as the doctrines of salvation, inspiration, and some issues of ecclesiology (the doctrine of the church) as well as individual piety. With regard to the doctrine of salvation, the Spirit represented the "subjective" side whereas Christology was the objective basis. With regard to Scripture, the Spirit played a crucial role in both inspiration and illumination of the Word of God. In various Christian traditions, from

6. Moltmann, *Spirit of Life*, p. 8.

mysticism to pietism to Classical Liberalism and beyond, the Spirit's work was seen mainly in relation to animating and refreshing one's inner spiritual life. Suffice it to say that the role of the Spirit in traditional theology was quite reserved and limited. It is this reductionism that has elicited a number of new proposals, and as a result, things are now changing rapidly.

While not leaving behind these emphases, today the Spirit is also connected with other theological topics such as creation, anthropology, Christology, and eschatology.[7] There is an attempt to give the Spirit a more integral and central role in theology. Political, social, environmental, liberationist, and other "public" issues[8] are being invoked by the theologians of the Spirit at the beginning of the third millennium. The Old Testament idea of the Spirit of God as the Spirit of life has gained a new significance;[9] one of the exciting results is a new dialogue between the Spirit and science.[10] In contrast to traditional pneumatologies, often perceived as dry and abstract, there is a new appreciation of the experience

7. Influential recent contributions include Moltmann, *Spirit of Life;* Moltmann, *The Source of Life: The Holy Spirit and the Theology of Life* (Minneapolis: Fortress, 1997); Michael Welker, *God the Spirit* (Minneapolis: Fortress, 1994); as well as Wolfhart Pannenberg, *Systematic Theology,* trans. Geoffrey W. Bromiley, 3 vols. (Grand Rapids: Eerdmans, 1991, 1994, 1998). While Pannenberg has not produced a separate monograph on pneumatology, his whole theological program is imbued by pneumatology as part of a thoroughgoing trinitarianism.

8. For political pneumatologies, see Geiko Müller-Fahrenholz, *God's Spirit: Transforming a World in Crisis,* trans. John Cumming (New York: Continuum, 1995); for "green" and eco-feminist pneumatologies, see Elizabeth A. Johnson, *Women, Earth and Creator Spirit* (New York: Paulist, 1993); for liberationist pneumatologies, see José Gomblin, *The Holy Spirit and Liberation,* trans. Paul Burns (Maryknoll, NY: Orbis Books, 1989); for a "pneumatology of work," see Miroslav Volf, *Work in the Spirit: Toward a Theology of Work* (New York/Oxford: Oxford University Press, 1991).

9. The main thesis of Moltmann's *Spirit of Life* is that the best way to discern the presence of the Spirit in the world is to work in support of life, growth, and development. The original subtitle in German, *Eine ganzheitliche Pneumatologie* ("holistic," "all-encompassing," or "comprehensive" pneumatology), expresses the main theme of the book better than the English subtitle *A Universal Affirmation.*

10. For some insights into the dialogue between the Spirit and science, see Pannenberg, *Systematic Theology,* vol. 2, esp. §2, "The Spirit of God and the Dynamic of Natural Occurrence"; Pannenberg, "The Doctrine of the Spirit and the Task of a Theology of Nature," chap. 5 in Pannenberg, *Toward a Theology of Nature: Essays on Science and Faith,* ed. Ted Peters (Louisville: Westminster John Knox, 1993); and Pannenberg, "God as Spirit — and Natural Science," *Zygon* 36, no. 4 (2001): 783-94. Process theology with its dynamic worldview has been fertile soil for the dialogue, as illustrated by the work of Joseph Bracken, S.J., *Society and Spirit: A Trinitarian Cosmology* (Selinsgrove, PA: Susquehanna University Press, 1991).

and spirituality of the Spirit. Also in contemporary pneumatology there is a desire to connect the Spirit with ethics and life, which is, after all, a thoroughly biblical idea. Furthermore, contemporary pneumatology both acknowledges and desires to relate itself to particular contexts, thus, for example, allowing women to express their experience of the Spirit in a unique way.[11] Contemporary pneumatology gives voices to the poor and oppressed, and to testimonies from Africa, Asia, and Latin America in a way never before in the history of reflection on the Spirit.[12] Last but not least: contemporary theology includes an enthusiasm over relating the Spirit of God to other religions; indeed, we can talk about the "turn to the Spirit" in the Christian theology of religions (as it is technically known).[13]

Pentecostal Pneumatology

The search for a Pentecostal pneumatology is an utterly complicated and complex task — even though an uninformed observer might assume that for a Spirit-movement such as this the task could be taken for granted. Whence the difficulty? The reasons are many:

First, unlike established Christian traditions such as Roman Catholicism, Pentecostalism cannot build on tradition for the simple reason that it came into existence only a century ago. Second, until recent years, Pentecostalism has not produced much theological literature; its contribution to Christian faith has been in the form of occasional pastoral and missional writings, testimonies, dreams, prophecies, and the like, which do not easily translate into an analytic, discursive theology.[14] Third, because

11. For feminist pneumatologies, see Elizabeth Johnson, *She Who Is: The Mystery of God in Feminist Theological Discourse* (New York: Crossroad, 1992); Rebecca Button Prichard, *Sensing the Spirit: The Holy Spirit in Feminist Perspective* (St. Louis: Chalice, 1999); and Nancy M. Victorin-Vangerud, *The Raging Hearth: Spirit in the Household of God* (St. Louis: Chalice, 2000).

12. For contributions to pneumatology from Asia, Africa, and Latin America, see Kärkkäinen, *Pneumatology*, chap. 6.

13. For a concise introduction, see Amos Yong, "The Turn to Pneumatology in Christian Theology of Religions: Conduit or Detour," *Journal of Ecumenical Studies* 35 (1998): 437-54.

14. This is of course not to say that Pentecostals have not produced theology. They have, but in forms that until recently have not been either appreciated or well known by the professional theological guild. Pentecostalism's way of doing theology — paralleling the way

Veli-Matti Kärkkäinen

Pentecostalism was birthed out of dynamic experience rather than a theological discovery,[15] it has liberally incorporated elements from a number of theological traditions and sources such as Methodist-Holiness movements, the Protestant Reformation, mystical-charismatic movements in the Roman Catholic and Eastern Orthodox churches, as well as black or African American spirituality.[16] Its theology is still in the making and represents a dynamic syncretistic exercise; the Pentecostal identity is best described in terms of spirituality rather than theology.[17] Fourth — against the assumptions of many — pneumatology does not necessarily represent the center of Pentecostal spirituality; the center is rather Christology. An emerging scholarly consensus holds that at the heart of Pentecostal spirituality lies the "Full Gospel," the idea of Jesus Christ in his fivefold role as

---

that much of non-Western Christianity is still doing it — has been oral rather than discursive. For the significance of orality to theology see Walter J. Ong, *Orality and Literacy: The Technologizing of the Word* (London and New York: Methuen, 1982) and in relation to Pentecostalism in particular, Walter J. Hollenweger, *Pentecostalism: Origins and Developments Worldwide* (Peabody, MA: Hendrickson, 1997), pp. 18-139 (this section, I, is titled "The Black Oral Root" [of worldwide Pentecostalism]).

15. Features such as orality of liturgy; narrativity of theology and witness; maximum participation at the level of reflection, prayer, and decision-making in a community characterized by inclusion and reconciliation; inclusion of dreams and visions in personal and public forms of worship, and a holistic understanding of the body-mind relationship, reflected in the ministry of healing by prayer, were formative during the emergence of the movement. W. J. Hollenweger, "After Twenty Years' Research on Pentecostalism," *International Review of Missions* 75 (January 1986): 6. Hollenweger (*Pentecostalism*, p. 551) has insisted that it was the early years of the emerging Pentecostal movement that gave the movement its *prodigium*. The first decade of the movement, says Hollenweger, forms the heart, not the infancy, of Pentecostal spirituality. See also Steven J. Land, *Pentecostal Spirituality: A Passion for the Kingdom* (Sheffield: Sheffield Academic Press, 1993), pp. 14, 47.

16. Hollenweger (*Pentecostalism*) has summarized the "roots" of Pentecostalism in these terms: (1) the black oral root; (2) the Catholic root, (3) the evangelical root, (4) the critical root, (5) the ecumenical root. This typology serves as the structure of his book. For a brief discussion, see his "Verheissung und Verhängnis der Pfingstbewegung," *Evangelische Theologie* 53 (1993): 265-88.

17. For discussion of Pentecostal identity, see V.-M. Kärkkäinen, "Free Churches, Ecumenism, and Pentecostalism," in *Toward a Pneumatological Theology*, ed. Amos Yong (Lanham, MD: University Press of America, 2002), chap. 4. For a fine account of key themes and orientations in Pentecostal spirituality, see Russell P. Spittler, "Spirituality, Pentecostal and Charismatic," in *The New International Dictionary of Pentecostal and Charismatic Movements*, ed. Stanley M. Burgess and Eduard M. van der Maas, rev. and expanded ed. (Grand Rapids: Zondervan, 2002), pp. 1096-1102.

Savior, Sanctifier, Baptizer with the Spirit, Healer, and Soon-Coming King.[18] The gateway to the work and experience of the Spirit among Pentecostals is thus the work of Christ.

The final challenge is undoubtedly the most radical one to any theologian attempting an outline of Pentecostal pneumatology, namely, the diversity of Pentecostalism — to the point that one should probably speak of Pentecostalisms (plural). The diversity arises in two dimensions: the cultural and the theologico-ecumenical. Pentecostalism, unlike any other contemporary religious movement, Christian or non-Christian, is spread across most cultures, linguistic barriers, and social locations.[19] Related to this is the theological and ecumenical diversity, which simply means that there are several more or less distinct Pentecostalisms — in the current typology, as noted in the introductory chapter; we can speak of classical Pentecostalism, the charismatic movements (within the established churches), and the so-called neo-charismatic movements, an extremely diverse and complex phenomenon in itself.

This means simply that both Pentecostals themselves as well as outside theological observers have not reached an agreement on *the* Pentecostal view of the Spirit and the Spirit's role in the world. Let me take a few obvious examples that have direct bearing upon my topic. African Pentecostalism gleans from the African spirit world[20] similarly to the way Latin American Pentecostalism conceptually encounters folk Catholicism and spiritism;[21] some Korean Pentecostals have made use of shamanistic traditions in the culture,[22] and so on.[23] Not all Pentecostal theologians,

18. The classic study is Donald W. Dayton, *Theological Roots of Pentecostalism* (Grand Rapids: Zondervan, 1987).

19. The diversity is well documented. For an up-to-date account, see, e.g., the annual statistic lists in the January issue of *International Bulletin of Missionary Research*, compiled by David B. Barrett and Todd M. Johnson.

20. See Ogbu Kalu's chapter 8 above for a careful discussion of Pentecostalism's heritage in traditional African religiosity. Helpful also is, e.g., Allan H. Anderson, *Moya: The Holy Spirit in an African Context* (Pretoria: University of South Africa Press, 1991); Anderson, "Pentecostal Pneumatology and African Power Concepts: Continuity or Change?" *Missionalia* 19 (1990): 65-74.

21. See, e.g., Hollenweger, *Pentecostalism*, chap. 7 (on Mexico) and chap. 10 (on Chile).

22. See Koo D. Yun's chapter 6 above and, e.g., Yoo Boo-Woong, *Korean Pentecostalism: Its History and Theology*, Studies in the Intercultural History of Christianity 52 (Frankfurt: Peter Lang, 1988).

23. See further, Allan H. Anderson and Walter J. Hollenweger, eds., *Pentecostals After a*

however, are willing to admit that these non-White, non-Western Pentecostalisms with their contextualized and "syncretistic" pneumatologies represent genuine Pentecostalism. The dispute continues and is not likely to find a resolution.[24]

So, here we are: Who are the theological spokespersons for global Pentecostalisms and charismatic movements and their understanding of the work of the Spirit in the world and among religions? To further complicate the issue, it is to be noted that "[i]n Third World Pentecostalism, experience and practice are usually far more important than dogma. Pentecostalism today is in any case both fundamentally and dominantly a *Third World* phenomenon. In spite of its significant growth in North America, less than a quarter of its members in the world today are white, and this proportion continues to decrease."[25]

This extended prolegomena to the search for Pentecostal pneumatology is not here for intra-Pentecostal debate or primarily for methodological reasons. In my understanding, it has everything to do with the

---

Century: Global Perspectives on a Movement in Transition, Journal of Pentecostal Theology Supplement 15 (Sheffield: Sheffield Academic Press, 1999).

24. The American Assemblies of God historian/theologian Gary McGee speaks of those whose "classification garners together a bewildering array of indigenous churches reflecting varying degrees of syncretism along with classical Pentecostal and Charismatic constituencies" and who are "loading the terms . . . with this much diversity." He implies that such groups as Zionists in Southern Africa, Kimbanguists in Central Africa, and Spiritual Baptists in Trinidad should not be termed Pentecostal at all (McGee, "Pentecostal Missiology: Moving beyond Triumphalism to Face the Issues," *Pneuma: The Journal of the Society for Pentecostal Studies* 16, no. 2 [1994]: 276-77). An opposing view is represented by the South African expert on Pentecostalism, Allan H. Anderson, *Bazalwane: African Pentecostals in South Africa* (Pretoria: University of South Africa Press, 1992), pp. 2-6. An inclusive view is championed also by the sociologist of religion Karla Poewe, who has suggested that "charismatic Christianity" is a fitting term for all Christian movements throughout history that have emphasized "religious or spiritual experiences and the activities of the Holy Spirit." In this term she includes "present-day Pentecostalism, the charismatic, renewal, and third wave movements, African Independent Churches (AICs), independent Pentecostal churches, and the New Independent Churches (NICs) or ministries worldwide." http://www.geocities .com/ccom_ctbi/ccom_AGM_files/020913-15_CCOM_AGM_Allan_Anderson.htm-_edn30; Karla Poewe, "Introduction: The Nature, Globality, and History of Charismatic Christianity," in *Charismatic Christianity as a Global Culture*, ed. Karla Poewe (Columbia: University of South Carolina Press, 1994), p. 2.

25. Allan H. Anderson, "The Pentecostal Gospel and Third World Cultures," paper read at the Annual Meeting of the Society for Pentecostal Studies, Springfield, Missouri, 16 March 1999 (http://artsweb.bham.ac.uk/aanderson/; accessed 21 August 2006), n.p.

material content of the presentation. Consequently, to dismiss it and immediately jump into *a* presentation of Pentecostal pneumatology — as if that would qualify for *the* Pentecostal view — would not only be naïve but also counterproductive for the purposes of this project, namely, to study Pentecostal/charismatic movements in their global diversity and multiformity.

To stick to this methodological principle, I will further specify my presentation in the following way: the rest of this essay will delve deeper into classical Pentecostalism's view of the Spirit and the Spirit's role in the world with a view to registering its unique features vis-à-vis and differences from the charismatic movements' views on the one hand and more indigenous non-Western Pentecostals' and neo-charismatics' views on the other hand. This means that I will mainly concentrate on giving a fair account of Pentecostal churches' understanding of the Spirit and bring in the contributions from the other two categories as they highlight the differences. At the same time, I will also keep my eye on the location of Pentecostal pneumatology in relation to the mainline pneumatological developments.

Distinctive Features of Pentecostal Pneumatology

It seems to me the most foundational feature and far-reaching contribution of Pentecostal views of the Spirit is what Pentecostals call "empowerment" and the Harvard theologian Harvey Cox names "primal spirituality." With this term Cox refers to the largely unprocessed central core of humanity where an unending struggle for a sense of destiny and significance rages. For Cox, Pentecostalism represents a spiritual restoration of significance and purpose to lift the people from despair and hopelessness.[26] Whereas for most other Christians the presence of the Spirit is just that, *presence,* for Pentecostals the presence of the Spirit in their midst implies *empowerment.*[27] While this empowerment often manifests itself in

26. Harvey Cox, *Fire from Heaven: The Rise of Pentecostal Spirituality and the Reshaping of Religion in the Twenty-first Century* (Reading, MA: Addison-Wesley, 1995), pp. 81ff.

27. In this distinction I am indebted to the Benedictine Catholic expert on Pentecostal/charismatic movements, Fr. Kilian McDonnell, OSB. I was unable to track down the exact quotation. First I heard it from him in the weekly theological discussions during the academic year 1997-98 while I was Resident Scholar at the Institute for Ecumenical and Cultural Research that Fr. Kilian has founded and was president of at that time.

spiritual gifts such as speaking in tongues, prophecy, or healings, it is still felt and sought for by Pentecostals even when those manifestations are absent. The main function of the Pentecostal worship service, then, is to provide a setting for an encounter with Jesus, the embodiment of the Full Gospel (as explained above) to receive the (em)power(ment) of the Spirit.[28] As important as sermon, hymns, and liturgy are, they are only secondary to the meeting with the Lord.

Pentecostalism has thus offered a grassroots challenge to established churches and theologies, especially those endorsing the so-called cessationist principle, which holds that miracles or extraordinary charismata ceased at or near the end of the apostolic age. Often ridiculed for emotionalism, Pentecostals introduced a dynamic, enthusiastic type of spirituality and worship life to the contemporary church, emphasizing the possibility of experiencing God mystically. Pentecostals dubbed this initial empowerment experience Spirit baptism.[29] While it was the experience rather than doctrine that came first, a novel and disputed doctrinal understanding of Spirit baptism emerged in the early years of the movement. While never uniformly formulated or followed by the worldwide movement, it is only fair to say that for the large majority of Pentecostals, this view came to be known as the "initial physical evidence." This simply means Pentecostals expect an external sign or marker of the reception of Spirit baptism, namely, speaking in tongues *(glossolalia)*. Pentecostals claim this doctrine comes from the book of Acts, their favorite book, and from contemporary experience.[30] Theologically the initial evidence doc-

---

28. In the words of Daniel Albrecht, the researcher of Pentecostal spirituality and ritual, "In a very real sense the Sunday services of . . . [Pentecostal] churches are designed to provide a context for a mystical *encounter,* an experience with the divine. This encounter is mediated by the sense of the immediate divine presence. The primary rites of worship and altar/response are particularly structured to sensitize the congregants to the presence of the divine and to stimulate conscious experience of God. . . . The gestures, ritual actions, and symbols all function within this context to speak of the manifest presence." Daniel E. Albrecht, "Pentecostal Spirituality: Looking through the Lens of Ritual," *Pneuma: The Journal of the Society for Pentecostal Studies* 14, no. 2 (1996): 21. See also Albrecht, *Rites in the Spirit: A Ritual Approach to Pentecostal/Charismatic Spirituality* (Sheffield: Sheffield Academic Press, 1999).

29. See Frank Macchia's chapter 1 above for a fine discussion of the theological and spiritual meaning of Spirit baptism to Pentecostals.

30. Pentecostal biblical scholarship has devoted much effort in studying Lukan pneumatology. Some of the first studies were Roger Stronstadt, *A Charismatic Theology of*

trine functions "sacramentally": it is an external confirmation of the inner grace received from God's Spirit. Pentecostals do not, of course, call it "sacramental," nor do they necessarily affirm the connection.[31]

Other gifts of the Spirit such as prophesying, prayer for healing, and works of miracles are enthusiastically embraced and sought for by Pentecostals. Belief in the capacity of the Spirit to bring about healing, whether physical or mental, is one of the hallmarks of Pentecostalism.[32] In this, Pentecostals echo the postmodern insistence on a holistic understanding of the body-mind relationship.[33] A related belief is the capacity to fight "spiritual warfare" and exorcise demonic spirits, if necessary. This is a significant part of Pentecostal spirituality, especially outside the West.[34]

Two interrelated features need to be added to aptly characterize the distinctives of any Pentecostal view of the Spirit, namely, eschatology and missionary enthusiasm; these also bear directly on their view of the Spirit's role among religions. From the beginning, Pentecostals were convinced that the twentieth-century outpouring of the Spirit marked the beginning

---

St. Luke (Peabody, MA: Hendrickson, 1984); and Robert Menzies, *The Development of Early Christian Pneumatology with Special Reference to Luke-Acts* (Sheffield: Sheffield Academic Press, 1991).

31. Both Pentecostal and non-Pentecostal theologians have made the connection between *glossolalia* and sacrament(al). The Catholic Heribert Mühlen, in the beginning stages of the International Dialogue between the Roman Catholics and Pentecostals (started in 1972 and still going on), called the charism of speaking in tongues in Pentecostalism a "substitute sacrament," a "physical experience" of the powerful presence of the Holy Spirit. He argues further that to emphasize "physical signs" such as the "signs" pointing to the presence of God is not necessarily foreign to Catholic sacramentalism — with phenomena like prayer for the gift of tears in the Roman Missal. Heribert Mühlen, "Charismatic and Sacramental Understanding of the Church: Dogmatic Aspects of Charismatic Renewal," *One in Christ* 12 (1976): 344-45. Similarly, the Pentecostal theologian Frank Macchia makes the connection when he asks, "May not Rahner's view of 'sacrament' help Pentecostals to understand why they regard tongues as such a significant medium for the realization of God's presence to empower believers for service?" Frank Macchia, "Tongues as a Sign: Towards a Sacramental Understanding of Pentecostal Experience," *Pneuma* 15, no. 1 (1993): 63.

32. See Margaret Poloma's comprehensive treatment above of the theology and practice of healing in Pentecostalism.

33. See further, Hollenweger, *Pentecostalism*, chap. 18.

34. See further, Amos Yong, "The Demonic in Pentecostal-Charismatic Christianity and in the Religious Consciousness of Asia," in *Asian and Pentecostal: The Charismatic Face of Christianity in Asia,* ed. Allan Anderson and Edmond Tang (London: Regnum International; Baguio City, Philippines: Asia Pacific Theological Seminary Press, 2005), pp. 93-127.

of the return of Jesus Christ to establish the kingdom. In the meantime, based on biblical promises such as Acts 1:8, Christians were supposed to be empowered by the Spirit to bring the gospel to all nations. As a result of this "eschatological urgency,"[35] a massive missionary and evangelistic enterprise emerged, a main factor in the continuing rapid growth of the movement. While at times Pentecostals find suspect "liberal" churches' emphasis on the "social gospel" at the expense of the proclamation, Pentecostals never withdrew from significant efforts to address physical needs even when at times those efforts were considered to be door-openers for evangelization.[36]

The Pentecostal theologian Amos Yong summarizes succinctly the nature of Pentecostal pneumatology and also points to its relation to other pneumatologies:

> In Pentecostalism, as in most conservative, traditionalist, and evangelical Christian traditions, the orthodox doctrine of the Holy Spirit as divine person continues to prevail. Yet Pentecostals go beyond many of their orthodox Christian kindred to say that the Holy Spirit continues to act in the world and interact personally with human beings and communities. In this tradition, then, there is the ongoing expectation of the Holy Spirit's answer to intercessory prayer, of the Spirit's continual and personal intervention in the affairs of the world and in the lives of believers even when not specifically prayed for, and of the Spirit's manifestation in the charismatic or spiritual gifts (as enumerated by St. Paul in 1 Corinthians 12:4-7). Of course, amidst all that occurs in Pentecostal circles are some rather fantastic accounts . . . and discerning between the

35. See the important study of the significance of eschatology to the formation of Pentecostal theology: D. William Faupel, *The Everlasting Gospel: The Significance of Eschatology in the Development of Pentecostal Thought* (Sheffield: Sheffield Academic Press, 1996). An interesting dialogue with mainline theologies is offered by Peter Althouse, *Spirit of the Last Days: Pentecostal Eschatology in Conversation with Jürgen Moltmann*, Journal of Pentecostal Theology Supplement (London: T. & T. Clark, 2004).

36. The chapters by Wonsuk Ma (chap. 3) and Doug Petersen (chap. 4) above give specific examples and theological rationale for Pentecostal social engagement in the Asian and Latin American contexts respectively. See also V.-M. Kärkkäinen, "Are Pentecostals Oblivious to Social Justice? Theological and Ecumenical Perspectives," *Missionalia* 29, no. 3 (2001): 387-404; Kärkkäinen, "Spirituality as a Resource for Social Justice: Reflections from the Roman Catholic-Pentecostal Dialogue," *Asian Journal of Pentecostal Theology* 6, no. 1 (2003): 75-88.

valid and the spurious is not always easy. Pentecostals face the tension of (on the one hand) accepting a rather traditional supernaturalistic worldview along with at least some of the more embarrassing claims that come with it resulting in their being excluded from scholarly or academic conversation, or (on the other hand) attempting to reinterpret Pentecostal testimonies within a more naturalistic framework so as to be able to proceed acceptably with rigorous scientific inquiry into Pentecostal spirituality and experience.[37]

Pentecostal Pneumatology in the Matrix of Contemporary Pneumatologies

So, how does classical Pentecostal pneumatology fare in comparison with mainline Christian doctrines of the Spirit, on the one hand, and with charismatic and neo-charismatic views, on the other hand?

Undoubtedly, Pentecostalism's belief in the ongoing, dynamic work of the Spirit in the world is in keeping with the contemporary postmodern dynamic worldview. Furthermore, Pentecostalism's embrace of a holistic view of the work of the Spirit, including healing and deliverance from evil powers, echoes the holistic approach of current trends.[38] In all of this, Pentecostal pneumatology with mainline doctrines of the Spirit offers a needed critique of traditional approaches. What distinguishes Pentecostals' understanding of the work of the Spirit from their mainline counterparts' is the reluctance to consider the role of the Spirit in relation to science (with the exception of the recently launched Pentecostalism and Science project under the leadership of A. Yong and James K. Smith), politics, environment, issues of equality, and similar public matters. Whether

37. Amos Yong, "'The Spirit Hovers over the World': Toward a Typology of 'Spirit' in the Religion and Science Dialogue," *The Digest: Transdisciplinary Approaches to Foundational Questions* 4, no. 12 (2004): n.p. (http://www.metanexus.net/digest/2004_10_27.htm; accessed 21 August 2006).

38. It is ironic that some of the trailblazers of the new holistic understanding of the Spirit of God, such as W. Pannenberg, totally miss the topic of healing and exorcisms in their pneumatology (and consequently, anthropology and ecclesiology). See further, V.-M. Kärkkäinen, "The Working of the Spirit of God in Creation and in the People of God: The Pneumatology of Wolfhart Pannenberg," *Pneuma: The Journal of the Society for Pentecostal Studies* 26, no. 1 (Fall 2004): 17-35. In contrast to Pannenberg, Moltmann (*Spirit of Life,* chap. 9) discusses these topics in his pneumatology.

this neglect by Pentecostals reflects the mindset of religious and theological conservatism or the alleged nonbiblical basis of the above-mentioned enterprises, or just lack of interest for other reasons, is yet to be determined. There seems to be little, if anything, in the structure and orientation of Pentecostal spirituality that seems to oppose tackling scientific, political, and public issues. As will be noted in the following, the theology of religions question has not been on the radar screen of Pentecostals either when thinking of the Spirit's role in the world.

When compared to non-Western Pentecostal and charismatic/neo-charismatic Christians' views of the Spirit, something similar comes to the fore: while sharing a lot in common — from an underlying charismatic spirituality to an expectation of the miraculous as part of the Christian's everyday life — it is also clear that classical Pentecostal pneumatologies shy away from political, social justice, environmental, and similar pursuits. Non-Western Pentecostal and charismatic movements are much less likely to define themselves in terms of the doctrine of initial evidence[39] and more liberally incorporate insights from various local sources, unless they are tutored by the "missionary parents" from the West.

The South African charismatic Reformed theologian Henry I. Lederle strikes a note that challenges Pentecostals who have been slower to reflect on the wider ministry of the Spirit in the world:

> For too long the Spirit and his work has been conceived of in too limited a sense. There was a capitulation at the beginning of the modern era in which faith became restricted to the private devotional life and the latter was then described as "spiritual." The Spirit should not be limited to spiritual experiences and charisms — even though it needs to be recognized that this element still awaits acknowledgment in much of Christianity. We need, however, to set our sights much higher. Not only the reality discovered by Pentecostalism needs to be reclaimed but also the cosmic dimensions of the Spirit's work. The Spirit is at work in the world and should not be degraded to an ornament of piety.[40]

---

39. Robert Mapes Anderson, *Vision of the Disinherited: The Making of American Pentecostalism* (Peabody, MA: Hendrickson, 1979), p. 4.

40. H. I. Lederle, *Treasures Old and New: Interpretations of Spirit-Baptism in the Charismatic Renewal Movement* (Peabody, MA: Hendrickson, 1988), p. 338. See also Nigel Wright, "A Pilgrimage in Renewal," in *Charismatic Renewal: The Search for a Theology*, ed. T. Smail, A. Walker, and N. Wright (London: SPCK, 1993), p. 31.

An illustration of the difference of ethos between classical Pentecostalisms' and charismatic movements' approaches to the Spirit's role in the world is a consultation on charismatic theology sponsored by the World Council of Churches at Geneva in 1980.[41] The theological task force identified three arenas of the work of the Spirit in the world:[42] (1) an ecclesiological approach: the Spirit works for the unity and united witness of all churches; (2) a cosmological approach: the Spirit renews creation and bestows fullness of life; this encompasses physical healing and healing of social relationships as well; (3) a sacramental approach: the Spirit is mediated through personal conversion, baptism, confirmation, and ordination as sacramental theologies renew their focus on the Spirit. Similarly, in the Two Thirds World pneumatologies, the holistic, cosmic orientation is often evident, of which African Independent Church pneumatologies are an excellent case study. According to M. L. Daneel, there are four basic orientations to the role of the Spirit in this understanding: (1) The Holy Spirit as Savior of Humankind; (2) The Spirit as Healer and Protector; (3) The Spirit of Justice and Liberation; (4) The Earthkeeping Spirit.[43] These orientations clearly go beyond and challenge Western Pentecostal views.

The Spirit and Religions in a Pentecostal Outlook

As mentioned above, Christian theology of religions has taken several significant turns. The last one, the "turn to the Spirit," by any account should fit in Pentecostal spirituality and theology. Indeed, as the charismatic theologian Clark Pinnock states,

> One might expect the Pentecostals to develop a Spirit-oriented theology of mission and world religions, because of their openness to religious experience, their sensitivity to the oppressed of the Third World where

41. The conference proceedings can be found in Arnold Bittlinger, ed., *The Church Is Charismatic* (Geneva: World Council of Churches, 1981).

42. "Towards a Church Renewed and United in the Spirit," in Bittlinger, *The Church Is Charismatic*, pp. 21-28.

43. M. L. Daneel, "African Independent Church Pneumatology and the Salvation of All Creation," in *All Together in One Place: Theological Papers from the Brighton Conference on World Evangelization*, ed. P. Hocken and H. D. Hunter (Sheffield: Sheffield Academic Press, 1992), pp. 96-126; see also Derek B. Mutungu's "A Response to M. L. Daneel," in the same collection, pp. 127-31.

they have experienced much of their growth, and their awareness of the ways of the Spirit as well as dogma.[44]

This has not, however, been the case for the most part.[45] While Pentecostals have excelled in missionary activities with impressive results by any standards, their thinking about the ministry of the Spirit in the world lags behind.[46] Not only that, but — aligning with the more conservative wing of the church — they have also been the first to raise doubts about any kind of saving role of the Spirit apart from the proclamation of the gospel. Most often Pentecostals have succumbed to the standard conservative/fundamentalist view of limiting the Spirit's saving work to the church (except for the work of the Spirit preparing one to receive the gospel).[47] A case in point is the recent warning from an official of the Assemblies of God, the

44. Clark Pinnock, *Flame of Love: A Theology of the Holy Spirit* (Downers Grove, IL: InterVarsity Press, 1996), p. 274.

45. For a helpful history of Pentecostal views of religions, see Amos Yong, *Discerning the Spirit(s): A Pentecostal-Charismatic Contribution to Christian Theology of Religions* (Sheffield: Sheffield Academic Press, 2000), pp. 185-97; on Charismatic Christians' views, see pp. 107-206; see also V.-M. Kärkkäinen, "Toward a Pneumatological Theology of Religion: Pentecostal-Charismatic Contributions," *International Review of Mission* 41, no. 361 (April 2002): 187-98.

46. For discussion of Pentecostal missiology and the Spirit's role therein, see Hollenweger, *Pentecostalism*, pp. 288-306; V.-M. Kärkkäinen, "'Truth on Fire': Pentecostal Theology of Mission and the Challenges of a New Millennium," *Asian Journal of Pentecostal Theology* 3, no. 1 (2000): 33-60; Kärkkäinen, "Mission, Spirit, and Eschatology: An Outline of a Pentecostal-Charismatic Theology of Mission," *Mission Studies* 16-1, no. 31 (1999): 73-94; Kärkkäinen, "Pentecostal Missiology in Ecumenical Perspective: Contributions, Challenges, Controversies," *International Review of Mission* 88, no. 350 (1999): 207-25; and Kärkkäinen, "Missiology, Pentecostal and Charismatic," in *The New International Dictionary of Pentecostal and Charismatic Movements,* ed. Stanley M. Burgess and Eduard M. van der Maas, rev. and expanded ed. (Grand Rapids: Zondervan, 2002), pp. 877-85.

47. A quick survey of Pentecostal manuals shows this clearly: Ernest S. Williams, *Systematic Theology,* 3 vols. (Springfield, MO: Gospel Publishing, 1953), vol. 3, p. 15; Ned D. Sauls, *Pentecostal Doctrines: A Wesleyan Approach* (Dunn, NC: Heritage Press, 1979), p. 54; Guy P. Duffield and Nathaniel M. Van Cleave, *Foundations of Pentecostal Theology* (Los Angeles: L.I.F.E. Bible College, 1983), pp. 268-70; Aaron M. Wilson, *Basic Bible Truth: A Doctrinal Study of the Pentecostal Church of God* (Joplin, MO: Messenger Publishing, 1987), p. 115; Mark D. McLean, "The Holy Spirit," in *Systematic Theology: A Pentecostal Perspective,* ed. Stanley M. Horton (Springfield, MO: Logion Press, 1994), p. 392. For this bibliographical note I am indebted to Cecil M. Robeck, "A Pentecostal Assessment of 'Towards a Common Understanding and Vision' of the WCC," *Mid-Stream* 37, no. 1 (1998): 31 n. 40.

largest white Pentecostal denomination in the United States. According to this statement, a pluralistic approach to theology of religions poses a threefold problem: (1) it is contrary to Scripture; (2) it replaces the obligation for world evangelism; and (3) those who fail to fulfill the Great Commission are ultimately not living under the Lordship of Christ.[48]

The location of Pentecostalism in the camp of conservative Christians, especially in the United States and many parts of Europe and as a result of aggressive missionary work also in many former mission lands, explains to a large extent the reservation about considering the Spirit's role in relation to religions. The alliance with fundamentalism, however, is a complicated and in a way self-contradictory development. Among all Christians, it is the fundamentalists who have most vocally opposed the Pentecostal claim for the continuing miraculous work of the Spirit. Similarly, the rather fundamentalistic understanding of revelation and inspiration they inherited may be at odds with a Pentecostal worldview.[49]

Since the 1970s, Pentecostals have had several significant ecumenical encounters and dialogues with the Roman Catholics,[50] the Reformed, and the World Council of Churches that have pushed them to reconsider and refine their understanding of the role of the Spirit in relation to religions.[51] The Catholic dialogue included a tentative discussion on the pos-

---

48. Harold Carpenter, "Tolerance or Irresponsibility: The Problem of Pluralism in Missions," *Advance* 31, no. 2 (1995): 19.

49. For an important discussion, see Gerald T. Sheppard, "Pentecostalism and the Hermeneutics of Dispensationalism: The Anatomy of an Uneasy Relationship," *Pneuma: The Journal of the Society for Pentecostal Studies* 6, no. 2 (1984): 5-34.

50. On the most longstanding and theologically most significant dialogue, see further, V.-M. Kärkkäinen, *Spiritus ubi vult spirat: Pneumatology in Roman Catholic-Pentecostal Dialogue (1972-1989)* (Helsinki: Luther Agricola-Society, 1998) and *Ad ultimum terrae: Evangelization, Proselytism, and Common Witness in the Roman Catholic-Pentecostal Dialogue 1990-1997*, Studies in the Intercultural History of Christianity 117 (Frankfurt: Peter Lang, 1999). For a scrutiny of specific missiological aspects, see V.-M. Kärkkäinen, "'An Exercise on the Frontiers of Ecumenism': Almost Thirty Years of the Roman Catholic-Pentecostal Dialogue," *Exchange: Journal of Missiological and Ecumenical Research* 29, no. 2 (2000): 156-71; Kärkkäinen, "Evangelization, Proselytism and Common Witness: Roman Catholic-Pentecostal Dialogue on Mission (1991-1997)," *International Bulletin of Missionary Research* 25, no. 1 (2001): 16-23.

51. Despite the longstanding ecumenical dialogues, probably the majority of Pentecostals to this day are at best ignorant of and at worst hostile to ecumenism for its alleged liberal theological agenda, compromising doctrinal purity, and similar reasons — again, gleaning from the typical fundamentalistic-conservative reasoning.

sibility of salvation in the early years of the process, and no unanimity was reached. Although both Catholics and Pentecostals believe that "ever since the creation of the world, the visible existence of God and his everlasting power have been clearly seen by the mind's understanding of created things" (cf. Rom. 1:20; Ps. 19:1-4), their perspectives radically diverged over the existence and/or meaning of salvific elements found in non-Christian religions.[52] Pentecostals insisted that there cannot be salvation outside the church.[53] Most Pentecostals limit the saving work of the Spirit to the church and its proclamation of the gospel, although they acknowledge the work of the Holy Spirit in the world, convincing people of sin.[54] The rationale for this more exclusivist attitude is found in the fallen state of humankind and in a literal reading of the New Testament, which for Pentecostals does not give much hope for non-Christians: "There was no unanimity whether non-Christians may receive the life of the Holy Spirit.... The classical Pentecostal participants do not accept ... [the Roman Catholic Church's inclusivistic stance according to which non-Christians may be saved under certain conditions] but retain their interpretation of the Scripture that non-Christians are excluded from the life of the Spirit: 'Truly, truly I say unto you, unless one is born anew, he cannot see the Kingdom of God' (John 3:3)."[55] Furthermore, Pentecostals, like many of the early Christians, tend to point out the demonic elements in other religions rather than common denominators.[56]

Even those Pentecostals who, similarly to Roman Catholics, maintain that the Holy Spirit is at work in non-Christian religions, preparing individual hearts for an eventual exposure to the gospel of Jesus Christ,[57] do not usually draw the conclusion that therefore large masses of people outside of the hearing of the gospel would be saved. In the Reformed-Pentecostal dia-

---

52. *Final Report 1991-1997*, #20. *Final Report* refers to the documents of the International Roman Catholic-Pentecostal Dialogue, unless otherwise indicated. "Perspectives on *Koinonia*: The Report from the Third Quinquennium of *The Dialogue* Between the Pontifical Council for Promoting Christian Unity of the Roman Catholic Church and Some Classical Pentecostal Churches and Leaders, 1985-1989," *Information Service* 75 (1990): 179-91; *PNEUMA: The Journal of the Society for Pentecostal Studies* 12, no. 2 (1990): 117-42.

53. *Final Report 1978-1982*, #14.

54. *Final Report 1991-1997*, #20.

55. *Final Report 1978-1982*, #14.

56. *Final Report 1991-1997*, #21.

57. *Final Report 1991-1997*, #21.

logue, likewise, a very reserved opinion about the possibility of salvation outside the Christian faith was expressed.[58] However, there is often an openness to acknowledging high morality and devotion among followers of other religions, and in some cases even a willingness to learn from them.[59]

As in the theology of religions in general, new developments are underway among some younger-generation Pentecostal theologians who are reconsidering the role of God's Spirit among the spirits in religions. Several reasons have been listed as to why Pentecostals and charismatics should engage the urgent task of a theology of religions: their international roots and global presence; the need to tackle present missiological issues such as syncretism, the denunciation of local traditions as a sign of a dualistic approach to questions regarding the gospel and culture, and the balance between gospel proclamation and work for social justice, to name a few of the most obvious.[60]

Recent Pentecostal Attempts Toward an Inclusivistic View of the Spirit Among Religions

It is no surprise that the leading Pentecostal theologian of religions, Amos Yong, comes from Asia (Chinese Malaysian origin); he has worked for years to construct a responsible Pentecostal theology of religions based on pneumatological and Trinitarian resources.[61] In his last monograph, fit-

---

58. "Word and Spirit, Church and World," *Final Report of the International Pentecostal-Reformed Dialogue* (Geneva: WARC, 2000), p. 12: "On the whole, Pentecostals do not acknowledge the presence of salvific elements in non-Christian religions because they view this as contrary to the teaching of the Bible. The church is called to discern the spirits through the charism of the Holy Spirit informed by the Word of God (1 Cor. 12:10; 14:29; cf. 1 Thess. 5:19-21; 1 John 4:2-3). Pentecostals, like many of the early Christians, are sensitive to the elements in other religions that oppose biblical teaching. They are, therefore, encouraged to receive the guidance of the Holy Spirit."

59. For details, see Yong, *Discerning the Spirit(s)*, pp. 187-97. For Anderson's wide and varied publications, see, e.g., *Bazalwane*. For interesting perspectives into Asian Pentecostalism and its attempts to appreciate cultural and religious elements of other faiths, see Julie Ma, "A Comparison of Two Worldviews: Kankana-Ey and Pentecostals," in *Pentecostalism in Context: Essays in Honor of William M. Menzies,* ed. W. Ma and R. P. Menzies (Sheffield: Sheffield Academic Press, 1997), pp. 265-90.

60. Yong, *Discerning the Spirit(s)*, pp. 206-15.

61. For starters, see his chapter 11 below on Pentecostalism's relation to Buddhism.

tingly titled *The Spirit Poured Out on All Flesh: Pentecostalism and the Possibility of Global Theology,* in chapter six, titled "The Holy Spirit and Spirits," he issues a call to all Pentecostals to work towards a public theology by engaging Pentecostal pneumatology with interfaith dialogue. His thesis is that "a pneumatologically driven theology is more conducive to engaging [interfaith issues] . . . in our time than previous approaches. . . . [R]eligions are neither accidents of history nor encroachments on divine providence but are, in various ways, instruments of the Holy Spirit working out the divine purposes in the world and that the unevangelized, if saved at all, are saved through the work of Christ by the Spirit (even if mediated through the religious beliefs and practices available to them)."[62] For him, a Pentecostal/charismatic theology of religions can be best defined "as the effort to understand both the immensely differentiated experiences of faith and the multifaceted phenomena of religious traditions and systems that is informed by experiences of the Spirit in the light of Scripture, and vice versa."[63] Moreover, this endeavor should be attempted without giving up the priority of evangelism on the one hand or, on the other hand, commitment to the authority of Scripture.[64]

Unlike Pentecostal theologians of former generations, Yong carries on a critical dialogue with and gleans from the whole variety of theological voices from Karl Rahner to Paul Tillich and others who have created "foundational pneumatologies." Yong's underlying thesis is that a Pentecostal pneumatological approach to religions should be based on a foundational concept of the Spirit as divine presence. He argues that it is possible to conceptualize divine presence and activity in the world without denying the reality of divine absence. Since these categories are potentially universal, they can be considered central elements of a more universal the-

---

62. Amos Yong, *The Spirit Poured Out on All Flesh: Pentecostalism and the Possibility of Global Theology* (Grand Rapids: Baker Academic, 2005), pp. 235-36. For earlier works to the same effect, see Yong's *Beyond the Impasse: Toward a Pneumatological Theology of Religions* (Grand Rapids: Baker Academic, 2003); *Discerning the Spirit(s)*; "A P(new)matological Paradigm for Christian Mission in a Religiously Plural World," *Missiology: An International Review* 33, no. 2 (2005): 175-91; "'Not Knowing Where the Spirit Blows . . .': On Envisioning a Pentecostal-Charismatic Theology of Religions," *Journal of Pentecostal Theology* 14 (April 1999): 81-112; "Whither Theological Inclusivism? The Development and Critique of an Evangelical Theology of Religions," *Evangelical Quarterly* 71, no. 4 (1999): 327-48.
63. Yong, *Discerning the Spirit(s)*, p. 24.
64. Yong, *Discerning the Spirit(s)*, pp. 24-25.

ology of the Spirit in the world.[65] Interestingly, regarding the challenge of theology of religions Yong also enlists the services of various resources among Pentecostals such as the Spirit-inspired religious experience in the form of glossolalia and other gifts as a token of the presence of the Spirit in believers' lives; the "Pentecostal pragmatism" that expects the miraculous from God but at the same time is committed to activism and service in the world; and spiritual discernment and a responsible recognition of and response to the demonic.[66] As a case study to test his ideas, Yong considers Umbanda, an Afro-Brazilian tradition, and its relation to Pentecostalism.[67] Revisiting his homeland's Buddhist background in a study underway, Yong also wonders if "provisionally, at least, the Holy Spirit could be discerned to be present and active even in Buddhist rituals opposing the world's forces of destruction insofar as the biblical fruits of the Spirit, for example, could be detected."[68]

Yong's Pentecostal and pneumatological interfaith ideas are in the making, and their wider reception and ability to inspire a reconsideration of issues is yet to be seen. Another Pentecostal theologian, the Hispanic Samuel Solivan, should be noted. Solivan has outlined five principles for Pentecostals for participation in interreligious dialogue: (1) the fact that the Holy Spirit is the one who leads Christians to all truth; (2) the importance of identification with the poor of the world and need to bring their distinctive voice into the dialogue; (3) the conviction of the prevenient workings of the Holy Spirit in every human being; (4) the empowerment of believers for witness by the Spirit; and (5) the diverse and pluralistic character of the Spirit's manifestations across racial, class, gender, lan-

---

65. Yong, *Discerning the Spirit(s)*, chap. 4; Yong, *Beyond the Impasse*, chap. 3; and *The Spirit Poured Out*, chap. 6.

66. Yong, *Discerning the Spirit(s)*, chap. 7. He takes up and adapts the basic categories suggested by Harvey Cox in his widely acclaimed *Fire from Heaven*.

67. Yong, *Discerning the Spirit(s)*, chap. 7.

68. Amos Yong, *Does the Wind Blow the Middle Way? Pneumatology and the Buddhist-Christian Dialogue* (unpublished manuscript, 2004), p. 266. This idea reminds me of the parallel suggestion by the Vietnamese Buddhist teacher Thich Nhat Hanh (*Living Buddha, Living Christ* [New York: Riverhead Books, 1994], 14, 20): "To me, mindfulness is very much like the Holy Spirit. Both are agents of healing. When you have mindfulness, you have love and understanding, you see more deeply, you can heal the wounds in your own mind. . . . Mindfulness helps us touch nirvana, and the Holy Spirit offers us a door to the Trinity." See also Amos Yong, "The Holy Spirit and the World Religions: On the Christian Discernment of Spirit(s) 'After' Buddhism," *Buddhist-Christian Studies* 24 (2004): 191-207.

guage, and religious boundaries.[69] On this foundation, as a Pentecostal pastor and academic theologian, Solivan is led to "examine the diverse ways the Holy Spirit is at work among other people of faith."[70] Yet he does so critically since there are always pitfalls — such as relativization of the truth — in an approach to mission in which dialogue is the *main* vehicle.[71]

My own work in the field of interfaith studies has focused on developing a Trinitarian understanding of the role of the Spirit in the world. Unlike Yong, Solivan, and other Pentecostal colleagues,[72] my own dialogue partners have been Protestant and Catholic colleagues outside Pentecostalism.[73]

Challenges from Charismatic Theologies

Moving in the same direction as Yong are several charismatic theologians of religions, the most well known of whom is the Canadian Baptist Clark Pinnock, who, like his younger Pentecostal colleague, has written extensively on pneumatology and a pneumatological approach to religions. Having first constructed a more inclusivistic Christological approach to religions,[74] during the past decade he has focused much of his

69. Samuel Solivan, "Interreligious Dialogue: An Hispanic American Pentecostal Perspective," in *Grounds for Understanding: Ecumenical Responses to Religious Pluralism,* ed. S. Mark Heim (Grand Rapids: Eerdmans, 1998), pp. 37-45.

70. Solivan, "Interreligious Dialogue," p. 43.

71. Solivan, "Interreligious Dialogue," p. 44.

72. See Tony Richie, "'Azusa Era Optimism': Bishop J. H. King's Pentecostal Theology of Religions as a Possible Paradigm for Today," *Journal of Pentecostal Theology* 14, no. 2 (Fall 2006): 247-60, and my response to Richie in the same journal, 15, no. 2 (April 2007): 263-68.

73. V.-M. Kärkkäinen, *Trinity and Religious Pluralism;* "'How to Speak of the Spirit Among Religions': Trinitarian 'Rules' for a Pneumatological Theology of Religions," *International Bulletin of Missionary Research* 30, no. 3 (July 2006): 121-27; "The Uniqueness of Christ and Trinitarian Faith," in *Christ the One and Only: A Global Affirmation of the Uniqueness of Jesus Christ,* ed. Sung Wook Chung (Exeter: Paternoster/Grand Rapids: Baker, 2005), pp. 111-35; Kärkkäinen, "Trinity and Religions: On the Way to a Trinitarian Theology of Religions for Evangelicals," *Missiology: An International Review* 33, no. 2 (April 2005): 159-74; Kärkkäinen, "'How to Speak of the Spirit among Religions': Trinitarian Prolegomena for a Pneumatological Theology of Religions," in *The Work of the Spirit: Pneumatology and Pentecostalism,* ed. Michael Welker (Grand Rapids: Eerdmans, 2006), pp. 47-70.

74. Clark H. Pinnock, *A Wideness in God's Mercy: The Finality of Jesus Christ in a World of Religions* (Grand Rapids: Zondervan, 1992); Pinnock, "The Finality of Jesus Christ in a World of Religions," in *Christian Faith and Practice in the Modern World: Theology from an*

energies on working towards a pneumatological and Trinitarian open-ness to religions.[75]

His main thesis is that a pneumatological approach resists the "fewness view" according to which only a few will be saved.[76] Going against this kind of restrictivism is not only God's nature as Father and the universality of the atonement of Christ, but also the ever-present Spirit, "who can foster transforming friendship with God anywhere and everywhere."[77] Pinnock's gateway to an appreciation of a more unlimited ministry of the Spirit is the "cosmic range to the operations of the Spirit."[78] Emphasis on the Spirit's work in salvation should not be read as a denial of his work in creation on which it is based, as too often has been the case.[79] As Pinnock reminds us, "Spirit is the ecstasy of divine life, the overabundance of joy, that gives birth to the universe and ever works to bring about a fullness of unity."[80]

In Lieu of Conclusions: Tasks for Further Study and Reflection

All theology is contextual and "locational." It is thus necessary to speak of Pentecostalisms — and consequently, of Pentecostal pneumatologies (plu-ral) — in order to resist reductionism. Classical Pentecostalism's location in the theologically (and in the American scene, often politically and so-

---

Evangelical Point of View, ed. M. A. Noll and D. F. Wells (Grand Rapids: Eerdmans, 1988), pp. 152-68; Pinnock, "Toward an Evangelical Theology of Religions," *Journal of the Evangelical Theological Society* 33 (1990): 359-68.

75. Pinnock, *Flame of Love;* Pinnock, "Evangelism and Other Living Faiths: An Evangel-ical Charismatic Perspective," in *All Together in One Place: Theological Papers from the Brigh-ton Conference on World Evangelism,* ed. P. Hocken and H. D. Hunter (Sheffield: Sheffield Academic Press, 1992), pp. 208-18; Pinnock, "An Inclusivist View," in *More Than One Way? Four Views of Salvation in a Pluralistic World,* ed. D. L. Ockholm and T. R. Phillips (Grand Rapids: Zondervan, 1995), pp. 93-148.

76. Pinnock, *Flame of Love,* pp. 185-215.

77. Pinnock, *Flame of Love,* pp. 186-87.

78. Pinnock, *Flame of Love,* p. 49. In an ecumenical spirit, Pinnock quotes here in ap-proval from Pope John Paul II, who speaks of "the breath of life which causes all creation, all history, to flow together to its ultimate end, in the infinite ocean of God."

79. Pinnock, *Flame of Love,* p. 51. A case in point is evangelical theologian W. H. Griffith Thomas (*The Holy Spirit of God* [Grand Rapids: Eerdmans, 1964], pp. 187, 196, 201), who pre-fers to bypass the cosmic activities of the Spirit as he sees them threatening the uniqueness of the gospel.

80. Pinnock, *Flame of Love,* p. 48.

cially) conservative camp has significantly shaped its view of the Spirit and the Spirit's work in the world. The pneumatology of the Pentecostal denominations, with their predominantly White American and European origins, is characterized by openness to the continuing, dynamic, and miraculous work of the Spirit in the church and in the lives of individual believers. Their pneumatology of religions, in contrast, is characterized by serious reservations about any kind of salvific role of the Spirit apart from the preaching of the gospel. Furthermore, classical Pentecostals' interests have not turned to reflect on the role of the Spirit in the world apart from the church in areas such as politics, science, and the environment. Their charismatic counterparts derive their pneumatologies in general and pneumatologies of religions in particular from the theologies of their respective churches — whether contemporary Roman Catholic or mainline Protestant churches' inclusivism — and are at times critical of classical Pentecostalism's exclusivism. Charismatic pneumatologies reflect the orientations of other mainline theologies in their desire to move beyond the domain of individual believers and churches to consider the Spirit's role more inclusively and holistically.

It seems to me the dividing line here has little to do with pneumatology per se and everything to do with underlying theological and biblical orientations, whether conservative-fundamentalist or mainline. Pluralistic pneumatologies, quite widely embraced by many in the mainline academia, are pretty much unknown in the whole Pentecostal/charismatic constituency even when using the most inclusive definition. An interesting research task would be to further study the locatedness of pneumatology in given theological and ecclesiastical contexts. This kind of study would give us an opportunity to test the hypothesis that a Pentecostal-type pneumatology — perhaps better than any other spirituality — can fit in more than one type of theological outlook. Support for that suggestion can be found in the more general observation that it is Pentecostalism's ingenuity to be able to find a dwelling place in so many different Christian families. How else can you explain the presence of Pentecostalism among the most fundamentalistic American Southerners, liberationist Latin American Catholics, mainline British Anglicans, and so on? Or where else can you find worship patterns from structured high-church liturgies to the most spontaneous independent churches' enthusiasm?

The research task can also be formulated like this: What, if any, is the underlying spiritual common denominator that despite radical ecclesiastical, cultural, theological, and socio-political differences, still makes it reasonable to speak of Pentecostalism as a generic term? Does it have to do with their understanding of the Spirit?[81]

This takes me to another query relevant to the purposes of the present study project: What are the connections, if any, between the Pentecostal "primal spirituality" and spiritualities of religions, especially those of Asian cultures? It seems to me that Pentecostal pneumatology — even when its potential to pursue that question seems to be trapped in a particular fundamentalistic-conservative milieu — has striking similarities with living religions such as Hinduism and Buddhism in their resistance to modernity's reductionistic, over-rationalistic, and at times dualistic worldview. The movement towards a post-/late-modern dynamic worldview with its willingness to reassess the canons of modernity has certainly opened up mainline Christian pneumatologies to a more holistic, dynamic reflection on the Spirit. Pentecostalism has that kind of undergirding primal spirituality as a wonderful asset. It is yet to be seen if suggestions such as those by Yong will elicit a wide-ranging resurgence of Pentecostal reflection or if that task will be left only for charismatic and neo-charismatic movements.

Another study task pertinent to the current study project would be to examine the issue of contextualization from the perspective of pneumatology and pneumatology of religions. As is well known, Pentecostals have been entrepreneurial in their approach to church structures, methods of mission and evangelism, styles of worship, and training of leaders, to take a few of the most obvious examples. Pentecostals have also been enthusiastic about applying whatever methods seem to work in their approach to other cultures and religions in mission work. And this is despite their at times quite conservative theological outlook. I wonder if any of the entrepreneurial, explorative, and risk-taking mentality could be channeled into Pentecostal reflection on pneumatology. Pentecostals have never eschewed controversies or avoided conflicts with views (such as cessationism) they deem wrong and limiting to the free flow of the Spirit. What would a Pentecostal pneumatology of religions look like when done with the radical

81. Daniel Albrecht (*Rites in the Spirit: A Ritual Approach to Pentecostal/Charismatic Spirituality* [Sheffield: Sheffield Academic Press, 1999], p. 28) speaks of an "underlying or core spirituality" among various types of Pentecostalisms. In addition to speaking of primal spirituality, Harvey Cox also speaks of "primal piety" (*Fire from Heaven*, pp. 99ff.) and "primal hope" (pp. 111-22) in relation to distinctive Pentecostal spirituality.

boldness with which some other Pentecostal views were advanced in the beginning decades of the movement?

One more challenging and probably somewhat controversial task lies ahead of us as we think of the potential of a Pentecostal pneumatology of religions.[82] What would be some of the ways to enhance dialogue within the wider Pentecostal family on the one hand and in relation to mainline theologies, on the other hand? I am reminded of the highly unexpected and ironic attitude of Pentecostals toward the emergence in the mainline churches of the charismatic movements in the early 1960s. While an outsider would assume that the spread of Pentecostal-type spirituality among established churches would have been seen as a sign and gift from God by classical Pentecostals, it brought to the surface the kinds of questions I have raised in discussing the task of identifying Pentecostal views. Pentecostalisms, no less than other Christian movements, are not free from the temptation to domesticate the Spirit. What will be the shape of a Pentecostal pneumatology of religions when Asian, African, and Latin American Pentecostal theologians — who already now represent the majority of the Pentecostal constituency — are enlisted side by side with their American and European colleagues in a common search?

According to the ancient biblical witness, *spiritus ubi vult spirat* ("The wind blows wherever it pleases" John 3:8 NIV). To quote the programmatic monograph title on the pneumatological theology of religions, could Pentecostals of all stripes, along with their mainline counterparts, join hands and minds in *Discerning the Spirit(s)*?[83]

---

82. See Tony Richie's discussion in chapter 12 focusing on the theology of religions of a Pentecostal pioneer, Bishop King.

83. Yong, *Discerning the Spirit(s)*.

CHAPTER 10

Deliverance as a Way of Confronting Witchcraft in Contemporary Africa: Ghana as a Case Study

Opoku Onyinah

Introduction

It is no longer news that the center of gravity of Christianity has shifted from the West to the Two-Thirds World — Asia, South America, and Africa. The reasons for this shift are varied and complex. However, the reasons for the growth of Christianity in Africa significantly include the way Africans have attempted to deal with their threatening fears, especially witchcraft. Witchcraft has been a prevailing belief in African cultures and has continually posed problems for the African people groups.

Following Evans-Pritchard's research in witchcraft among the Azande of Congo and his advancement of the misfortune or the explanation theory, the African phenomena of witchcraft have become prominent on the agenda of anthropologists. Significant are the works of Clyde Mitchell, Middleton and Winter, Max Marwick, Mary Douglas, and others who theorized the function of witchcraft as a release of tension within certain types of African social structure.[1] The studies of S. F. Nadel, M. Gluckman,

---

1. J. Clyde Mitchell, *The Yao Village: A Study in the Social Structure of a Nyassaland Tribe* (Manchester: Manchester University Press, 1956); John Middleton and E. H. Winter, eds., *Witchcraft and Sorcery in East Africa* (London: Routledge and Kegan Paul, 1963); Max G. Marwick, *Sorcery in Its Social Setting: A Study of the Northern Rhodesian Cewa* (Manchester: Manchester University Press, 1965); Mary Douglas, ed., *Witchcraft Confession and Accusations* (London: Tavistock, 1970).

Originally published in *Asian Journal of Pentecostal Studies* 5, no. 1 (2002): 107-34.

and Hans Debrunner also demonstrate that witchcraft belief is the outcome of social instability, such as famine, rapid change, oppression, and economic distress.[2] Other works, such as Margaret Field's case studies and analysis of so-called witches in Ghana, reveal how witchcraft is rooted in the psychological reactions of those suffering from ill health, misfortunes, and inability to control their destinies.[3]

These interpretations led some anthropologists and missionaries to think witchcraft belief was only superstition to be dispelled with modernity. Thus Parrinder argues, "an enlightened religion, education, medicine and better social and racial conditions will help to dispel witchcraft beliefs."[4] Unfortunately Parrinder lived to become "a false prophet" in the sense that, although an enlightened religion, that is, Christianity, has grown in Africa, belief in witchcraft has survived and even been revived.

The contemporary studies on witchcraft in Africa, such as those of Peter Geschiere, Birgit Meyer, Jean and John Comaroff, show that the concept is no longer "traditional" but operates as an important aspect of "modernity."[5] In some of these presentations witchcraft provides images of defining modernity through the local consumption of global commodities;[6] they show how witchcraft is domesticated in personal

2. S. F. Nadel, "Witchcraft in Four African Societies: An Essay in Comparison," in *Witchcraft and Sorcery,* ed. Max G. Marwick (London: Penguin Books, 1952), pp. 286-99 (286); M. Gluckman, *Customs and Conflicts in Africa* (Oxford: Blackwell, 1959), p. 101; Hans W. Debrunner, *Witchcraft in Ghana: A Study on the Belief in Destructive Witches and Its Effects on the Akan Tribes* (Accra: Presbyterian Book Depot, 1959).

3. Margaret J. Field, *Religion and Medicine of the Ga People* (London: Oxford University Press, 1937); Field, *Search for Security: An Ethno-Psychiatric Study of Rural Ghana* (London: Faber & Faber, 1960).

4. George Parrinder, *Witchcraft: A Critical Study of the Belief in Witchcraft from the Records of Witch Hunting in Europe Yesterday and Africa Today* (Harmondsworth: Penguin Books, 1958), pp. 202-3.

5. Peter Geschiere, *The Modernity of Witchcraft: Politics and the Occult in Postcolonial Africa* (London: University Press of Virginia, 1997); Birgit Meyer, *Translating the Devil: Religion and Modernity Among the Ewe in Ghana* (Edinburgh: Edinburgh University Press, 1999); Meyer, "Make a Complete Break with the Past: Memory and Post-Colonial Modernity in Ghanaian Pentecostalist Discourse," *Journal of Religion in Africa* 28, no. 3 (1998): 316-49; Meyer, "Commodities and Power of Prayer: Pentecostalist Attitudes Toward Consumption in Contemporary Ghana," *Development and Change* 29 (1998): 751-76; Jean Comaroff and John Comaroff, eds., *Modernity and Its Malcontents: Ritual and Power in Postcolonial Africa* (Chicago: University of Chicago Press, 1993).

6. Jane Parish, "The Dynamics of Witchcraft and Indigenous Shrines Among the

violence[7] and also how the phenomenon is involved in politics.[8] For the African, such images are real and deadly. For example, Geschiere has shown how in the Maka area in Cameroon the state courts have started to convict so-called witches.[9] Furthermore, in her work among the Tonga speakers in Gwembe Valley in a southern province in Zambia, where fathers are often accused of witchcraft, Elisabeth Colson has demonstrated how the accused really do suffer and in one case a man had to hang himself to avoid such suffering.[10] In the 2001 election in Ghana, George Ayittey reported that one parliamentary candidate, professor Philip Kofi Amoah, complained after he had been hit in the face by a crow that some people were out to fight him spiritually because of the inroad to success he was making.[11] According to Ayittey, the professor soon complained of dizziness and died on his way to the hospital.

As it was done in the past, protection from witchcraft activities has become a common concern. Formerly, such protection was sought from the priests of the gods or from sorcerers and medicine men. From the early part of the twentieth century, a variety of exorcistic activities have dominated African states. Even when the colonial regimes suppressed witchcraft activities within the anti-witchcraft shrine because they thought they hampered progress, they reemerged within the African Initiated Churches and later in a form of movement within the classical Pentecostal churches.[12] As soon as one of these movements expends itself, another of a similar nature springs up with a larger following. As a result, at present, almost all churches include exorcistic activities, referred to as "deliverance"

Akan," *Africa* 69, no. 3 (1999): 427-47; Elizabeth Colson, "The Father as Witch," *Africa* 70, no. 3 (2000): 333-58.

7. Peter Geschiere and Cyprian Fisiy, "Domesticating Personal Violence: Witchcraft, Courts and Confessions in Cameroon," *Africa* 64, no. 2 (1994): 323-41; Comaroff and Comaroff, *Modernity and Its Malcontents.*

8. Geschiere, *The Modernity of Witchcraft;* Birgit Meyer, "Money, Power and Morality in Popular Ghanaian Cinema," a paper presented at the consultation Religion and Media, Accra, May 21-27, 2000.

9. Geschiere and Fisiy, "Domesticating Personal Violence," p. 323.

10. Colson, "The Father as Witch," pp. 333-58.

11. George Ayittey, "How Ghana Was Saved," *Ghana Review International* 77 (February 2001): 17-19.

12. By classical Pentecostal churches this paper refers to Pentecostals who put stress on speaking in tongues and may have either direct or remote relations with the Azusa Street revival.

in their programs, since failure to do so amounts to losing members to churches that include such activities.[13] It is apparent now that Christianity in Africa has been pentecostalized.

The main agenda of this sort of pentecostalization is deliverance, which is based on the fear of spirit forces, especially witchcraft. Jane Parish struggles with the right terminology for describing such a deliverance center at Dorman in Ghana. She calls it *aduruyefo* (medicine maker), but her presentation, which included accounts of the warding off of evil spirits from so-called contaminated Bibles, involvement in intensive prayers, and invocation of the Holy Spirit, indicates that she was talking about a Christian prayer center. She mistakenly thought that it was an anti-witchcraft shrine.[14]

This study attempts to explore how deliverance ministry has replaced the anti-witchcraft shrines and the exorcistic activities of the African Initiated Churches. Using Ghana as a case study, I evaluate this ministry to find out its positive and negative effects. Most of the research on which this work is based was carried out among Ghanaian Christians between 1997 and 1999. These include interviews I conducted with pastors, exorcists, traditional priests, so-called witches, and delivered witches. The data also includes a survey I conducted in 1999 among 1201 participants across Ghana concerning the belief in the traditional spirit-world. The survey showed relatively even distribution across educational and occupational categories and age. However, many people who filled out the forms were male from Pentecostal denominations. My prior experience as a Ghanaian Pentecostal pastor since 1976 also gives flavor to this work.

Pentecostalism in Ghana

The Missionaries' Struggle with the Ghanaian Situation

Although the initial attempt to evangelize Ghana by the Roman Catholic Mission in the fifteenth century was a failure, Christianity was firmly established in the mid-1800s through the enterprising missionary activities

---

13. See Opoku Onyinah, "Matthew Speaks to Ghanaian Healing Situations," *Journal of Pentecostal Theology* 10, no. 1 (2001): 120-43.

14. Parish, "Dynamics of Witchcraft," pp. 432-33.

of the Basel Mission (1845), the Bremen Mission (1847), the Wesleyan Methodist (1840), and the Catholic Mission (second attempt in 1880).[15] A survey conducted by Operation World and published in 2001 showed that 64 percent of Ghanaians were Christians.[16]

As an effort to evangelize and civilize the indigenous people, on the one hand, the missionaries taught that the belief in spirit-forces such as the gods, fetishism, dwarfs, and witchcraft was superstitious. Yet, on the other hand, they also presented the devil and demons as the power behind these spirit-forces.[17] By the introduction of a personalized devil and the association of the gods with demons, the missionaries strengthened the belief in witchcraft, yet they failed to provide for the holistic needs of the people. For the Ghanaian, these images were real life-threatening forces.[18] Many people held that the power of the gods and the other spirit forces, which could be used either for good or evil purposes, operated through human intermediaries, namely, traditional priests. Yet the human intermediaries often allied themselves with witches. Witches were thought to feed on human flesh and drink human blood, inflict material losses and diseases on people, and make people ignoble through their misdeeds. Consequently, all misfortunes were thought to be the work of witches. Therefore people became preoccupied with finding out from the traditional priests the supernatural causes of misfortunes if initial attempts to find a cure failed. Tutelage under the gods was thought to be the best way of protection. Thus as Kalu says of the logic of covenant making among the Igbo of Nigeria[19] and as Meyer observes about the images of evil among the Ewes of Ghana, these life-threatening forces can be considered representations of particular fears that, in turn, are centered around the Ghanaian cultural hermeneutics.

Since the missionaries were unable to deal with the situation satisfac-

15. Peter Bernard Clarke, *West Africa and Christianity: A Study of Religious Development from the 15th to 20th Century* (London: Edward Arnold, 1986), pp. 7-26, 41-42, 57-62.

16. Patrick Johnstone and Jason Mandryk with Robyn Johnstone, *Operation World: 21st Century Edition*, 6th edition (Carlisle: Paternoster Lifestyle, 2001), p. 275.

17. For discussion on the missionaries' encounter with the Ghanaian people, see Harris W. Mobley, *The Ghanaian's Image of the Missionary: An Analysis of the Published Critiques of Christian Missionaries by Ghanaians, 1897-1965* (Leiden: E. J. Brill, 1970).

18. Margaret J. Field, *Search for Security: An Ethno-Psychiatric Study of Rural Ghana* (London: Faber & Faber, 1960).

19. Ogbu U. Kalu, *The Embattled God: Christianization of Igboland, 1841-1991* (Lagos: Minaj Publishers, 1996), pp. 29-49.

torily, there emerged a prophetic ministry in Ghana which announced a new dawn of Christianity whose fulfillment was seen in the African Initiated Churches, called "spiritual churches" in Ghana.[20] Healing and exorcism were central in their services. Although these churches attracted lots of adherents, there were weaknesses, such as lack of theological framework and accountability from the ministers, which led some to become involved in questionable practices such as exploitation and immorality.[21] They caused a decline and paved the way for the popularity of the classical Pentecostal churches.

The Pentecostal Response

The origins of classical Pentecostal churches[22] in Ghana can be traced back to Apostle Anim, who upon receipt of a magazine called *Sword of the Spirit* from the Faith Tabernacle Church[23] in 1917, began preaching healing in Christ. Consequently, a new movement began. His desire to know more about the baptism of the Holy Spirit finally linked him with the Apostolic Church of Bradford, England, which sent James McKeown to assist him in 1937.[24]

Anim's stance on medicine later caused a split between him and McKeown. Whereas McKeown believed in the use of medicine in addition to prayer, Anim rejected all types of aids, including medicine.[25] Eventually,

20. This study uses the term "spiritual churches" in reference to these churches.

21. For instance, see Albert Watson, "Menace of Spiritual Churches," *Daily Graphic* (Accra), May 1976, p. 5; Peter P. Dery, "Traditional Healing and Spiritual Healing in Ghana," *Ghana Bulletin of Theology* 4, no. 4 (1973): 53-64.

22. By classical Pentecostal churches this study refers to Pentecostals that have their origins directly or indirectly in the Azusa Street (Los Angeles, USA) revival.

23. Faith Tabernacle Church was not a Pentecostal movement in the strictest sense, but combined an emphasis on healing with its primary aim of cultivating and protecting the inner holiness of the sect as a distinctive community. For further reading, see Turner and Peel, who give a good background of this sect: Harold W. Turner, *History of an African Independent Church I: The Church of the Lord (Aladura)* (Oxford: Clarendon, 1967), pp. 10-26; J. D. Y. Peel, *Aladura: A Religious Movement among the Yoruba* (London: Oxford University Press, 1968), pp. 63-71.

24. Christine Leonard, *A Giant in Ghana: 3000 Churches in 50 Years: The Story of James McKeown and the Church of Pentecost* (Chichester: New Wine Press, 1989), p. 27.

25. Leonard, *A Giant in Ghana*, p. 34.

Anim named his group "Christ Apostolic Church," while McKeown's group remained as the "Apostolic Church." McKeown's church, the Apostolic Church, grew faster. But this was later split in 1953 and again in 1962. The churches established by Anim and McKeown, the Apostolic Church and the Church of Pentecost, the Christ Apostolic Church, and the Assemblies of God, were the main Pentecostal churches in Ghana until the 1970s. The Pentecostal practices of deliverance have been developing gradually since 1937.

These developments have been necessary, since originally classical Pentecostalism had not been encouraging deliverance ministry, which had been a very important issue of African traditional religions. Although the British sociologist Stephen Hunt observes that "the growth and appeal of deliverance has come with the expansion of the 'classical' Pentecostal movement at the beginning of the twentieth century,"[26] at this period the emphasis was on speaking in tongues as an initial evidence of the baptism of the Holy Spirit and also as a powerful weapon for evangelism. Healing and exorcism were to accompany the Holy Spirit baptism. From this perspective, some early Pentecostals opposed those who attempted to make deliverance a specialty.[27]

The Ghanaian Pentecostal churches held a similar position until the visit of the Latter Rain team from the U.S.A. to Ghana (and Nigeria) in 1953. The Latter Rain movement bore many similarities to the early Pentecostal movement that originated at the Azusa Street revival, yet it emerged with the aim of revitalizing Pentecostalism, since they felt that Pentecostalism was experiencing a current dryness of faith. Among other things, the Latter Rain emphasized deliverance and was opposed to the establishment of human organization.[28] After their visit, lay prophets and prophetesses emerged who began to exorcise people from afflicting spirits. But some misunderstanding between them and the leadership made their ministry short-lived. By the end of 1958, all those lay exorcists had left the classical Pentecostal churches to establish their own ministries, laying emphasis on healing and exorcism.

26. Stephen Hunt, "Managing the Demonic: Some Aspects of the Neo-Pentecostal Deliverance Ministry," *Journal of Contemporary Religion* 13, no. 2 (1998): 215-30 (216).

27. Hunt, "Managing the Demonic," p. 217; Steven S. Carter, "Demon Possession and the Christian," *Asian Journal of Pentecostal Studies* 3, no. 1 (2000): 19.

28. M. Richard Riss, "Latter Rain Movement," in *Dictionary of Pentecostal and Charismatic Movements*, ed. S. M. Burgess and G. B. McGee (Grand Rapids: Regency Reference Library, 1988), pp. 532-34 (532).

Two trends developed within Ghanaian Christianity during the 1970s and 1980s, which eventually led to the formation of a distinct theology. First, the books and cassettes from some Western preachers, especially Americans, including Oral Roberts, Kenneth Hagin, Kenneth Copeland, Reinhard Bonke, and later Benny Hinn, were used to enhance the preaching of many ministers. Often sermons by the pastors in Ghana and other parts of Africa were derived from materials drawn from these ministers, especially Roberts's seed faith principle, which was centered on prosperity, and Hagin's faith healing. The second trend (during the later part of the 1980s) flowed from an interest in books and cassettes (both video and audio) that sought to increase people's awareness of demons and how to exorcise them. Prominent among these materials were the books and cassettes of the British evangelist Derek Prince,[29] who visited Ghana in 1987 on the ticket of the Ghana Pentecostal Council.[30]

Prince asserts that a person can be a Christian, baptized in the Holy Spirit and speak in tongues, yet still have demons, ancestral and other curses in his or her life, until the Holy Spirit reveals them to be dealt with.[31] Dwelling heavily on Matthew 11:12, among other quotations, Prince argues that casting out a demon or renouncing a curse can be a lengthy process, and it is only forceful men who can lay hold of it.[32] Prince's stance is similar to ministers such as Basham, Dickason, Kraft, Koch, Bubeck, Wimber, and MacNutt.[33] This view was significantly different from that of

29. The books of Derek Prince that will be examined include *Blessings or Cursing* (Milton Keynes, UK: Word Publishing, 1990); *From Cursing to Blessing* (Fort Lauderdale, FL: Derek Prince Ministries, 1986); *They Shall Expel Demons: What You Need to Know About Demons: Your Invisible Enemies* (Harpenden, UK: Derek Prince Ministries, 1998).

30. The Ghana Pentecostal Council comprises most of the Pentecostal and charismatic churches in Ghana.

31. Prince, *Blessings or Cursing*, pp. 9-10; *From Cursing to Blessing*, pp. 8, 28, 36-37; *They Shall Expel Demons*, pp. 155-69.

32. Prince, *Blessings or Cursing*, pp. 190-98; *They Shall Expel Demons*, p. 235.

33. D. Basham, *Can a Christian Have a Demon?* (Monroeville, PA: Whitaker House, 1971); C. Fred Dickason, *Demon Possession and the Christian* (Chicago: Moody Press, 1987); C. H. Kraft, *Defeating Dark Angels* (Kent: Sovereign World, 1993); K. Koch, *Occult Bondage and Deliverance* (Grand Rapids: Kregel, 1970); *Demonology Past and Present* (Grand Rapids: Kregel, 1973); M. Bubeck, *The Adversary* (Chicago: Moody Press, 1987); J. Wimber and K. Springer, *Power Evangelism,* new edition (London: Hodder & Stoughton, 1992), pp. 168-69, 176-77; see also *Power Healing* (San Francisco: Harper & Row, 1987); Francis MacNutt, *Deliverance from Evil Spirits: A Practical Manual* (London: Hodder & Stoughton, 1995).

classical Pentecostals, who had refused to accept the possibility of a Christian being possessed by a demon. However, since Prince's theory appealed to the Ghanaian worldview, some Pentecostals as well as other Christians accepted it. Consequently, some Christians, both intellectuals and non-intellectuals, began to reinterpret these teachings in culturally relevant ways and put them into practice. What was going on in Ghana was also taking place in other parts of Africa.[34] The outcome of this reformulation is what this paper refers to as "witchdemonology."[35]

Witchdemonology in Ghanaian Context: A Field Study

Toward a Terminological Clarification

The study uses the term "witchdemonology" instead of the usual Western terms "demonology" and "witchcraft," because first, the traditional definitions of the terms "demonology" and "witchcraft" do not fit into the Ghanaian situation.[36] Second, the understanding and practices in the Ghanaian context, as will soon be presented, is a synthesis of both the Western and the Ghanaian concepts, especially that of the Ghanaian traditional religions where the witch is always the focus.[37] Thus the term "witchdemonology" is used in this study to describe the beliefs and practices of deliverance ministries in Ghana. These include witchcraft, demonology, ancestral curses, and exorcism.

The concept of "witchdemonology" is strongly based on the Ghanaian cosmology. To throw more light on this, I shall call on data from the survey

34. Symons Onyango, *Set Free from Demons: A Testimony to the Power of God to Deliver the Demon Possessed* (Nairobi: Evangel, 1979); Kaniaki and Mukendi, *Snatched from Satan's Claws: An Amazing Deliverance by Christ* (Nairobi: Enkei Media Service, 1991); Iyke Nathan Uzora, *Occult Grand Master Now in Christ* (Benin City: Osabu, 1993).

35. See Opoku Onyinah, "Contemporary 'Witchdemonology' in Africa," *International Review of Mission* 93, no. 370/371 (2004): 330-45.

36. For example, in the West the definition of witchcraft includes the worship of Satan and the practice of magic and sorcery. See Jeffrey Burton Russell, *A History of Witchcraft* (London: Thames & Hudson, 1980), p. 8. The definition of demonology also includes "malevolent spirits having supernatural powers and dedicated to destruction." Hans Holzer, *Encyclopedia of Witchcraft and Demonology* (London: Octopus Books, 1974), p. 195.

37. Ghanaian terms usually used for witchcraft are *bayie* (Akan), *aye* (Ga), *adze* (Ewe), and *anyen* (Fanti).

I conducted in 1999 of 1201 participants. For the question, "Is witchcraft real?" 91.7% said yes, 7.7% said no, and 0.7% were not sure. On educational background, 100% of all those who held a first degree said yes, while 85% of those who did not have any official schooling said yes and 15% said no.

The terms "witch" and "witchcraft" are used synonymously with the terms "demon," "demonology," and "evil spirit." Demon possession is described as a demon coming to live in a person without consent. It is considered a covenant of soul and spirit without the person's permission. Witchcraft is taken as an advanced form of spirit possession. Against this background, it is assumed that almost all traditional priests are witches.

The origin of demons is linked with the fallen angels. It is held that these beings (fallen angels) with disembodied spirits, found themselves in rivers, seas, mountains, rocks, trees, and in humans, and that these have become the gods of the Africans. All Africans are therefore under a curse, because their ancestors worshiped the gods.

Ancestral curse is a new "doctrine" that has emerged with "witch-demonology." Although this concept has its basis in traditional beliefs, the emphasis was not based on curses, but on blessings.[38] Yet the Pentecostal concept of the ancestral curse is the belief that the consequences of the sins committed by the progenitors are recurrent in their family lines. The effects of these curses in a person's life include chronic diseases or hereditary diseases, mental breakdowns, emotional excesses, allergies, repeated miscarriages, repeated unnatural deaths such as in suicides and accidents, continuing financial insufficiencies, frequent breakdown of marriages, and abnormal behavior such as extreme tantrums or extreme reservedness.

Linked with the origin of demons/gods and ancestral curses is the strong belief in the territorial spirit, specifically promoted by the "third-wave" theologian Peter Wagner.[39] This is the notion that the demons assume a hierarchy with powers of greater and lesser ranks having specific geographical assignments. The proponents of "witchdemonology" have as-

38. People who were venerated as ancestors, the living dead, were those who led prospering and meaningful lives; these people, thought to be closer to the Supreme Being, were to intercede for the living. People who broke taboos, offended the ancestors, or committed specific sins could bring curses upon the state, but sacrifices were offered to appease the responsible gods and thereby retract the curse forever.

39. E.g., C. Peter Wagner, ed., *Engaging the Enemy: How to Fight and Defeat Territorial Spirits* (Ventura, CA: Regal, 1993); idem, *Confronting the Powers: How the New Testament Church Experienced the Power of Strategic Level Spiritual Warfare* (Ventura, CA: Regal, 1996).

sumed that the real sources of African problems are the controlling powers of various territorial spirits, such as poverty and idolatry. This is to say that Africa's problems do not just depend upon scientific and modern development. Taking a cue from Wagner, some African scholars such as Oshun and "evangelist" Nwankpa have stressed the need to wage "spiritual warfare" against these spiritual enemies to break free the African continent.[40]

It is believed that there are signs, which hint that a person is demonized or a witch. One of the surest signs proponents of this ministry offer is that such people are especially uneasy in the presence of "spiritual people."

There are many ways through which demons are said to enter people and be passed on to their families or others. The term for this process is demonic "doorway" or "opening." Idolatry of any kind is said to be a major opening. Other demonic doorways that deliverance exponents assume include sinful deeds (Luke 22:3);[41] involvement in any other religion apart from the "one prescribed by the Lord," that is, evangelical Christianity; and any type of emotional pressure from childhood experiences (James 3:16). It is also propounded that demons may enter human beings through emotional traumas like the death of a loved one, surviving a car accident, or murder. Some believe those who watch such incidents on television are also vulnerable to demonic entry.

It is assumed that all evil acts have their demonic counterparts. For example, a demon of fornication enters the one who fornicates while the demon of lust enters the person who watches a pornographic video or pictures. While the Bible reveals the seriousness of sin and the need to overcome it through Christ (e.g., Eph. 4:25-32), this theology claims that all evil acts and experiences come from demons. The logical inference is that demons are at work any time there is evil behavior or sickness in the lives of both Christians and non-Christians.

---

40. See Emeka Nwankpa, *Redeeming the Land: Interceding for the Nations* (Achimota: African Christian Press, 1994), p. 9; Chris O. Oshun, "Spirits and Healing in a Depressed Economy: The Case of Nigeria," *Mission Studies* 25, no. 1 (1998): 32-52 (33).

41. Visits to places considered "worldly" such as the disco and pop concerts are classified as examples of these doorways. It can be a single sinful act or the persistent practice of it (habit) that opens the way for demons. For example, while it is held that a single act of adultery, homosexuality, lesbianism, sexual abuse, or a premeditated lie may open the door for demons, it is the repeated acts of masturbation, fornication, pornography, exaggeration in conversation that open the way for demons.

The discourse so far indicates that everyone, including Christians, could be a witch, demon possessed, or inherit ancestral curses. It is purported that in addition to salvation, every African Christian needs deliverance from witchcraft, demons, ancestral curses, or diseases, before they will be set free. In my survey, when asked the question, "Considering the Ghanaian background, does every Christian need deliverance?" 55.1% said yes, 41.2% said no, and 3.7% had no idea. It is not uncommon for those who answered "no" and "no idea" to seek explanations in ancestral curses when they are faced with problems that seem prolonged and that baffle their minds. Therefore, prayer groups have been formed within the churches to cater to this need. Within some churches, residential prayer centers have been established to accommodate the sick.[42] Deliverance becomes a major activity in these churches. In such centers, the leaders prescribe specific days of fasting and prayer to the clients. So-called witches are chained until they are delivered or otherwise.

Deliverance Session

There are two types of deliverance offered: mass and personal. Mass deliverance, which is our focus, begins like the normal Pentecostal type of service, but the focus is on testimonies and preaching about the works of demons and how God's power can set people free from them.

Before the main deliverance session, some clients might have already contacted the exorcists in their homes. Often people are required to complete a form with exhaustive questionnaires, seeking information about the background of the person, after which an interview is conducted to find out the supernatural causation of problems. People who have contacted the exorcists already as well as others who need deliverance are asked to move to the front of the congregation and form queues. The instructions differ from person to person. But often following Evangelist Tabiri's innovation of "breaking,"[43] instructions are given to participants to write on the piece of paper names of parents and family members

42. Cf. Margaret M. Poloma, "Old Wine, New Wineskins: The Rise of Healing Rooms in Revival," *Pneuma* 28, no. 1 (2006): 72-88.

43. Tabiri was a prayer-center leader who was officially ordained as an evangelist by the Church of Pentecost.

known to them and keep them for the breaking rituals.[44] After the initial instructions, the congregation sings with much expectancy, accompanied by clapping and musical instruments. The leader may then pray and also give instructions on how to pray. Prayer is often said repeatedly with gestures to "break," "bind," "bomb," "trample" on them, "whip with canes," "burn with the fire of God,"[45] "strike with the axe of God," "cast out demons," and "break" curses. As these are done with gestures, for example, the words *bombowon, shooto won* (bomb or shoot them) are usually followed by the sound *poo, poo, pee, pee* with the paper in their hands. Some leaders sell special canes at church for the purpose of caning the witches spiritually.[46] The "blood of Jesus" and "the name of Jesus" are used repeatedly to rebuke witches and all evil powers.

Meanwhile, the team members move among the people and lay hands on them. As the prayer goes on, people begin to sob, groan, shout, roar, fall down, and struggle on the ground. The leaders pay special attention to those who show such signs without falling down, by commanding and sometimes pushing them. Unlike some Western charismatics, especially the Catholic charismatics who, according to Csordas, consider falling down as resting in the Spirit,[47] falling down is interpreted here as a manifestation of demons. Therefore, when one struggles or falls down, some of the team members continue to cast, bind, or break the power of evil in that person. When there is resistance, the leader engages in dialogue with the person, asking the name of the demon. Sometimes people begin to speak in different forms, which indicate that some spirits have taken over. They become points of attraction and the leaders engage in active dialogue with them.

As the process of deliverance goes on, people may cough, vomit, or urinate. Through the teachings of deliverance proponents such as Prince, it has come to be accepted that demons may go out through any one of the orifices in the human body.[48] Thus these acts are considered signs of successful deliverance. The process may take two to three hours, until the

44. After the rituals, such papers are burnt or destroyed as signs of breaking.

45. Here *Onyamegya* (God's fire) is called from heaven to burn the witch.

46. Note the action is done in the absence of the witch, which is believed to be the person's enemy. This means that though the action is done physically, none are whipped.

47. Thomas Csordas, *The Sacred Self: A Cultural Phenomenology of Charismatic Healing* (Berkeley: University of California Press, 1994), p. 272.

48. Prince, *They Shall Expel Demons*, p. 233.

commotion cools down. But this is not the end of the session. The leader may call those with specific needs and pray for groups in turn.

After this, the leader often requests testimonies of deliverance and healing from the members. Thereafter, the leader may instruct the participants to go out delivered. However, since it is claimed that a person needs constant deliverance, the leader may instruct them on how to do self-deliverance.

With the self-deliverance, the person will have to be his/her own exorcist. The process is similar to the mass deliverance. The prayer of deliverance differs from person to person. However, often there is personal affirmation of one's faith in Christ, confession of any known sin, repentance of all sins, forgiveness of other people's sin, breaking with satanic contact, and finally a commanding prayer.

Clearly, the methodology for the deliverance session is a mixture of a wide range of practices, including African traditional, spiritual churches, and biblical. For example, like the traditional shrines and the spiritual churches, psychology is implied in the confession of witches, the drumming, and the repetition of the songs that build up pressure on the people before deliverance is carried on. Again, like the spiritual churches, "magico-religious methodology" is apparent in the repetition of the "prayer languages" during deliverance. In addition to these, the techniques of hypnotherapy are applied indirectly during the teaching and testimonies around demons and deliverance. The use of psychoanalysis is also evident in the questionnaires and the interviews conducted by the exorcists before and during deliverance. The fasting, prayers, and commands are the reinterpretations of some scripture verses and how Jesus dealt with the demonic (e.g., Matt. 17:21 AV; Mark 5:1-20).

Theological Reflections on Witchdemonology: Emancipation or Servitude

Interpretation

The discussion so far shows that the concept of "witchdemonology" gets its demonization foundation from the missionaries' interpretation of African traditional beliefs and practices and other religions. Yet it departs from the missionaries' interpretation when it comes to the concept of power and deliverance where it derives its demonization strength from the ministries and materials of the North American deliverance exponents. Gifford observes, "Undoubtedly the U.S. charismatic demonology has traditional African beliefs; but the demonology of Africa's contemporary charismatic churches may well be getting its special character through the power of American literature."[49] What comes out here is that in the attempts to appropriate foreign Christian materials for their use, the proponents of "witchdemonology" are concerned about demonization, especially of the African traditional practices, and how to exorcise such demonized individuals, which they believe are threats to their successful living. Yet by putting such emphasis on demonization and deliverance, the proponents of this ministry have been too harsh on other religions and rejected their own cultures.

Many scholars such as Gifford,[50] Dijk,[51] Marshall,[52] Hackett,[53] and Schoffeleers[54] have observed this strong position which neo-Pentecostals have taken. Hackett, for example, describes this position as "somewhat merciless toward 'traditional and ancestral beliefs' and practices."[55] Meyer feels the scholars have played down the role that demonology played in the spiritual churches. She writes, "They drew a much stricter boundary between non-Christian religion and Christianity than earlier studies of such churches might suggest."[56] But Meyer's point is weak here, since her works continually appear to communicate the Pentecostals' "rigid stance towards traditional religion"[57] more than the scholars mentioned.[58]

49. Steve Brouwer, Paul Gifford, and Susan D. Rose, *Exporting the American Gospel: Global Christian Fundamentalism* (New York: Routledge, 1996), p. 170.

50. Paul Gifford, "Ghanaian Charismatic Churches," *Journal of African Religion* 64, no. 3 (1994): 241-65; Brouwer, Gifford, and Rose, *Exporting the American Gospel*, pp. 151-78; Paul Gifford, *African Christianity: Its Public Role* (London: Hurst & Company, 1998).

51. Rijk A. van Dijk, "From Camp to Encompassment: Discourses of Transsubjectivity in the Ghanaian Pentecostal Diaspora," *Journal of Religion in Africa* 27, no. 4 (1997): 1-25.

52. Ruth Marshall-Fratani, "Mediating the Global and the Local in Nigerian Pentecostalism," *Journal of Religion in Africa* 28, no. 3 (1998): 278-315.

53. Rosalind I. J. Hackett, "Charismatic/Pentecostal Appropriation of Media Technologies in Nigeria and Ghana," *Journal of Religion in Africa* 28, no. 3 (1998): 258-77.

54. Matthew Schoffeleers, "Ritual Healing and Political Acquiescence: The Case of Zionist Churches in Southern Africa," *Africa* 1 (1991): 1-25.

55. Hackett, "Charismatic/Pentecostal Appropriation," p. 261.

56. Meyer, *Translating the Devil*, p. 174.

57. Birgit Meyer, "'Delivered from the Powers of Darkness': Confessions about Satanic Riches in Christian Ghana," *Africa* 65, no. 2 (1995): 236-55 (244).

58. Meyer, "'Delivered from the Powers of Darkness'"; Meyer, "Make a Complete Break"; Meyer, *Translating the Devil*, pp. 153, 173.

This study identifies with those scholars who assess that neo-Pentecostals recognize more demons than the spiritual churches. The reason is that whereas both accepted the African worldview and dealt with it accordingly, the spiritual churches did not promote the issue of the ancestral curses, complete severance from festivals, and family gathering. For these spiritual churches, throwing away idols and stopping the worship of them was enough.[59] But neo-Pentecostals or proponents of "witchdemonology" not only advocate complete abstinence from traditional practices, they also see demons associated with them and "impose" deliverance for all adherents to the traditional ways.

From this perspective — i.e., the neo-Pentecostals' emphasis on ancestral curses and deliverance — Meyer has postulated that, for neo-Pentecostals, to "become modern individuals" means breaking with the past.[60] By this, Meyer identifies with many of the current anthropologists such as Comaroff and Comaroff, Geschiere, Colson, and Parish, whose works in Africa have demonstrated that "witchcraft is a finely calibrated gauge of the impact of global cultural and economic forces on local relations."[61] That this partly holds for the deliverance ministry in Ghana is seen in the fact that 23 percent of those who expressed the reasons for visiting prayer centers during my survey included those who wanted success at business or prosperity in another area. Yet make no mistake here, the quest for wholeness (e.g., prosperity, dignity, health, fertility, and security) has its basis in the Ghanaian cultures, yet within the cultures, such a desire was to enable one to support the extended family. Thus Meyer, as well as the above-listed anthropologists, does well to unearth the ultimate outcome of the deliverance ministry, that is, promotion of individualism as against the interest of the traditional extended family system. Nevertheless, this assertion does not take into account the main reason why many clients consult exorcists. As discovered through my fieldwork, the rationale behind consultation is often toward *abisa*, that is, the desire to find the cause of one's problems. Deliverance often becomes a remedy after diagnoses have been made.

59. See, for example, Christian G. Kwami Baëta, *Prophetism in Ghana: A Study of "Spiritual Churches"* (London: SCM Press, 1962), pp. 29-30.

60. E.g., Meyer, "Make a Complete Break," p. 102; Meyer, *Translating the Devil*, pp. 215-16.

61. Comaroff and Comaroff, *Modernity and Its Malcontents*, p. xxviii; Geschiere, *The Modernity of Witchcraft*; Colson, "The Father as Witch," pp. 333-58; Parish, "The Dynamics of Witchcraft."

Beside this point, the scholars mentioned and others including Kamphausen, Asamoah-Gyadu, and Meyer herself elsewhere see deliverance ministry as a response to modernity, where individual riches and foreign commodities are often seen as of demonic origin, which need to be exorcised.[62] Kamphausen, for example, notes, "The hermeneutical key to the decoding of the Pentecostal symbolic system seems to be implied in the concept of Western commodities being of strange origin."[63] Thus "[becoming a] modern individual" cannot be the real concern of the deliverance advocates.

Consequently, there is a paradox in the neo-Pentecostals' concept of "witchdemonology." On the one hand, neo-Pentecostals are seen as carrying the message of the missionaries by considering traditional practices as demonic, and on the other hand, they reject the missionary interpretation that belief in witchcraft and demonology is superstitious, and carry on the practices of anti-witchcraft shrines by exorcising anything that gives them cause to doubt their origins and authentication. Thus "witchdemonology" cannot be placed under modernity (or mission Christianity), neither can it be identified as premodernity (or traditional religion). Clearly it derives its strength from postmodernity, where part of the traditional religion and part of Christianity can peacefully coexist as a coherent theology.[64] "Witchdemonology" is a synthesis of both. One indication that postmodernity is a possible way of explaining the acceptability of deliverance within the churches in Ghana is that whereas exorcism had been featuring prominently in the history of the churches in Ghana, it had not come into the limelight. But within

62. J. K. Asamoah-Gyadu, "Renewal Within African Christianity" (Ph.D. thesis, University of Birmingham, 2000), p. 276; Meyer, "Commodities and Power of Prayer."

63. Erhard Kamphausen, "Pentecostalism and De-Fetishism: A Ghanaian Case Study," a paper presented at the International Theological Consultation of the Six Member Churches of the Bremen Mission, Ghana Ho, February 23-26, 1999, p. 9.

64. This assertion becomes apparent if various analyses of postmodernity by some scholars are taken into consideration. For example, Lyotard highlights fantasy as a major feature, and Barnes sees myth as having an acceptable place in this concept. Thus, deliverance with its fantasies and mythologies clearly has its strength from postmodern philosophy. Jean-François Lyotard, "What Is Postmodernism?," and Roland Barthes, "Myth Today," both in *Art in Theory: An Anthropology of Changing Ideas*, ed. Charles Harrison and Paul Wood (Oxford: Blackwell, 1990), pp. 1009-15 (1009) and pp. 687-93, respectively. Furthermore, the writing of current anthropologists such as Geschiere, Jean and John Comaroff, which have been cited already, show that ambiguity, which is neither African nor European, features prominently in modern African witchcraft beliefs.

the postmodern world, where "homogeneous plurality within fragmentation of cultures, traditions, ideologies, forms of life, language games, or life
worlds"[65] is a key feature, deliverance with all its contradictions is welcomed.
With the emphasis on biblical text, therefore, the desire of the Pentecostals
cannot be associated with just "[becoming a] modern individual." Rather it
can better be associated with what Cox calls "primal spirituality," which he
explains as the "largely unprocessed nucleus of the psyche in which the unending struggles for a sense of purpose and significance goes on."[66] Cox
rightly observes that this is found in Pentecostalism worldwide and also un-
derlies original biblical spirituality.[67] A nuance of Cox's assertion, "the sacred self," is what Csordas proposes as the center of charismatic healing and
deliverance ministry in North America.[68] Thus Csordas sees an inquiry into
the sacred and the search for meaning as the underlying factors of charismatic healing and deliverance ministry. Not coincidentally, this sort of "primal spirituality" intersects with the African traditional spirituality. For example, in Ghana it goes well with *abisa* (consultation) and the rituals that
may follow. Therefore, "witchdemonology" has come to stay among Ghanaian and African Christianity.

Emancipation

The positive aspects of the theology of "witchdemonology" are seen in several ways:

First, it offers its adherents the opportunity to oscillate between the
traditional and Christian beliefs and practices. Here people are able to express their fears in witchcraft and other life-threatening forces and seek
protection from them. For those who think that ancestral spirits are ham-
pering their progress in this modern world, they have the opportunity to
be "exorcised." Some people see this way of "deliverance" as cheaper than
the expenses incurred in counseling that will be offered in the Western
framework.

65. Philip Sampson, "The Rise of Postmodernity," in *Faith and Modernity,* ed. Philip
Sampson, Vinay Samuel, and Chris Sugden (Oxford: Regnum, 1994), pp. 29-57 (41).

66. Harvey Cox, *Fire from Heaven: The Rise of Pentecostal Spirituality and the Reshaping
of Religion in the Twenty-first Century* (Reading, MA: Addison-Wesley, 1995), pp. 60-61, 81.

67. Cox, *Fire from Heaven,* pp. 213, 228, 243.

68. Csordas, *The Sacred Self,* pp. 15-24.

Second, it offers women equal access to places of leadership among some classical Pentecostals, who have refused to ordain women into the pastorate. Women who exhibit charisma can establish prayer centers.

Third, the proliferation of the deliverance ministry has caused the classical Pentecostals and other churches to reconsider their beliefs and practices. The prayer centers are characterized by many reports of miraculous phenomena, as against few in the conventional church services.

Fourth, many new people, ranging from top government officials to the very low in society, join Pentecostal and other churches through the "witchdemonology" ministry.

Servitude

The positive side of this theology of "witchdemonology" does not, however, preclude a negative assessment of it. The negative aspects include the following:

First, accusations of witchcraft absolve people from acknowledging the responsibility for their wrongdoing, their sins, and their inadequacies, and blaming someone else, often a poor person, who becomes the enemy of the whole community. Yet the Pentecostals claim to support the oppressive and the poor in society.[69] Thus Shorter rightly sees witchcraft accusation as "auto-salvation or self-justification."[70]

Second, the teachings on witchcraft and demons, coupled with testimonies from "exorcised witches," subject congregants to pressures quite disproportionate to the phenomena described. Thus people are psychologically led to confess anti-social behaviors and nocturnal emissions that baffle their understanding as witchcraft activities. These confessions can attract stigmatization from other members of society, and thus instead of deliverance and healing that leads to liberation, the physical and psychological conditions of such people are worsened and in extreme cases lead to death.

Third, many of the symptoms taken as witchcraft or spirit possession

---

69. E.g., Cheryl Bridges Johns, *Pentecostal Formation: A Pedagogy Among the Poor* (Sheffield: Sheffield Academic Press, 1993), pp. 46-61, 138-40.

70. Aylward Shorter, *Jesus and the Witchdoctor: An Approach to Healing and Wholeness* (London: G. Chapman; Maryknoll, NY: Orbis Books, 1985), p. 96.

can be explained by medical science.[71] In such cases repeated deliverances worsen the person's condition.

Fourth, the socio-economic factor in Africa causes many people to begin prayer centers just as means of financial support. Since there is no training, certification, or formal recognition from a body of Christians required to begin a prayer center, charlatans and the unemployed who have strong personalities can easily claim spiritual encounters and begin centers with a profit motive in mind. Linked with this socio-economic factor are the deliverance teachings at the centers, which consider health and wholeness as the result of obedience to biblical principles on blessing, to the neglect of biblical principles about suffering (e.g., Luke 13:1-5; Rom. 8:35-39; 2 Cor. 12:7-12).

Fifth, by the demonization of all other faiths apart from the evangelical/Pentecostals', in this pluralistic world, neo-Pentecostals deter healthy ecumenism and often cause unnecessary tension between Pentecostalism and other faiths.

Sixth, the process of deliverance, which often involves breaking links with families, eventually divides the traditional extended family system and promotes individualism.

Seventh, the theology of "witchdemonology" reinforces the "primitive animistic" belief system that keeps communities in servile fearfulness and hampers progress. During my fieldwork, there were many instances where people had stopped building houses in their hometowns for fear of witches.

Eighth, the uncritical approach adopted by both proponents and adherents of this ministry encourages dubious people to deceive others with their exaggerated or fabricated testimonies. People who attempt to challenge some of the testimonies are branded as skeptics. Besides, it is assumed that theologians cannot understand "spiritual things," and by implication cannot teach such people. The major problem with this is that such exorcists can lead genuine people to doom, just like the massacre of over 780 members of the Church of the Ten Commandments in Uganda in the year 2000 and other cult-inspired deaths elsewhere in the world.[72]

---

71. For examples, seizures may be symptoms of epilepsy. Personality changes can be psychological malfunctions or mental disorders such as hysteria, schizophrenia, or paranoia. Habitual behaviors, such as sexual desire, tantrums, and extreme quietness may be temperamental traits or associated with past memories.

72. "Cult Massacre," *Metro* (local paper in Birmingham, UK), July 21, 2000, put the death toll at 780.

Conclusion

Deliverance in contemporary Africa has been shown to be based on the persistent belief in witchcraft and other spirit forces, culminating in the formation of a theology called "witchdemonology." Using Ghanaian situations as an example, it has been demonstrated that the theology of "witchdemonology" is based on the synthesis of both African traditional religion and Christianity. Important aspects of this theology were seen as the attempts to identify and exorcise demonic forces in people's lives (whether in an individual's life or at a corporate level) in order for them to succeed in the contemporary world. The complex problems that one encounters in evaluating this theology of "witchdemonology" are evident after considering both the positive and the negative effects. On the one hand, through a synthesis of both old and new patterns, it takes the culture of the people into consideration by dealing with related beliefs and threatening fears in their newly acquired faith. As Meyer concludes, "in contrast to the 'mission-church Christianity,' . . . [it] offers the possibility of approaching in the safe context of deliverance what people seek to leave behind but still disturbs them."[73] Gifford also concludes that deliverance is relatively harmless.[74] From this positive assessment, then, the theology of "witchdemonology" represents a remarkable contribution to a paradigm shift in Christianity in Africa. In a way, it is a further attempt to contextualize the gospel to the African people, in addition to the efforts made by the Independent Churches and the exponents of African theology.

Nevertheless, assessment of the negative effects makes this ministry quite alarming. Its preoccupation with demons and witches shows that it is an affirmation of the old order. Its practitioners appear to have fallen into the weaknesses of the anti-witchcraft shrines and some of the African Independent Churches. Similar to what Sundkler observes about the Bantu prophets in South Africa, their assertions and promises are "more high sounding than they are sound."[75] The approach may fit well into the African cultural milieu, but the emphasis is a threat to the progress of Christianity and modernity in Africa. In spite of the rapid growth of their ap-

73. Meyer, *Translating the Devil*, p. 216.

74. Gifford, *African Christianity*, pp. 107-8.

75. Bengt G. M. Sundkler, *Bantu Prophets in South Africa*, 2nd edition (Oxford: Oxford University Press, 1961), p. 236.

proach, they cannot bring the African out of the fear of witchcraft and other supernatural powers. This does not mean that this ministry should be suppressed. The discussion so far reveals that this ministry has been progressive among the African peoples. Suppression has never been successful. Rather, this is to suggest that it is an incomplete ministry that needs theological analysis of the spirit-world to complement it. This theological analysis, therefore, needs to be the concern of African Pentecostal theologians.

CHAPTER 11

From Azusa Street to the Bo Tree and Back: Strange Babblings and Interreligious Interpretations in the Pentecostal Encounter with Buddhism

Amos Yong

Introduction

What has Azusa Street to do with the Bodhi tree? What indeed has the 1906 revival in Los Angeles to do with the famous Bo tree in Bodh Gaya (in the state of Bihar, India) under which Siddhartha Gautama was said to have found awakening?[1] And what, if anything at all, has the Pentecostalism that emerged from the Azusa Street revival to do with the Buddhism that developed out of Gautama Buddha's experience of enlightenment?

In the following I respond to these questions in three parts. First, I sketch the various levels of the Pentecostal encounter with Buddhism. Second, I turn to a discussion and critical analysis of the theological assumptions that are inevitably in play whenever we on the Pentecostal side think about other religions, including Buddhism. Finally, assuming the validity of these questions is defended, at least in a preliminary manner, in the preceding two parts, I attempt a thought experiment regarding how a Pentecostal dialogue with Buddhism might proceed. My goal is to see if we can understand why the questions in the opening paragraph above are not as far-fetched as on first hearing, and then show how we might begin to respond to them. If by the end of this essay the reader is led both to see the

---

1. The Bo tree also now flourishes throughout Sri Lanka, where it is considered a sacred site representing the Buddha's enlightenment; see Tessa J. Bartholomeusz, *Women Under the Bō Tree: Buddhist Nuns in Sri Lanka*, Cambridge Studies in Religious Traditions 5 (Cambridge: Cambridge University Press, 1994), p. 98.

value of these questions and to have posed new ones as a result of interacting with them, then I would consider my efforts in these pages to have been successful.

Pentecostalism and Buddhism — What Encounters?

If there is a feeling so far that the juxtaposing of "Pentecostalism" and "Buddhism" seems strange and awkward, there are some very good reasons why this is the case, and these have to do with the fact that the traditional "encounters" between these two traditions have been more along the lines of "confrontation" than "dialogue." In this section, I will unpack three levels of the Pentecostal encounter with Buddhism: the evangelistic level focused on conversion; the social level focused on socio-economic and political engagement; and the dialogical level focused on mutual enrichment. While I wish to defend the appropriateness of various (but not all) aspects of these three levels of encounter, I will also suggest Pentecostal mission is better conceived if broadly understood to include all three of these spheres of activity, rather than if narrowly defined according to traditional terms.

Pentecostal Mission: Encountering Buddhism "In the Trenches"

Pentecostalism is well known as a missionary movement.[2] Like many other conservative Protestant missionary movements, most Pentecostals have considered other religions to be false, and their adherents to be lost unless converted to faith in Christ.[3] For these reasons, Pentecostals have generally ap-

---

2. Thus Steven Land calls Pentecostalism an "end time missionary fellowship"; see his *Pentecostal Spirituality: A Passion for the Kingdom*, Journal of Pentecostal Theology Supplement Series 1 (Sheffield: Sheffield Academic Press, 1993), esp. chap. 3. Cf. also James R. Goff Jr., *Fields White unto Harvest: Charles F. Parham and the Missionary Origins of Pentecostalism* (Fayetteville: University of Arkansas Press, 1988); and L. Grant McClung, *Azusa Street and Beyond: Pentecostal Missions and Church Growth in the 20th Century* (South Plainfield, NJ: Bridge, 1986).

3. The work of classical Pentecostal theologian Bishop J. H. King (Pentecostal Holiness Church) bears this out, although there is also surprising openness in his thought to the possibility that God may be at work in the lives of people in other religions unbeknownst to

proached other religions with a certain degree of wariness, concerned about not being misled with regard to the truth on the one hand, but also about needing to defend their Christian faith from the misunderstandings, misconceptions, and falsehoods of non-Christian religions on the other hand.

However, most Pentecostals do not approach their missionary calling through emphasizing such a defensive-minded posture. Rather, motivated by their conviction that the gift of the Holy Spirit has empowered them to bear Christian witness to the ends of the earth (cf. Acts 1:8), Pentecostals generally are more inclined to embrace any opportunity to give their testimony than they are to engage in apologetics or polemical debate. Hence Pentecostal missionary rhetoric against other faiths is more often found in "in-house" publications designed to highlight conversion testimonies of those in other religions to Christian faith and to encourage sending churches to support their missionaries who are ministering to people in other religions.

There is, however, another level of Pentecostal confrontation with the religions that involves their views about spiritual warfare and power encounter.[4] At the doctrinal level, many Pentecostals believe that there are "territorial spirits" that rule certain regions of the world, and often they would view these as demonic entities that are associated with other religions. In the latter case, there might be some Pentecostals who believe that the non-Christian religious institution in a local area is the means through which a territorial demon exercises a controlling power over its practitioners. These convictions are often manifest in the following types of practices: power encounters and exorcisms when dealing with individuals who are believed to be oppressed or possessed by demonic entities; prayers for healing when dealing with sick or diseased individuals; and spiritual warfare waged by congregations against rulers, authorities, "the cosmic powers of this present darkness, [and] spiritual forces of evil in the heavenly places" (Eph. 6:12). Even if the other religious traditions are not specifically named, it is often assumed they are included under what is addressed by such apostolic language.

them; see Tony Richie, "Azusa-era Optimism: Bishop J. H. King's Pentecostal Theology of Religions as a Possible Paradigm for Today," *Journal of Pentecostal Theology* 14, no. 2 (April 2006): 247-60.

4. I discuss the Pentecostal spiritual warfare worldview in my *Discerning the Spirit(s): A Pentecostal-Charismatic Contribution to Christian Theology of Religions,* Journal of Pentecostal Theology Supplement Series 20 (Sheffield: Sheffield Academic Press, 2000), pp. 238-43.

In general, the Pentecostal encounter with Buddhism has featured all of these more confrontational styles. Pentecostals in predominantly Buddhist regions of the world like Sri Lanka, Myanmar, Thailand, and other parts of Southeast Asia, and the East Asian world of China and Japan, have emphasized each of these mission strategies: evangelism leading to conversion, miracles, and healing of the sick, emphasis on the empowering and life-transforming baptism of the Holy Spirit and other spiritual gifts, and exorcisms and power encounters.[5] This is the case also in animistic contexts, where Buddhist, Islamic, or other world-religious traditions have long been overlaid on indigenous beliefs and practices.[6] In these locales, in addition to the other standard evangelistic approaches, Pentecostals wage spiritual warfare against what they call the witchcraft of animistic religiosity.

Now it should not be forgotten that Buddhism is in some respects just as much of a missionary religion as is Pentecostal Christianity.[7] So while Pentecostals understand Buddhism according to their own Pentecostal categories, so also do Buddhists view all non-Buddhist beliefs and practices according to various Buddhist frames of reference.[8] Hence wherever Buddhists have traveled to spread the Dharma — from the original Bo tree

---

5. For preliminary studies, see Mark R. Mullins, "Japanese Pentecostalism and the World of the Dead: A Study of Cultural Adaptation in Iesu no Mitama Kyokai," *Japanese Journal of Religious Studies* 17 (1990): 353-74; G. P. V. Somaratna, "Madame Anna E. Lewini's Mission to Sri Lanka," *Indian Church History Review* 30 (1996): 22-32; Chin Khua Khai, "Pentecostalism in Myanmar," *Cyberjournal for Pentecostal-Charismatic Research* 10 (2001), http://www.pctii.org/cyberj/cyber10.html; and Joshua (pseudonym), "Pentecostalism in Vietnam: A History of the Assemblies of God," *Asian Journal of Pentecostal Studies* 4, no. 2 (2001): 307-26.

6. See the discussion of Julie C. Ma, *When the Spirit Meets the Spirits: Pentecostal Ministry Among the Kankana-ey Tribe in the Philippines,* Studies in the Intercultural History of Christianity 118 (Frankfurt am Main: Peter Lang, 2000).

7. See Frank Whaling, "A Comparative Religious Study of Missionary Transplantation in Buddhism, Christianity, and Islam," *International Review of Mission* 70 (1981): 314-33, esp. 319-24; Charles S. Prebish and Martin Baumann, eds., *Western Dharma: Buddhism Beyond Asia* (Berkeley: University of California Press, 2002); Judith Snodgrass, *Presenting Japanese Buddhism to the West: Orientalism, Occidentalism, and the Columbian Exposition* (Chapel Hill, NC, and London: University of North Carolina Press, 2003); Linda Learman, ed., *Buddhist Missionaries in the Era of Globalization* (Honolulu: University of Hawaii Press, 2005); and Lawrence Sutin, *All Is Change: The Two-Thousand-Year Journey of Buddhism in the West* (New York: Little, Brown & Co., 2006).

8. As documented by Kristin Beise Kiblinger, *Buddhist Inclusivism: Attitudes Towards Religious Others* (Burlington, VT: Ashgate, 2005).

southward initially, and then eastward, to the point of crossing the Pacific Ocean and arriving in the Western Hemisphere — they have sought to make sense of what they encountered in terms they were familiar with.

In some cases, the two missionary religious traditions have confronted one another with greater force and intensity, resulting in "clashes" of various sorts. In Sri Lanka, for example, the growth of evangelical and Pentecostal forms of Christianity amidst a revitalized and nationalistic Sinhalese Buddhist majority has led to the Buddhist charge that Christians engage in unfair proselytizing activities to gain converts. The Buddhist response has included a series of efforts to pass laws against such proselytism.[9] There have been few, if any, winners in the confrontation between aggressive Pentecostal evangelism and Sinhalese Buddhist chauvinism.

Pentecostal Social Engagement: Encountering Buddhism "On the Ground"

Although confrontation has been all too prevalent in the Pentecostal encounter with Buddhism, it has not been the only mode of interaction. Less well known are Pentecostal social ministries. Because of the central place of Jesus as healer in Pentecostal theology and praxis, many Pentecostals have connected their healing ministries with mission projects focused on meeting the needs of the body. In general, then, Pentecostal missions have always included social relief projects such as rescue missions, hospitals, and orphanages.[10] To be sure, mission work along these lines has usually emphasized that Pentecostal ministry to the body serves the more ultimate purposes of ministering to the souls of humankind: Jesus heals bodies and remakes whole lives as means of turning hearts toward him. Yet there has also been a growing realization that rather than viewing these foci of the material-social and the spiritual in hierarchical terms, a more holistic Pentecostal theology of mission is urgent.[11]

---

9. See Mahinda Deegalle, "JHU Politics for Peace and a Righteous State," in *Buddhism, Conflict and Violence in Modern Sri Lanka*, ed. Mahinda Deegalle (London and New York: Routledge, 2006), pp. 233-54, esp. 244 and 251.

10. Douglas Petersen, *Not by Might Nor by Power: A Pentecostal Theology of Social Concern in Latin America* (Oxford: Regnum, 1996), esp. chaps. 4-5.

11. Andy Lord, *Spirit-Shaped Mission: A Holistic Charismatic Missiology* (Waynesboro, GA: Paternoster, 2005).

What does this mean for the Pentecostal encounter with world religions in general and with Buddhism in particular? Again, Pentecostals generally do not "target" people of other faiths specifically.[12] Rather, their missionary ventures are designed to engage people with recognized needs as Pentecostals see them: the sick, the poor, and hungry, etc., who have not yet been evangelized. Hence more often than not, Pentecostal social relief projects encounter neither the Buddhist *Sangha* nor the Buddhist intellectual elite, but rather the Buddhist layperson or the popular Buddhist practitioner who may or may not understand herself primarily in Buddhist terms. Hence in many of these cases, conversions to Pentecostal Christianity are considered by the Buddhist hierarchy to be based on unethical evangelistic practices: nominal Buddhists convert because (the charge goes) they are given gifts, promised material gain, or drawn into (unsuspecting) relationships with Western missionaries and their organizational agencies.

Certainly Pentecostal missionary impulses continue to be revised in reaction to these accusations. Depending on the socio-political context, Pentecostal social ministries may be less aggressively tied in with their evangelistic activities. Yet in times of genuine crisis and tragedy, as in the tsunami of December 2004, for instance, it is not uncommon to find Pentecostals working as neighbors or as part of relief agencies with people of other faiths.[13] In the case of the relief efforts in Sri Lanka, interfaith cooperation was widespread (even if there was an outcry against some evangelical groups, including Pentecostals, that linked aid and assistance with conversion activities). In most cases, however, Pentecostal collaboration with people of other faiths in general and with Buddhists more specifically is not widely publicized. Pentecostals who might be sympathetic to interfaith social projects would not want to be misunderstood by their fellow members to be either compromising their Christian convictions or "consorting" with "the enemy."

---

12. The exception might be Pentecostal missions to specifically Islamic countries, although even then, the goal is to missionize *people* in general, rather than *Muslims* in particular; see, e.g., Malek Sobhi, "Islam Encountering Gospel Power," in *Called and Empowered: Global Mission in Pentecostal Perspective*, ed. Murray W. Dempster, Byron D. Klaus, and Douglas Petersen (Peabody, MA: Hendrickson, 1991), pp. 180-97.

13. Post-tsunami relief efforts evidenced "countless experiences of grassroots hospitality" between Buddhists and Christians; see Paul Jeffrey, "A Great Leveler: Sri Lanka's Factions Deal with the Tsunami," *Christian Century* 122, no. 3 (February 8, 2005): 8-10.

Buddhist forms of social activism, however, differ from their Pentecostal counterparts at least along two lines. First, there has been the emergence of "Engaged Buddhism" around the world that has been shaped more or less by Christian social gospel and liberation theologies.[14] These are led primarily by Buddhist intellectuals and activists and are focused as much, if not more, on transforming the structural conditions that cause social, economic, and political inequities. At these levels there is little interaction with Pentecostals, who for the most part are uninvolved in these arenas, having left these tasks to mainline Protestant and Roman Catholic initiatives.

A second type of Buddhist social engagement can be seen in a movement like the Sarvodaya Shramadana (meaning, literally, universal awakening gift of labor) in Sri Lanka.[15] Having gained Non-Governmental Organization (NGO) status in 1972, Sarvodaya has been from its inception a grassroots association committed to empowering local villages in their fight against poverty. But since the beginning of the civil war a few decades ago between the Sinhalese-dominated government and a radical Tamil minority, Sarvodaya has also embraced the further goal of mobilizing a nonviolent vision for the reconciliation and healing of the island nation. Now because Sarvodaya's ecumenical and interfaith spirituality enables Muslims, Hindus (Tamils), and Christians (especially mainline Protestant churches) to cooperate with the majority Buddhist (Sinhalese) work force, Pentecostals are all the more unlikely to be publicly identified with Sarvodaya projects and initiatives. So even if Pentecostals might agree with the explicitly articulated goals of the local village development and uplift, there are these three "strikes" — the Buddhist ideology, the ecumenical

14. For introductions, see Christopher S. Queen and Sallie B. King, eds., *Engaged Buddhism: Buddhist Liberation Movements in Asia* (Albany: State University of New York Press, 1996); and Christopher S. Queen, ed., *Engaged Buddhism in the West* (Boston: Wisdom, 2000).

15. For an overview, see John R. Williams, "Religion, Ethics and Development: An Analysis of the Sarvodaya Shramadana Movement of Sri Lanka," *Canadian Journal of Development Studies* 5, no. 1 (1984): 157-67; and George D. Bond, "Sarvodaya Shramadana's Quest for Peace," in *Action Dharma: New Studies in Engaged Buddhism*, ed. Christopher Queen, Charles Prebish, and Damien Keown (New York and London: RoutledgeCurzon, 2003), pp. 128-35. Sarvodaya was founded in 1958 by a science teacher, A. T. Ariyaratne; for a recent statement of his vision for the movement, see his "Healing Divided Societies: A Sri Lankan Experience," in *Religion and Culture in Asia Pacific: Violence or Healing?* ed. Joseph A. Camilleri (Melbourne: Vista Publications, 2001), pp. 47-55.

spirituality, and the socio-economic focus — that prevent their being formally associated with Sarvodaya.

In short, both Pentecostalism and Buddhism are committed to social transformation. However, their visions for social engagement differ, and so far they appear to be dis-engaged from one another, working at best on parallel tracks and at worst on unrelated projects. Is it possible that there might be a pooling of resources and a mutual tackling of common causes? We will return to this question later.

Pentecostalism and Interreligious Dialogue: A Conversation with Buddhism?

So far we have discussed the phenomenology of the Pentecostal encounter with Buddhism in terms of confrontation and social dis-engagement. In an age of increasing interreligious dialogue, is there anything that might be said about Pentecostalism and Buddhism along these lines? I suggest that there is growing "dialogue" at both the lay and academic levels.

At the level of the average Pentecostal layperson, it was unlikely in former times that they would have had acquaintances or friends from other faiths. Before the age of globalization, Buddhists were either abroad or in their own ethnic (Asian) enclaves (for those in non-Buddhist regions of the world) or were viewed merely as "objects" of evangelization. Since the mid-1960s, however, Pentecostal Christians around the world have more and more frequently found people of other faiths, including Buddhists, as schoolmates, neighbors, co-workers, and fellow citizens.[16] Coming to know actual practitioners of other religions in person, including Buddhists, challenges stereotypes, corrects misunderstandings, and transforms perceptions. Part of the result of our incredibly shrinking global village is that Buddhists are less and less the "exotic," "strange," or "dangerous" other. Instead, there is a growing "dialogue of life" that occurs when acquaintances evolve gradually into friendships, when collegiality breeds familiarity, and when common causes nurture trust across ethnic, cultural, and religious lines. To be sure, there are still many sectarian (meant as a so-

16. For an overview of these developments in North America, see Terry C. Muck, *Alien Gods on American Turf: How World Religions Are Evangelizing Your Neighborhood* (Wheaton, IL: Victor/Christianity Today, 1991).

ciological descriptor rather than pejoratively) Pentecostals who may reject public schools, friendships with unbelievers, or ecumenical initiatives, and for them, Buddhists and people of other faiths remain categorized primarily as those in need of evangelization.

For other Pentecostals, however, knowing people of other faiths in person changes the way one relates to them. Evangelism remains important, albeit in a different key. In some Pentecostal and charismatic circles, especially those related to the Emerging church, there is a more dialogical approach: yes, Christians share their stories and bear interpersonal witness to Christ; but yes, Christians also listen to the testimonies of religious others in an environment of mutuality and hospitality.[17] Whereas in former times, any efforts to learn about the religious "other" would have been for the purposes of more effective evangelism, in these Emerging church contexts the point is the establishing of authentic relationships. There is the recognition that Christians need to earn the right to be heard in a postmodern and pluralistic religious world, and that there is a disingenuousness about listening to the religious "other" only because one is motivated to undermine their religiosity through polemical apologetics.[18]

In the academic context, it should be noted that Pentecostals have only in the last generation begun to attain terminal degrees, first in history in the 1960s, then in biblical studies in the 1970s-80s, and now in theology since the 1990s.[19] Theological studies in the last two decades, however, have become increasingly multidisciplinary, pluralistic, and, perhaps most importantly, intertwined with the academic study of religion (known formerly as the history of religions — *Religionswissenschaft* — and now also as the discipline of religious studies).[20] These developments have impacted academic Pentecostalism in at least two ways.

17. See Eddie Gibbs and Ryan K. Bolger, *Emerging Churches: Creating Christian Community in Postmodern Cultures* (Grand Rapids: Baker Academic, 2005), chap. 6.

18. This was the lesson learned by Asian Christians from their nineteenth-century colonial experience; see, e.g., the account by Elizabeth J. Harris, *Theravada Buddhism and the British Encounter: Religious, Missionary and Colonial Experience in Nineteenth-Century Sri Lanka* (New York and London: Routledge, 2006).

19. I trace this development in my "Pentecostalism and the Theological Academy," *Theology Today* 64, no. 2 (2007): 148-57.

20. For introductory discussions, see Willi Braun and Russell T. McCutcheon, eds., *Guide to the Study of Religion* (New York and London: Cassell, 2000); and Linell Elizabeth Cady and Delwin Brown, eds., *Religious Studies, Theology, and the University: Conflicting Maps, Changing Terrain* (Albany: State University of New York Press, 2002).

First, the academic study of theology and, concomitantly, of religion, has begun to transform Pentecostal self-understanding. This is because Pentecostals have discovered that (a) it is less possible in the academic context to define oneself as being of "genuine faith" and others as being of "false religiousness"; (b) the categories applied to the history of religion are just as applicable to one's home religion; and (c) it has been left to scholars of religion to defend the *sui generis* nature of religion against those in other disciplines who might tend to reduce religion to biological, neurological, psychological, social, or other categories, and on this front, they (Pentecostals) make common cause with scholars who are also people of other religious faiths. In other words, if in the study of theology the lines between those who are "insiders" and "outsiders" are blurred in an ecumenical context, then in the study of religion these same lines are not so easily drawn in an interreligious context.

Secondly, and most obviously, the academic study of theology and, concomitantly, of religion, has begun to transform Pentecostal understanding of other religious traditions. Whereas before there was simply a dichotomy between "us" (Pentecostal Christians) and "them" (all those in all other religions, perhaps even including all other "Christians" insofar as they were not Pentecostals!), now there is a growing realization of the complexity of the category of "religion." Whereas before Muslims, or Hindus, or Buddhists, etc., were simply religious others, now there is an increasing recognition that there are varieties of Muslims, Hindus, Buddhists, etc., and that there are even some who consider themselves Muslim-Christians, or Hindu-Christians, or Buddhist-Christians, etc.[21] Whereas before Buddhists, etc., were simply "lost" and in need of evangelization, now there is the acknowledgment that even if that were the case, Pentecostal Christians might still be able to learn from Buddhism, etc., in particular and from their Buddhist, etc., interlocutors and dialogue partners in general. In short, academic Pentecostal perspectives about the religions in general and about Buddhism and Buddhists in particular are much more complicated than before, but these developments are occurring alongside what is happening at the lay level rather than taking place only in the so-called ivory towers of the academy.

In the preceding, I have presented what might be called a phenomen-

---

21. See Catherine Cornille, ed., *Many Mansions: Multiple Religious Belonging and Christian Identity* (Maryknoll, NY: Orbis Books, 2002).

ology of the Pentecostal encounter with Buddhism through the lenses of three modes of engagement: evangelism, social action, and dialogue. Elsewhere, I have argued that the Christian mission should be understood to include all three of these activities, each representing a spectrum of possible approaches.[22] But why has Pentecostalism emphasized the first over the other two? What are some of the commitments that have shaped and will continue to shape Pentecostal mission priorities and activities? These are theological questions that have been hinted at so far, but deserve more explicit articulation.

Pentecostalism and Buddhism: What Is the Question?

I now turn more specifically to theological matters, not only because I am a systematic theologian, but because there are many Pentecostals who would see no need for discussion about the relationship between Pentecostalism and Buddhism apart from certain well-established mission-focused objectives. In this section, I want to clarify what is at stake theologically in thinking about the relationship between Pentecostalism and Buddhism. To do so, I suggest that there are at least three levels of pertinent questions: that concerning the Christian understanding of salvation (soteriology), that concerning the Christian understanding of the religions (theology of religions), and that concerning the Christian understanding of Buddhism in particular (theology of Buddhism). Let us take each in turn.

Pentecostalism and Buddhism: The Question of Salvation

I submit that perhaps the most important question to Pentecostals is the one that asks about what will happen to their Buddhist neighbors, co-workers, acquaintances, and to all Buddhists who are unevangelized if they were to die without having come to faith in Christ. This is fundamentally *the* Pentecostal question, and it is essentially soteriological. Pentecostals are missionaries and evangelists because of their conviction that people

22. See Amos Yong, *The Spirit of Hospitality: Pentecost and Christian Practices in a World of Many Faiths* (Maryknoll, NY: Orbis Books, 2008), esp. chaps. 3 and 5.

are lost apart from hearing, receiving, and confessing the gospel, the good news about Jesus the Christ.

At this level, Pentecostals are not concerned about Buddhists as Buddhists; rather, they are concerned about Buddhists as people who are lost apart from the gospel. Hence in this framework, it is not that people are Buddhists that is important; in fact, what matters is not that anyone is a Buddhist, or a Muslim, or a Jew, or even an agnostic, but that each of these types of individuals is Christ-less. The unique calling and mission of each Pentecostal is to bear witness to Christ to the ends of the earth, and for this purpose, God has poured out his Spirit for precisely this purpose. Theologically speaking, then, I suggest that the underlying question for most Pentecostals when Buddhism, or any other religious tradition, is mentioned concerns their theology of the unevangelized.

Elsewhere, I have argued that it is such a theology of the unevangelized that has produced the dominant categories of exclusivism (salvation is available only in and to those who join the home religion), inclusivism (salvation is made available to those outside the home religion, albeit only through means derived from the home religion), and pluralism (salvation is available in every religion, analogously to the religions being different treks converging at the top of the same mountain).[23] Most Pentecostals are exclusivists in terms of their conviction that salvation is found only in Christ, and that all those who perish apart from Christ are condemned to an eternity separated from God. For this reason, Pentecostals take their missionary mandate very seriously. They believe that the eternal fate of people in other religions depends on Christian obedience to the Great Commission.

It is beyond the scope of this essay to explain why I do not think that Pentecostal theology is inherently or necessarily exclusivistic.[24] At the same time, I don't believe that abandoning the exclusivistic position leads to the abandonment of Christian mission as many fear. Rather, as I have already suggested above, Pentecostal mission is both multidimensional and multifaceted. Further, this does not mean that Pentecostals cease to be concerned about the salvation of others. Instead, if salvation is understood

23. See Amos Yong, *Beyond the Impasse: Toward a Pneumatological Theology of Religions* (Grand Rapids: Baker Academic, 2003), pp. 22-29; cf. my more recent assessment in "The Spirit, Christian Practices, and the Religions: Theology of Religions in Pentecostal and Pneumatological Perspective," *Asbury Journal* 62, no. 2 (2007): 5-31.

24. A book-length argument can be distilled from my *The Spirit Poured Out on All Flesh: Pentecostalism and the Possibility of Global Theology* (Grand Rapids: Baker Academic, 2005).

holistically to include a this-worldly dimension anticipating the next world, then the soteriological concern remains in place, though its scope is broadened. Finally, I am not undermining the Pentecostal commitment to bear witness through the empowerment of the Holy Spirit. On the contrary, it is precisely the power of the Spirit that is needed for Pentecostal witness to be borne not only in evangelism but also in social engagement and interreligious dialogue.

Pentecostalism and Buddhism: The Question of Theology of Religions

A related but yet distinct question concerns the Pentecostal understanding of "religion." Pentecostals have a pre-understanding about what "religion" means, so that to talk about "Pentecostalism and Buddhism" in the same sentence already presumes a certain (mostly implicit) Pentecostal theology of religions. Let me unpack this notion along two lines.

First, many Pentecostals contrast their Christian *faith* with other *religions*. By this, they are convinced that: (a) only Christian faith saves, and other religions do not; (b) Christian faith is a gift whereby God seeks out and reaches down to humankind, whereas other religions derive from human efforts to seek out and reach up to God; and (c) Christian faith is based on a personal and living relationship every human being can have with God in Christ, while other religions involve lifeless rituals devoid of divine presence or agency.[25] Insofar as Pentecostals associate Buddhism with religion, to that same extent each of these assumptions would apply to the Pentecostal perspective on the Buddhist tradition.

Second, while other religions are at best human efforts to search after and reach out to God, they are at worst demonic mechanisms designed to deceive, oppress, and mislead humankind, and to keep them from moving out of the darkness and into the light.[26] In this worst-case scenario, many Pentecostals contrast the divine source of Christian faith with the demonic

---

25. The second point was adapted by the wider conservative Protestant churches, including Pentecostalism, from Karl Barth, although most adherents of these churches would not recognize or know Barth's name.

26. See my "'The Light Shines in the Darkness': Johannine Dualism and the Challenge of Christian Theology of Religions Today," *Journal of the American Academy of Religion* 89, no. 1 (2009): 31-56.

origins of other religions. Again, inasmuch as Pentecostals classify Buddhism as a subcategory of religion, to that same degree they would assume Buddhism to be a tool of the Devil and his demons.

In either case, such a Pentecostal theology of religion in general or of Buddhism in particular may reveal more about the Pentecostal self-understanding than about either religion in general or about Buddhism in particular. What is important to note is that Pentecostals already have a negative definition of "religion" that contrasts to their positive self-understanding. At the popular or lay level, it is not uncommon for Pentecostals to say that theirs is a "relationship" (with Jesus) rather than a "religion" (which has negative, ritualistic, or institutionalistic connotations). I submit that such a dichotomous theological view derives in part from and in turn illuminates the apocalyptic, sectarian, and dualistic worldview that early modern Pentecostals uncritically borrowed from their dispensationalist and fundamentalist forebears. Again, it would take us too far afield to argue this point here.[27] Suffice it to say that Pentecostalism itself has now been acknowledged even by its own scholars and theologians to be "a religion."[28] Further, as a bona fide religion, Pentecostalism comes with the full spectrum of religious artifacts — the good, the bad, and the ugly[29] — and hence is in that sense not much different from any other religious tradition. But finally, and most important theologically, if in fact Pentecostals believe that salvation comes through God alone and embrace the Barthian (and Pauline) insight that salvation is a gift from God, then they also need to insist on another Barthian claim: that every religion, including the Pentecostal religion(!), is itself fallen and in need of Christ's redemption.[30]

Once these shifts are made, then Pentecostals are free to move from an a priori definition of religion to an a posteriori one. In this case, they

27. For a preliminary argument, see Gerald T. Sheppard, "Pentecostalism and the Hermeneutics of Dispensationalism: Anatomy of an Uneasy Relationship," *Pneuma: The Journal of the Society for Pentecostal Studies* 6 (1984): 5-33.

28. As admitted in the subtitle of Byron D. Klaus and Murray W. Dempster, eds., *The Globalization of Pentecostalism: A Religion Made to Travel* (Oxford and Irvine, CA: Regnum, 1999).

29. See Anthea Butler, "Pentecostal Traditions We Should Pass On: The Good, the Bad, and the Ugly," *Pneuma: The Journal of the Society for Pentecostal Studies* 27, no. 2 (2005): 343-53.

30. For Barth on the religions, see Veli-Matti Kärkkäinen, *An Introduction to the Theology of Religions: Biblical, Historical and Contemporary Perspectives* (Downers Grove, IL: InterVarsity Press, 2003), chap. 18.

would be not only invited but also required to allow each religious tradition to define itself, rather than be defined only by others. In fact, this was precisely the Pentecostal stance over and against the dominant Christian traditions of the first part of the twentieth century, when Pentecostals were themselves said to be aberrations of Christian discipleship (at best) or demon-possessed (at worst).[31] It took a long time for these characterizations to be corrected and overcome, for Pentecostals to be afforded the opportunity to be heard, to give their own testimonies, and to describe themselves. Today, it would behoove Pentecostals to revisit their "theology of religions" and adopt a more empirical and critical perspective that actually pays attention to the "religion" part of that set of ideas. This would mean that Pentecostals would actually have to learn from religious others about how they understood themselves.

Pentecostalism and Buddhism: A Theology of Buddhism?

In the preceding discussion I have followed a trail that began with the question of the theology of the unevangelized, moved to the question of theology of religions in general, and then suggested the possibility of a theology of religion in particular. This raises the question about the possibility of a Pentecostal theology of Buddhism.

Now what is a Pentecostal theology of Buddhism? Such would be different from a Buddhist theology, which can be said to be a theology from a Buddhist perspective.[32] Rather, a Pentecostal theology of Buddhism would provide Pentecostal and theological perspectives on the phenomenon of Buddhism. Hence, as in any theological view, there are the biblical, historical, dogmatic, and ecclesial (in this case, Pentecostal) perspectives on the one hand, the perspectives derived from the "object" of the theological gaze on the other hand, and the dynamic, critical, and creative attempt to relate the two hands together.[33]

31. This is documented by Cecil M. Robeck Jr., *The Azusa Street Mission and Revival: The Birth of the Pentecostal Movement* (Nashville: Nelson Reference, 2006), esp. pp. 75-84.

32. E.g., Roger R. Jackson and John J. Makransky, eds., *Buddhist Theology: Critical Reflections by Contemporary Buddhist Scholars* (London: RoutledgeCurzon, 2003).

33. For an explication of my theological method and hermeneutics, see Yong, *Spirit-Word-Community: Theological Hermeneutics in Trinitarian Perspective* (Eugene, OR: Wipf & Stock, 2005).

In this case, our Pentecostal gazes are steadfast upon "Buddhism." What then would inform a potential Pentecostal theology of Buddhism? At the very least, multi- and interdisciplinary approaches should illumine the Buddhist tradition. Further, the internal diversity of the Buddhist tradition — the Theravada and Mahayana and the many traditions through which they are constituted; the Yogacara and Vajrayana; the various regional, local, and indigenous forms of global Buddhisms, etc. — should be well represented. And last but most important, the voices and perspectives of actual Buddhists should be consulted. Methodologically, any theology of Buddhism, including any Pentecostal theology of Buddhism, should register what is considered by Buddhists to be most important about their faith tradition, and should be recognizable and even acknowledged by Buddhists when described to them.[34] By doing this, Pentecostal laypeople and scholars would be doing nothing less than allowing Buddhists to "bear witness" to Buddhism on their own terms rather than impose a definition of Buddhism on them.

In this section, I have stepped back one level of abstraction from a phenomenology to a theology of the Pentecostal encounter with Buddhism. In the process, I have identified at least three levels of questions that may mark what Pentecostals think is at stake in the encounter: the question of salvation and the Great Commission; the question of theology of religions and of Christian and Pentecostal self-understanding in a pluralistic world; and the question of theology of Buddhism, and the possibilities for such a Pentecostal account. The reader might guess that I will say each of these levels of questioning is important. I would go further to say that how we respond at any one level will have implications for how we respond at other levels. But if this is the case, then is that not to insist that the Pentecostal confrontation with Buddhism must at some point be balanced out by a Pentecostal dialogue with Buddhism, by a listening to the "tongues" (testimonies) of Buddhists, and by attempting to decipher the coherence of their interpretations?

---

34. Such a methodological dictum derives from Wilfred Cantwell Smith, "Comparative Religion: Whither — and Why," in *The History of Religions: Essays in Methodology*, ed. Mircea Eliade and Joseph M. Kitagawa (Chicago: University of Chicago Press, 1959), p. 34, cited in Sheldon R. Isenberg, "Comparative Religion as an Ecumenical Process: Wilfred Cantwell Smith's *World Theology*," *Journal of Ecumenical Studies* 24, no. 4 (1987): 616-43, at 624.

Pentecostalism and Buddhism: Whither the Discussion?

In this final section, I wish to conduct a thought experiment involving a Pentecostal dialogue with Buddhism. I suggest that such a conversation might proceed "from below" (from the human condition), through the "heavens" (our cosmic environment), to the divine (or whatever Buddhists think ultimate reality is). Consider the following, however, to be no more than programmatic suggestions of possible bridges that might connect the two traditions, and over which some mutually beneficial exchange might transpire. It may be that the end of this discussion (and this essay) will reveal the thought experiment as unfruitful, or it may be that we find various other possibilities for the future of the Pentecostal encounter with Buddhism. Which shall it be?

Pneuma and Anatman: Potential Anthropological Common Ground?

In an earlier article, I have suggested that a pneumatological approach to theological anthropology may hold unforeseen possibilities for a dialogue with Buddhism.[35] Whereas popular interpretations of Buddhist views of the human person emphasize the doctrine of no-self (*anatta* in Pali, or *anatman* in Sanskrit) and hence tend to think of Buddhism in nihilistic terms, such a conclusion is premature. A more historically informed and philosophically nuanced reading of Buddhist sources reveals instead that the no-self teaching is embedded within a wider philosophical and soteriological framework featuring three fundamental doctrines: (a) that all things, including human persons, are transitory, and hence there are no immutable substances (or souls) devoid of change (in fact, by definition, any unchanging thing cannot be found in a dynamic world); (b) that all things, including human persons, arise interdependently with other causes and conditions, and hence are constituted by a web of dynamic relationships; and (c) that the claim that there are unchanging human souls is ac-

---

35. The following is a summary of an argument developed at length in Yong, "Christian and Buddhist Perspectives on Neuropsychology and the Human Person: *Pneuma* and *Pratityasamutpada*," *Zygon: Journal of Religion and Science* 40, no. 1 (2005): 143-65. I refer the reader to the scholarship cited in this article.

tually bad news, since escape from suffering *(dukkha)* would then be impossible. The key to Buddhist anthropology, I suggest, is its dynamic and relational ontology.

How might a pneumatological theology serve as a springboard for a Pentecostal dialogue with Buddhism? Three lines of initial response can be sketched. First, I would argue that Pentecostals are not intuitively Platonists who think of the human person in dualistic terms — e.g., as being constituted by minds or souls as distinct from bodies. Rather, given the Pentecostal emphasis on the healing of the body and the embodied and affective character of Pentecostal spirituality and piety (as seen in tongues as evidence of the Spirit, or in the dance and the shout, or in the phenomenon of "being slain in the Spirit"), I am convinced that Pentecostals operate instead with a more holistic theological anthropology. Such a holistic approach may allow Pentecostals to bypass the intractable debates in the history of Western philosophy and theology about whether human beings are monistic or dualistic (or even trichonomistic).[36]

Further, the Pentecostal imagination assumes there will also be a spiritual or pneumatological dimension to the human person. Pentecostals can agree that human beings are defined in some ways by their embodiment but reject the claim that they are reducible to their bodies.[37] Rather there is an emergent spiritual capacity that is pneumatologically shaped. At this pneumatological level, human beings are relational creatures, constituted by their relationships with others — at the personal, ecclesial, and social levels — with their environments, and with God.[38] Such a relational construct affords opportunities for dialogue with Buddhist views of human persons as interdependently originated.

Perhaps most intriguing, however, is that the Buddhist anthropology is

---

36. For a historical perspective, see Paul S. MacDonald, *History of the Concept of Mind: Speculations About Soul, Mind, and Spirit from Homer to Hume* (Aldershot, UK, and Burlington, VT: Ashgate, 2003); for an assessment of the conceptual issues, see Joel B. Green and Stuart L. Palmer, eds., *In Search of the Soul: Four Views of the Mind-Body Problem* (Downers Grove, IL: InterVarsity Press, 2005).

37. I suggest some ways for Pentecostals to defend this nonreductionist view in my "The Spirit and Creation: Possibilities and Challenges for a Dialogue Between Pentecostal Theology and the Sciences," *Journal of the European Pentecostal Theological Association* 25 (2005): 82-110, esp. 96-100.

38. I argue that pneumatology opens up to relationality in my *Spirit-Word-Community,* pp. 28-34.

interrelated with its soteriology. But whereas "salvation" in the Buddhist scheme of things involves liberation from negative karmic forces that produce suffering — e.g., through the Four Noble Truths: (a) there is suffering; (b) all suffering has a cause; (c) it is possible to identify the causes of suffering and cut them off at the root; (d) the beginnings of the cessation of suffering involve entry onto the Eightfold Path[39] — Christian salvation viewed through the Pentecostal lens involves the four- or fivefold gospel of Jesus as savior, healer, baptizer, sanctifier (for fivefold-ers), and coming king. But when set side by side with the relational Buddhist anthropology and its dynamic soteriology, the interesting question arises about whether or not the Pentecostal anthropology and soteriology is similarly structured.

The Spirit and the Spirits: Cosmological Convergences?

Rather than pursue this line of questioning further at this point, let me introduce another set of related considerations in search of other bridges for the Pentecostal dialogue with Buddhism: those related to their cosmological visions. The beginnings of any conversation along these lines must acknowledge that there are various views regarding the nature of the cosmos across the Buddhist spectrum: from what might be called demythologized accounts on the one side to popular or lay Buddhist beliefs and practices on the other, with official textual sources in between.[40] In the main, however, human beings live in a multilayered universe, in a middle level between animals, ghosts, and various hells beneath, and spirits, deities, and Buddhas above. What is distinct about the Buddhist view is that these innumerable levels "below" and "above" are interdependent (as is everything else in the Buddhist cosmology), and that there is an ongoing "movement"

39. I discuss the beliefs and practices related to Theravadan (South and Southeast Asian) Buddhism in another essay: Yong, "Technologies of Liberation: A Comparative Soteriology of Eastern Orthodoxy and Theravada Buddhism," *Dharma Deepika: A South Asian Journal of Missiological Research* 7, no. 1 (2003): 17-60, esp. 32-42.

40. There is a growing scholarly literature on this topic. For starters, see Francis Story, *Gods and the Universe in Buddhist Perspective: Essays on Buddhist Cosmology and Related Subjects* (Kandy, Sri Lanka: Buddhist Publication Society, 1972); Randy Kloetzli, *Buddhist Cosmology: From Single World System to Pure Land* (Delhi: Motilal Banarsidass, 1983); and Akira Sadakata, *Buddhist Cosmology: Philosophy and Origins*, trans. Gaynor Sekimori (Tokyo: Kosei, 1997).

of karmic forces which results in deities being "demoted" or ghosts being "promoted," etc., in future lives. So on the one hand Buddhists believe we inhabit a richly populated and fluid cosmos, but on the other hand, there are neither "substantive" or eternally unchanging selves anywhere, nor inaccessible realms cut off from the rest of the cosmic domains.

A Pentecostal dialogue with Buddhism on the nature of the cosmos can proceed in at least two directions. First, whereas there is a small minority of Buddhists who dismiss notions of ghosts, spirits, or deities, the majority will sense an affinity with most Pentecostals who also live in a multilevel universe. Pentecostals have rehabilitated what the Enlightenment and modernist mentality had dismissed: the angels, ghosts, and demons of the premodern world.[41] Most Pentecostals believe (as already noted above) that there is a spiritual realm consisting not only of angelic beings but also of spiritual rulers, authorities, and forces of evil in the heavenly places. It would be an interesting exercise to see how Pentecostal views regarding these "powers" compare and contrast with those of their Buddhist counterparts.

But second, Pentecostals are not as interested in theorizing (or even theologizing) about the powers as they are in engaging them and "putting them in their place." Such engagement takes various forms: prayer, fasting, exorcisms, and various modes of what Pentecostals call "spiritual warfare." Most Pentecostals may not be aware, however, that Buddhists of various stripes also engage in similar activities against the ghosts and devils of the preternatural world. Even more interesting is that their modes of engagement take many similar forms — scriptural chanting (from the Buddhist sutras), purification rites, and exorcisms — and appear to be successful with regard to meeting various material, existential, and spiritual needs.[42] Whereas some Pentecostals may surmise that these "success stories" are

41. Anthropologist Paul Hiebert calls this rationalist mistake "the flaw of the excluded middle," referring to this "space" between the terrestrial human domain and the realm of God; see Hiebert, *Anthropological Reflections on Missiological Issues* (Grand Rapids: Baker Books, 1994), esp. chap. 12.

42. Elsewhere, I discuss Buddhist exorcisms in detail (with thorough documentation), and compare them with Pentecostal practices; see my "The Demonic in Pentecostal-Charismatic Christianity and in the Religious Consciousness of Asia," in *Asian and Pentecostal: The Charismatic Face of Christianity in Asia*, ed. Allan Anderson and Edmond Tang (London: Regnum International; Baguio City, Philippines: Asia Pacific Theological Seminary Press, 2005), pp. 93-127.

deceptive ploys of the prince of darkness to keep people trapped in the "stronghold" that is the Buddhist religion, the words of Jesus seem to militate against such a possibility: "If Satan casts out Satan, he is divided against himself; how then will his kingdom stand?" (Matt. 12:26).

I am far from ready to make any dogmatic pronouncements on these matters. My goal in this essay is simply to make some suggestions about possible topics for dialogue between Pentecostals and Buddhists, and with regard to cosmology and the human mode of interacting with the spiritual realm, there may be much more to the Pentecostal-Buddhist conversation than on first appearance.[43]

Spirit and Sambhogakaya: *Pneumatology and Buddhology?*

In the end, however, Pentecostals are pneumatologically and theologically oriented. Put in Christian parlance, theirs is a Trinitarian vision of God as Father, Son, and Holy Spirit. In fact, it is precisely because Pentecostals presume a vivid and vibrant pneumatology in their piety, spirituality, and practices that they can be said also to hold a robust Trinitarian theology.[44]

At this level of theology proper, can Pentecostals have a dialogue with Buddhists who are known for their nontheistic views? A number of preliminary responses can be made. First, some Buddhists may be nontheistic, and even atheistic. However, it is important to recall that such atheism has been developed over the centuries principally in reaction against ancient Vedic and Brahmanic notions of Brahma and Atman. In that sense, Buddhist atheism may not be of the same type as Western atheisms forged against the monotheistic traditions. Further, I have already mentioned, at least at the

---

43. See also my essays, "Going Where the Spirit Goes . . . : Engaging the Spirit(s) in J. C. Ma's Pneumatological Missiology," *Journal of Pentecostal Theology* 10, no. 2 (April 2002): 110-28; and "Spirit Possession, the Living, and the Dead: A Review Essay and Response from a Pentecostal Perspective," *Dharma Deepika: A South Asian Journal of Missiological Research* 8, no. 2 (2004): 77-88, for further discussion of these matters. I am convinced that Pentecostals engaged in the task of rethinking their demonology for the twenty-first century can learn a great deal from the interreligious dialogue in general and from the Christian dialogue with Buddhism in particular.

44. I would consider even Oneness Pentecostals to be "robustly Trinitarian," not in the sense that they would defend the classical formulations of the ancient councils, but in the sense that they also have high views of Christ and the Spirit.

lay level, Buddhists live with a multiplicity of deities in the innumerable Buddha heavens. In this sense, Buddhism can be said to be both polytheistic (in many Theravadan forms) and even quasi-monotheistic (in some Mahayana strands of the tradition).[45]

Second and building on the first, some Buddhist commentators have gone so far as to talk about Buddhist monotheism.[46] The argument is that certain Buddhist notions of the Buddha take on monotheistic features in terms of the Buddha's omniscience, omnipotence, and omnipresence — all of which are characteristic features of Western monotheisms. I still think this nomenclature misleading, especially since Buddhism lacks a doctrine of creation that is central to the Western monotheistic accounts.[47] At the same time, Pentecostal Christians may find it interesting that there is a Trinitarian form to Buddhist devotion that is encapsulated in the doctrine of the three bodies *(trikaya)* of the Buddha: the "created body" *(nirmanakaya)* is the Buddha manifest in historical space and time; the "body of mutual enjoyment" *(sambhogakaya)* is the archetypal Buddha who "appears" in many different ideal forms and is known by different names in the various Buddhist traditions; and the "reality body" *(dharmakaya)* is the absolutely unconceptualizable and unlimited principle of Buddhahood.[48] Yet the three bodies are but varying aspects of the one Buddha: one in essence but three in form, nature, and activity. This corresponds in different respects both with the classical Trinitarian formulations of the patristic church, and (from a Oneness perspective) with the modalistic views of the third century.

Such a "trinitarianism" buddhology raises the obvious question: Are Pentecostal views of the Holy Spirit as the third person (for Trinitarians) or manifestation (for Oneness) of the Trinity comparable at all with any

45. See B. Alan Wallace, *Contemplative Science: Where Buddhism and Neuroscience Meet* (New York: Columbia University Press, 2007), chap. 5.

46. E.g., Wallace talks about "the monotheistic status of Vajrayana Buddhism"; see his *Contemplative Science,* pp. 99-106.

47. Recently, however, Perry Schmidt-Leukel, *Buddhism, Christianity and the Question of Creation: Karmic or Divine?* (Aldershot, UK, and Burlington, VT: Ashgate, 2006), has argued that Buddhists and Christians may not be as far apart on this important question as previously thought.

48. For brief discussions, see Beatrice Lane Suzuki, *Mahayana Buddhism: A Brief Outline,* 3rd ed. (1959; reprint, New York: Macmillan, 1969), pp. 52-63; and Yves Raguin, "Ultimate Reality and the 'Three Bodies' of Buddha," *Areopagus* 2, no. 1 (1988): 34-37.

aspect of the Buddhist *trikaya* doctrine? In a fascinating article on "The Holy Spirit Through a Buddhist Lens," Soho Machida does suggest that the trinitarian structures of Christian theology and Buddhist thought invite seeing the Holy Spirit as parallel to the *sambhogakaya*.[49] Now Machida makes this point nondogmatically, and actually spends the bulk of his essay presenting the Holy Spirit in terms of the Buddha's truth or Dharma. In fact, his main point is that Christian pneumatology can help invigorate Buddhist beliefs and practices in terms of the Spirit's role in rendering a certain level of immediacy and dynamism to the lived faith experience. Viewing the Holy Spirit qua Dharma may enable a more personal engagement with the Buddha and endow daily life with a more existentially palpable sense of Buddhist faith.[50]

Pentecostals are right to be doubtful that such proposals will convince Pentecostals and Buddhists that the Holy Spirit is equivalent to *sambhogakaya* or any of the other Buddha bodies. But rather than arguing for such identification, my goal throughout this essay has been to simply imagine how a Pentecostal dialogue with Buddhism might proceed and to lay out some bridges over which a meaningful discussion could ensue.

Anticipations, Instead of a Conclusion

There is no space to pursue these issues further in this paper. My goal has been to suggest that there are sufficient commonalities between Pentecostal and Buddhist anthropologies and cosmologies to at least begin a conversation. And, as we have seen, both anthropologies and cosmologies presume soteriologies and a theology (in the Pentecostal case) or a buddhology (in the Buddhist case). But even at this level, there may be surprising springboards for discussion that take us to the heart of what both sides consider to be ultimately true and important.

If such a dialogue were to commence, it will undoubtedly unearth substantive differences in the process. But that is the nature of the interre-

49. See Soho Machida, "The Holy Spirit Through a Buddhist Lens," *Buddhist-Christian Studies* 16 (1996): 87-98, esp. 91.

50. Here is one example of how the Buddhist-Christian dialogue may actually contribute to the revitalization of Buddhism. The classic text explaining and defending such a possibility going in both directions is John B. Cobb Jr., *Beyond Dialogue: Toward a Mutual Transformation of Christianity and Buddhism* (Philadelphia: Fortress, 1982).

ligious dialogue: not necessarily to find commonalities (although some will also emerge) but to understand differences (which have been perennially emphasized). It is the observation of such commonalities amidst differences that will perhaps enable Pentecostals and Buddhists to collaborate in socio-economic, political, and environmental projects for the common good. To be sure, there will need to be an extensive period of interpreting the strange tongues of each tradition so that dialogue partners can begin to grasp what it is that is being testified to. Along the way, there will be misunderstandings, mistranslations, and misinterpretations. However, these are corrected by staying the course and, from the Pentecostal side, believing that the charisms of the Spirit will ultimately enable communication to occur, not apart from but precisely in and through the diversity of languages, experiences, and commitments.[51]

Perhaps over the long run Pentecostals will themselves be transformed in the conversation as they come to know their dialogue partners. Perhaps it is also possible that in such a conversation, Pentecostals will learn how to bear witness in a more pneumatically inspired way to the Christ they love. The results of the dialogue may be unpredictable, but that has never deterred a people who are committed to following the wind of the Spirit, even if they "do not know where it comes from or where it goes" (John 3:8). The Spirit has carried Pentecostals from Azusa Street to the ends of the earth; perhaps soon Pentecostals will pause long enough under the Bo tree to engage those who have found refuge under its shade.[52]

---

51. As suggested by Pentecostal theologian Jean-Jacques Suurmond, who suggests that there is a correlation between the outpouring of the Spirit (on and since the Day of Pentecost) and the increased human capacity for cross-cultural and even interreligious understanding; see Suurmond, *Word and Spirit at Play: Towards a Charismatic Theology*, trans. John Bowden (Grand Rapids: Eerdmans, 1994), pp. 200-201.

52. My thanks to Jon Rice, Timothy Leung, Doc Hughes, and Veli-Matti Kärkkäinen.

CHAPTER 12

Azusa-Era Optimism: Bishop J. H. King's Pentecostal Theology of Religions as a Possible Paradigm for Today

Tony Richie

Introduction

The ideology and reality of religious pluralism currently challenges all Christians, including Pentecostals, to articulate an adequate theology of religions.[1] Joseph Hillary King (1869-1946) was an important Pentecostal pioneer who helped found and lead one of the oldest and strongest classical Pentecostal denominations. Both he and his church were directly and strongly influenced by the Azusa Street revival that began in Los Angeles, California, in 1906 under the leadership of William J. Seymour but soon spanned the globe with the power of a modern Pentecostal outpouring of the Holy Spirit (cf. Acts 2:1-4).[2] Well educated and widely traveled, especially for most Pentecostals at the time, King addressed theology of religions fairly often and in depth. Douglas Jacobsen says King's theology is at

1. Cf. Terry C. Muck, *Alien Gods on American Turf*, Christianity Today Series (Wheaton, IL: Scripture Press Publications, Inc., Victor Books, 1990); and Diana Eck, *A New Religious America: How a "Christian Country" Has Become the World's Most Religiously Diverse Nation* (San Francisco: HarperSanFrancisco, 2001).

2. See H. V. Synan, "King, Joseph Hillary," in *The New International Dictionary of Pentecostal and Charismatic Movements*, ed. Stanley M. Burgess and Eduard M. van der Maas, rev. and expanded ed. (Grand Rapids: Zondervan, 2002), pp. 822-23.

An earlier version of this essay appeared in *Journal of Pentecostal Theology* 14, no. 2 (April 2006): 247-60. For a follow-up to this chapter, see Veli-Matti Kärkkäinen's "A Response to Tony Richie's 'Azusa-era Optimism: Bishop J. H. King's Pentecostal Theology of Religions as a Possible Paradigm for Today,'" *Journal of Pentecostal Theology* 15, no. 2 (April 2007): 263-68.

its core "deeply and consistently optimistic," with "an air of graciousness and patience."[3] These appealing characteristics certainly appear in his theology of religions. J. H. King is a particularly apt example of an early Pentecostal's approach to Christian theology of religions. This chapter surveys salient features of King's theology of religions before offering suggestions about contemporary application.

A Guarded and Gracious Optimism

Bishop King's sophisticated and subtle theology of religions comes to us through his autobiography, a theological work, and a collection of essays and sermons that serve as sources for this brief survey.[4] King should in no wise be considered an advocate of the ideology of religious pluralism. He did not equally esteem other religions alongside Christianity. He could even be honestly hard on shortcomings and sins he saw in the religions. His autobiography records his reactions to world religions as he traveled internationally. In Japan he negatively assessed the dreary atmosphere surrounding Buddhist worship he observed firsthand at a local temple.[5] He later called another Buddhist festival a farce based on an impossible relic. King said, "All idolatry is an absolute farce and utterly empty. It is based on falsehood and centers on the personality of the devil."[6] In China he referred to the "dense heathenism" and "dense darkness" he encountered amid "millions of idol worshipers."[7] His study of Islam led him to label it a

---

3. Douglas Jacobsen, *Thinking in the Spirit: Theologies of the Early Pentecostal Movement* (Bloomington and Indianapolis: Indiana University Press, 2003), pp. 192-93. King does not give us a systematically developed theology of religions. He is not that kind of theological thinker. Nonetheless, following the implications of King's ideas leads us on a fairly sophisticated venture.

4. Bishop J. H. King, *Yet Speaketh* (Franklin Springs, GA: Publishing House of the Pentecostal Holiness Church, 1949); King, *From Passover to Pentecost*, 4th edition (Franklin Springs, GA: Advocate Press, 1976 [1911]); and *Christ — God's Love Gift: Selected Writings of J. H. King*, vol. 1 (Franklin Springs, GA: Advocate Press, 1969).

5. See King, *Yet Speaketh*, pp. 155-56, 158, and 160. My colleague and King scholar, Tony Moon (Emmanuel College), cautions me to keep this aspect of King's thought in mind. Whatever else it was, King's theology of religions was not a rosy-eyed optimism denying the dark and demonic elements often found in the religions.

6. King, *Yet Speaketh*, p. 222.

7. King, *Yet Speaketh*, pp. 166-67.

"militaristic religion" and a more "carnal" religion than Christianity.[8] Although he seemed intrigued by India itself, he still referred to it religiously as "that land of mysteries," "that dark land," and "that dark desolate land."[9] King particularly deplored the Hindu caste system and thought Hinduism "the greatest system of idolatry ever established upon earth."[10]

Furthermore, King sharply distinguished between religious zeal and systems spawned by the flesh and that which is of the Spirit.[11] He also critiqued the Jews of Jesus' day, though not so much for being outright wrong as for being too narrow-minded to know Christ when he appeared among them.[12] He stringently castigated religious prejudice of any kind, acknowledging its extensive and alarming existence among Pentecostals as well as among "Jesuits, bigoted Jews, and fanatical Mohammedans."[13] He also, however, avidly affirmed the "Jewishness" of both Jesus and Saul of Tarsus or Paul the apostle.[14] And in a subtle plea for tolerance, King strenuously warned against dangers of the irrational devotion of religious prejudice.[15]

But King benignly believed not all non-Christian religions are entirely bereft of true divine presence and influence. For example, he was convinced that "the Living God, who reigns on high, the Creator of all things" put into the heart of an advanced, upper-caste Hindu priest, the father of a girl named Ramabai, to radically depart from custom in educating his daughter. He thus unawares prepared her to receive Christ later in life.[16] King related the testimony of a young Mongolian man "who had walked over deserts and mountains for months and months in quest of the peace which his poor heathen heart longed to possess," and how "God in his

8. King, *Yet Speaketh*, pp. 169-70.

9. King, *Yet Speaketh*, pp. 179, 181, and 183.

10. King, *Yet Speaketh*, p. 184. King also criticized so-called Christians who behave like heathen and show "who the real heathen are after all" (pp. 199-200). Cf. Amos Yong on the importance of spiritual discernment regarding religions in *Discerning the Spirit(s): A Pentecostal-Charismatic Theology of Religions*, Journal of Pentecostal Theology Supplement Series (Sheffield: Sheffield Academic Press, 2000).

11. King, *From Passover*, pp. 29-30.

12. King, *From Passover*, pp. 142-44.

13. King, *From Passover*, p. 169.

14. King, *From Passover*, p. 171.

15. King, *From Passover*, pp. 142-45.

16. King, *Yet Speaketh*, p. 185. Cf. Keith J. White's outstanding overview of Pandita Ramabai's life and faith, "Jesus Was Her Guru," *Christian History and Biography* 87 (Summer 2005): 12-14, 16-18.

mysterious providence" led him to the missionaries "to find the way of peace and heavenly rest."[17] He also told of God giving visions and sending angels to heathen who had never heard the gospel so that they and their families might be converted to Christ.[18]

King went even farther than telling of amazing conversions. For example, he unstintingly applauded the Jews for being a means of advancing the knowledge of God among the peoples of this world.[19] Still more surprisingly, in South India he spoke of meeting a sophisticated "rajah" who so impressed him he said that one "would not take [him] to be a heathen in the common meaning of the term."[20] Yet he left no doubt that the sacrifice of Christ on the cross in his mind "was the greatest sacrifice of all time, the most stupendous accomplishment of all ages," and that "Christ alone was fully able to redeem the human race, and His resurrection was a demonstration that man had been liberated from all the effects of the fall." King was unquestionably completely convinced that Christ's "resurrection was the full beginning of the great new creation as an infinite movement."[21]

A Grounded Optimism

King effectively established his theology of religions on biblical and theological bases. Five ideas seem central and crucial: a cosmic Christology, a rather refined doctrine of universal atonement, the reality and efficacy of general revelation, a qualified acceptance of religious experience over rigid doctrinal propositionalism, and, though somewhat less directly, the dynamic and progressive nature of pneumatology and soteriology.

King's vision of Christ and his creation was grand and cosmic in scope. Even when he commented on texts usually considered more particularistic (e.g., John 14:6), King could uncover layers of universality and inclusiveness regarding the nature of divine revelation and redemption.[22] King's consistent Christological focus is clearly suggestive of a basic orientation to Christology. For him, everything from and of God comes in

17. King, *Yet Speaketh*, p. 204.
18. King, *Yet Speaketh*, p. 223.
19. King, *Yet Speaketh*, pp. 229-30.
20. King, *Yet Speaketh*, pp. 212-13.
21. King, *Yet Speaketh*, pp. 244, 257.
22. King, *Christ*, pp. 21-31, 43-61.

Christ — but not only in the historic, temporal Christ but also in the cosmic, eternal Christ.[23] J. H. King's theology of religions is illumined by a literally larger-than-life view of Christ. The lordship of Christ is not lessened but enlarged by a theology of religions affirming his cosmic presence and influence among all peoples.

Christ's atonement is at the heart of King's theology of religions. The atonement is the exact counterpart to the fall, reversing both its unconditional/universal and conditional/particular aspects. The atonement, as an eternal act in the mind of God, actually exceeds the temporal limits and effects of the fall (cf. 1 Peter 1:20; Rev. 13:8). God's original and eternal purpose for his creation will be accomplished by virtue of the atonement of Jesus Christ.[24] King quite consistently combined the concepts of the universality of the atonement and the necessity of Christ.[25] Of special note is King's distinction between the objective and unconditional and the subjective and conditional elements of the atonement. In this way partial benefits of the atonement may be applied to all without falling into the falsehood of universalism.[26] The same atoning act that assures infants do not die lost because of original sin also applies to heathen. Infants and heathen, then, are to a limited extent included in the general benefits of Christ's atonement.[27]

Building on biblical texts such as John 1:9 and Romans 1:19-20; 2:14-15, King spoke of "the effect of the atonement upon heathen hearts, preventing the absolute erasure of every trace of the divine image from their being," a fact "opening a way whereby truth may find its way into their conscience and reason."[28] Hence the reality and efficacy of general revelation, ideally complemented and completed by special revelation, appears. King's

---

23. King, *Christ*, pp. 89-97 and 105-11. I here use "cosmic" Christ in a fairly informal manner without referencing a quite formal use of that term by certain others (Samartha and Panikkar). In my mind, King's grand, all-encompassing view of Christ is quite properly described as cosmic.

24. King, *From Passover*, pp. 5-8, 101-4.

25. King, *From Passover*, pp. 39-40.

26. King, *From Passover*, p. 109; *Christ*, pp. 110-11.

27. King, *From Passover*, pp. 14, 16. Another early Pentecostal disapprovingly describes Augustinianism as a system that automatically places "all unbaptized infants and all heathen" "in a state of reprobation," thereby implying a more or less temporary state of probation for both infants and heathen. E. S. Williams, *Systematic Theology*, vol. 2 (Hot Springs, MO: Gospel Publishing House, 1991 [1953]), pp. 143, 145.

28. King, *From Passover*, pp. 101-2.

theology of revelation is important and positive regarding the religions. While in northern India Bishop King had opportunity to present a public lecture to English-speaking members of the Muslim populace. He chose to speak on "The Natural as That Which Leads to the Knowledge of God."[29] Invited to give the same lecture to an educated audience in another city he essentially explained "God's revelation through creation" of his unity and sovereignty to all humanity. When allowed to give a follow-up lecture to the same audience, he then built on the previous lecture to present the gospel of Christ and his personal testimony.[30]

King apparently considered general revelation to have efficacious salvific energy. He assumed the patriarch Abraham's conversion from idolatry began as a result of a study of general revelation that was later completed by a special revelation involving a personal appearance of "the God of glory."[31] Significantly, he nonetheless asserted that a Spirit-filled person does not depend on natural light alone, on "unaided reason," but upon "the illumination of the Spirit," a light that is "all heavenly in origin and nature."[32] A sort of revelatory scale may be surmised in these comments. Thus King was enabled to approve limited benefits of general revelation while arguing for the necessity of special revelation. In addition, the role of the Holy Spirit in revelation becomes increasingly apparent as one ascends the revelatory scale. God is nonetheless really at work redemptively along the entire revelatory continuum.

The manner in which Christology, the atonement, revelation, and religious experience came together in King is illustrated in the following extensive quote.

> The Atonement is parallel to the Fall. The fall is universal. Sin touches every living being. Not one has escaped. Wherever man is found, sin is

---

29. King, *Yet Speaketh*, pp. 194-95.

30. King, *Yet Speaketh*, pp. 196-97. Obviously King's optimistic theology of religions left ample room for evangelism and missions. Cf. Harold D. Hunter and Peter D. Hocken, eds., *All Together in One Place: Theological Papers from the Brighton Conference on World Evangelization*, Journal of Pentecostal Theology Supplement Series (Sheffield: Sheffield Academic Press, 1993); Clark H. Pinnock, "Evangelism and Other Living Faiths: An Evangelical Charismatic Perspective," in Hunter and Hocken, eds., *All Together in One Place*, pp. 208-14; and Anthony O. Gbuji, "Evangelization and Other Living Faiths: A Roman Catholic Perspective," in Hunter and Hocken, eds., *All Together in One Place*, pp. 215-18.

31. King, *From Passover*, p. 26; cf. *Yet Speaketh*, pp. 52 and 234.

32. King, *From Passover*, p. 125.

found. Wherever sin is found, there is some vague idea that there is some power that can remove it, or that there is some way to escape from its consequence. The atonement covers all the ground of sin. Millions know nothing of it, historically. Yet every one is mysteriously touched by the atonement in that aspect of it which is unconditionally applied. *There may be those who have the essential Christ that know nothing of the historic Christ.* They may have pressed, in heart, up through the mist of heathenism, and prayed to the God that made heaven and earth, and in this way touched the Christ and found peace. We do not know this to be true, but we infer the same from certain statements in the Word.[33]

Some may experience Christ, and the true God, beyond their actual level of intellectual understanding of the person and work of Christ.[34] King allowed for, even argued for, at least the possibility of some knowing Christ, and participating in God's grace through Christ, in some sense, apart from direct, personal acquaintance with the historical gospel proclamation of the church. While King was conscientiously not dogmatic about this doctrine, he clearly thought an optimistic theology of religions compatible with the biblical record and Pentecostal witness.

Finally, the dynamic and progressive nature of the pneumatology and soteriology of J. H. King may be applied to his theology of religions (though less directly).[35] As I see it, the strength of King's position is its ability to simultaneously perceive Christ in terms of both universality and

---

33. King, *From Passover*, p. 101 (italics added).

34. Pentecostal orthopathy allows for possibilities of at least some level of genuine religious experience among non-Christians. See my "Awe-Full Encounters: A Pentecostal Conversation with C. S. Lewis Concerning Spiritual Experience," *Journal of Pentecostal Theology* 14, no. 1 (2005): 99-122 (105-6).

35. Samuel Solivan suggests Pentecostals recognize the prevenient workings of the Holy Spirit in every human being as well as the diverse and pluralistic character of the Spirit's manifestations across religious boundaries, making a commitment to cautiously "examine the diverse ways the Spirit is at work among other people of faith." See Samuel Solivan, "Interreligious Dialogue: An Hispanic American Pentecostal Perspective," in *Grounds for Understanding: Ecumenical Responses to Religious Pluralism*, ed. S. Mark Heim (Grand Rapids: Eerdmans, 1998), pp. 37-45 (43). James Bowers observes that "Wesleyan-Pentecostals rarely if ever used Wesley's term 'prevenient grace,' but shared with him the belief that salvation began with the work of God's grace in the sinner." See "A Wesleyan-Pentecostal Approach to Christian Formation," *Journal of Pentecostal Theology* 6 (1995): 55-86 (64 n. 32). Conversion, though a definite experience, is also a dynamic process beginning before and continuing after justification/regeneration.

particularity ("the Son in eternity as well as the Messiah in time"[36]). Perhaps a weakness is the failure to adequately envision the Holy Spirit's involvement in the revelatory and redemptive reality that makes up the religions. But, then again, perhaps this is not so serious a shortcoming after all. King averred in no uncertain terms that the Holy Spirit is actively involved in everything Christ does in us. He said, "Everything divine in us is directly related to the Holy Spirit," adding that "Every work of grace must be wrought by Him [the Holy Spirit]. All communications from God to our hearts must be through His agency." He unreservedly insisted, "Rule Him [the Holy Spirit] out, and there is nothing left."[37] In this context he argued for distinct stages of Christian sonship, characterized by distinct relations with the Holy Spirit in each and allowing for ongoing development and perfection in time and eternity.[38] King does not directly relate his pneumatology and soteriology at this point to theology of religions. The context here is concerned with spirituality in the Christian sense. But it seems a small step to apply his dynamic and progressive Pentecostal pneumatology and soteriology beyond the pale of conventional Christianity.[39] If Christ and his atonement are foundational for theology of religions, if the Holy Spirit is involved in everything Christ does, and if the Holy Spirit's work even in Christians is dynamic and progressive, does it not follow that the Holy Spirit may be dynamically and progressively involved in a preliminary mode in applying Christ and the atonement in the experience of those we might call "pre-Christian"?[40] At the least, King's theology of religions implicitly draws on his Wesleyan-Pentecostal pneumatological-soteriological progressive dynamism.[41]

36. King, *Christ*, p. 122.

37. King, *Christ*, p. 136.

38. King, *Christ*, pp. 131-41.

39. As Veli-Matti Kärkkäinen argues in *Toward a Pneumatological Theology: Pentecostal and Ecumenical Perspectives on Ecclesiology, Soteriology, and Theology of Mission*, ed. Amos Yong (Lanham, MD: University Press of America, 2002), Pentecostal theology of religions should aim at developing dimensions of pneumatology without diminishing Christology (pp. 238-39).

40. Clark Pinnock speaks of "not-yet-Christians," *Flame of Love: A Theology of the Holy Spirit* (Downers Grove, IL: InterVarsity Press, 1994), pp. 213-14. Gerald McDermott's work on Jonathan Edwards's dispositional soteriology suggests similar directions. See his *Jonathan Edwards Confronts the Gods: Christian Theology, Enlightenment Reason, and Non-Christian Faiths* (Oxford: Oxford University Press, 2000).

41. King specifically and repeatedly identified John Wesley as a major source of his

A Guiding Optimism

Understanding King's underlying attitude toward other religions per se is especially important in our attempt to appropriate his thought for contemporary Pentecostal theology of religions. Here we must be careful not to read too much into scattered and sporadic statements. However, King does provide exciting possibilities. For example, he editorializes on whether Christianity is properly judged by and in the world of religions. He does not think Christianity is fairly evaluated by others. He opines that because of its "legitimate effects upon individuals" "the religion of Christ" may be assessed as "all that it claims to be — a religion from heaven — divinely perfect — profoundly holy and far superior to all earthly religions." He closes with a climactic chorus of its abundant blessings.[42] Yet there is more. King rather bluntly and boldly begins this editorial with a descriptive analysis of Christianity and pre-/non-Christian religions.

> Today represents, or embraces, the age of Christendom. It is the dispensation in which *Christianity as a distinct and powerful religion* exerts its influence as a moral force and asserts its sway in the wide world. From the days of Abel to the present *the religion of Christ has been the only divine agency for saving men from sin, but it was not understood and accepted as such, that is, as Christianity,* but as the religion of Jehovah, the God of Creation, as well as the God of Abraham, Isaac, and Jacob.[43]

King further declares that this religion of Christ "was largely hidden" during the days before Christ's incarnation or "his historic manifestation." The

---

thought. His theology exemplifies a Wesleyan-Pentecostal hermeneutic in action (cf. *From Passover*, pp. 64, 126, and 135). Kärkkäinen draws attention to the dynamic, developmental strain of pneumatological soteriology running through John Wesley, Eastern Orthodoxy, and Pentecostal-Holiness traditions in *Toward a Pneumatological Theology*, pp. 158-61. An exploration into how King's thought might relate to contemporary ecumenical trends, such as Roman Catholicism's Vatican II or evangelicalism's inclusivist Clark Pinnock, could also prove profitable. Kärkkäinen suggests that King represents "a creative combination" of different models stressing Christianity's "partial replacement" and "fulfillment" of other religions. See V.-M. Kärkkäinen, "A Response to Tony Richie's 'Azusa-era Optimism: Bishop J. H. King's Pentecostal Theology of Religions as a Possible Paradigm for Today,'" *Journal of Pentecostal Theology* 15, no. 2 (April 2007): 263-68.

42. King, "Today," *The Pentecostal Holiness Advocate* 9, no. 31 (December 3, 1925): 1, 8.
43. King, "Today," p. 1 (italics added).

religion of "the historic Christ" began in his earthly life and continues to the present and is properly "designated the religion of the Christ the Son of God." Since it "was revealed and established through his humanity . . . hence it is an intensely human-divine religion." First, note that King deliberately distinguished between Christendom/Christianity as "a distinct and powerful religion," or present-day sectarian system, and "the religion of Christ," or religion rooted in the person of Christ himself, transcending chronological and ecclesiastical definitions. Second, King ascribed saving efficacy to "the religion of Christ," not to the Christian religious system per se. Third, King's threefold description of "the religion of Christ" was all-encompassing in that it included divine and natural religion rooted in the person of Jehovah and his creation prior to and apart from the specific Judaic tradition. Fourth, King's explicit distinction elucidated earlier between the *essential* Christ and the *historic* Christ is also here quite clearly implicit; but here and now, and of supreme significance for our subject, applied not to a discussion of *individuals* but to that of *religions*. Fifth and finally, note that King, as a result of his incarnational theology, insisted that even historic Christianity is an intense combination of both human and divine elements rather than some kind of completely heavenly enterprise.

Subsequent statements in this same editorial confirm and augment the preceding points. King argues that "Great heathen religions" "embrace and endorse" essentially natural morality as it already exists in human nature, basically leaving people just as they are, while "the religion that comes down from above" or "the religion of the Son of God" effects radical individual and personal transformation through regeneration. Indeed, the moral state of those in "Heathen and unChristian [sic] religions" is satanic and sinful, while "Christianity is the only religion that has a real high moral standard." First, King apparently meant non-Christian religious morality is a mixture of the natural and the diabolical, and second, he indubitably affirmed the moral and spiritual superiority of Christianity because of its unparalleled power to change human lives.

Another piece of special interest for King's theology of religions is a short sermon on "Jonah's Gourd." King does not censure Jonah's reluctance to reach out to the divinely doomed heathen of Nineveh, but attempts to understand his apparent Jewish racial bias and religious prejudice. Nevertheless, King plainly asks, "Was Nineveh hopelessly doomed? Was there no way to avert the threatened punishment?" He boldly answers, "Yes, but Jonah did not see how it could be done." He speculates how Jonah may have reasoned that they "had no way to approach God" or they were without "a divine process . . . to obtain God's blessings."[44] But King declares that God said otherwise!

> If there be no Priest or sacrifice yet, God will accept their repentance as genuine, and lift the judgment hanging over them. *Forsaking sin is not dependent upon Priest and sacrifice.* Prayer can find its way to God without these. . . . God did not even ordain the Priesthood and sacrifices in Israel *as an absolute necessity.* Jonah . . . will see what may be termed *God's departure from His own way of accepting souls.* He will see that *God will pardon sin outside of the Jewish sacrificial system, and independent of it.*[45]

Now note King's honest and straightforward confession and declaration. He said, "That's a hard lesson to learn. Doubtless we need to see that *God can save people today in a manner contrary to the way we prescribe or point out.*"[46] Still not satisfied, King pushed Pentecostals even harder:

> The Lord not only taught Jonah a lesson *to enlarge his view of His mercy and compassion,* but was using him in a way to reveal great truths that should belong to *future generations . . . to establish rules of judgment.* . . . There were 120,000 inhabitants of Nineveh that did not know their right hand from their left. They were innocent. Should they be destroyed? *No.* Thus God's judgments are such that He will not punish *even among Gentile peoples* those who have not justly brought this upon them. God will not send the innocent to perdition.[47]

Then King turned the tables on the Christians! He speaks of "another rule of divine judgment" in which "those who accept of truth in a lower state and with less light" will on the day of judgment "condemn those who have far greater light and opportunity." King concludes by contending that Jonah's signatory status pointing to the death and resurrection of Christ also points to a promise that the Jewish people will eventually "repent and ac-

---

44. J. H. King, "Jonah's Gourd," *The Pentecostal Holiness Advocate* 20, no. 29 (November 19, 1936), pp. 1-2.

45. King, "Jonah's Gourd," p. 1 (italics added).

46. King, "Jonah's Gourd," p. 1 (italics added).

47. King, "Jonah's Gourd," p. 1 (italics added).

cept the will of God in Christ." In other words, "They will be brought out by God's power."[48]

First, note that King incontrovertibly taught that God's saving purpose and power are not limited to or by any religious sectarian system, including Judeo-Christian religion. Second, he applied his inclusive insights beyond the individual level to that of religious groups, again including those utterly outside the Judeo-Christian tradition. Third, he adamantly insisted that pre-Christian Jewish inclusivism serve as a continuing paradigm for future generations today too, rather than limiting it to pre-incarnation experience or history. Fourth, King declared that the standard of final judgment and punishment includes consideration of the correlation of religious ignorance and innocence with human conduct. Fifth and finally, in spite of, and perhaps because of, all of the above, King nevertheless assumed non-Christian religions should and really would somehow culminate in Christ, even if only eschatologically.

Here are a few results of my reading of King to date specifically regarding other religions. We must first ask whether we can reasonably conclude King is correct in his contention about the possibility of pre-/non-Christian religions containing the religion of Christ. While possibly none would deny the uniquely symbiotic status of Christianity's parent religion, nevertheless to actually call it "the religion of Christ" is still an exceedingly strong statement. Yet King does so, and that not without biblical precedent (Heb. 11:26). Therefore, a biblical basis for King's approach seems plausible. This also establishes a precedent for other religions to the extent that they share in the same principle (Gen. 20).

We may also suggest King's nascent theology of religions is explicitly Christological and implicitly pneumatological in a nicely nuanced way. In short, the unrestrained religion of Christ, that is, religion rooted in the person of Christ himself rather than any specific religious system, may be made actually present and potentially salvific in the midst of non-Christian religions through the mysterious operation of the omnipresent and ever-active Spirit of Christ (cf. Rom. 8:9). Significantly for ecclesiology and missiology, accepting King's proposal does not at all undermine the unique and necessary nature of Christianity and Christian mission. On the one hand, the religions are not inherently efficacious but only experience efficacious ingredients of divine grace and goodness. On the other hand,

48. King, "Jonah's Gourd," p. 8.

Christianity, as the specially revealed religion of Christ, has unique and necessary status. In fact, we can, with King, call Christianity "the only true religion" because it is the only religion fundamentally *founded* on Christ (1 Cor. 3:11). Yet this should never be taken to imply that no true religion of Christ in any manner or measure exists elsewhere. But it does mean no non-Christian religion can be correctly called "the only true religion" in the same sturdy sense as Christianity. Accordingly, a corollary consideration, as Amos Yong has often ably reminded us, is properly discerning God's genuine presence or absence versus the presence or absence of the demonic within non-Christian contexts.[49] In point of fact, and I personally think King would say "Amen," ought not even ecclesial *Christianity* examine itself in the light of its loyalty, or the lack thereof, to the real religion of *Christ?*

But just how far can we faithfully go in affirming other religions? If true to the tradition of King, we will be cautious at this point. Another early and important Pentecostal, Charles Parham, typically more daring and direct than King, contended that non-Christian religions may continue to serve providential purposes during the Christian dispensation and that their salvific status will be eschatologically determined through Christ's "inheritance" of the heathen.[50] But I am reluctant to tread beyond that point. Clark Pinnock is probably correct to conclude that while "redemptive bridges" appear in non-Christian cultures and religions, regarding the religions themselves as "vehicles of grace" would be unwise.[51] Here is a dilemma for Pentecostals. Simple blanket condemnations, as in fundamentalist exclusivism, or blank approbations, as in liberal pluralism, are much easier — but not accurate. Recognizing that religions are a mixed bag of blessings and curses, of light and darkness, of the divine and the demonic (and the just plain human!), and laboring to discern the difference is much more complex — but correct.

Summarily speaking, two points seem to stand out head and shoulders above all else: A theology of religions creatively continuous with the thought of early Pentecostal leader and thinker Bishop J. H. King optimistically affirms the potentially salvific presence of the religion of Christ in

49. See Yong, *Discerning the Spirit(s)*.

50. See Tony Richie, "Eschatological Inclusivism: Exploring Early Pentecostal Theology of Religions in Charles Fox Parham," *Journal of the European Pentecostal Theological Association* 27, no. 2 (2007): 137-52.

51. Pinnock, *Flame of Love*, pp. 200-208.

pre-/non-Christian religions through the power of the Holy Spirit, and the supreme status of Jesus Christ and incomparable superiority of the religion founded directly upon his person are unquestionable.

An Optimistic Pentecostal Theology of Religions Today

J. H. King's optimistic Pentecostal theology of religions suggests potential directions for developing a contemporary Pentecostal optimism regarding Christian theology of religions. Any assumption that earlier (older) Pentecostal resources on religions would be exclusively pessimistic is invalidated. This represents the most radical rationale of this research. Heretofore Pentecostal theology of religions has been primarily either drawing on conceptual categories from ecumenical sources or developing theological and philosophical insights of contemporary Pentecostal pneumatology.[52] As helpful and needful as these are, and they are extremely so, the developing possibility of mining our own historical Pentecostal resources is especially exciting.

The example of J. H. King's early Pentecostal theology of religions indicates Pentecostals have a heritage of optimism that perhaps has been denied or ignored.[53] As contemporary Pentecostals confronted with a culture of religious pluralism, we need to acquaint ourselves with this optimistic element in order to help prepare ourselves to deal with the current scenario in a manner consistent with our original identity. Pentecostalism, of course, either in the past or present, is not necessarily monolithic in nature; great variety and diversity exist about details on most issues.[54] But whatever overall attitude the majority movement eventually adopts regarding theology of religions, it needs to include awareness of the optimistic thread in our historic theology. I strongly suggest that Pentecostals be-

52. E.g., Veli-Matti Kärkkäinen's *An Introduction to the Theology of Religions: Biblical, Historical, and Contemporary Perspectives* (Downers Grove, IL: InterVarsity Press, 2003) or *Trinity and Religious Pluralism: The Doctrine of the Trinity in Christian Theology of Religions* (Burlington, VT: Ashgate, 2004) and Amos Yong's *Discerning the Spirit(s)*.

53. Charles Parham and G. T. Haywood, Azusa-era Pentecostals, also advocated an open attitude toward adherents of other religions; see Jacobsen, *Thinking in the Spirit*, pp. 41, 212. Cf. Yong's discussion of generally negative Pentecostal rhetoric on the religions, *Discerning the Spirit(s)*, pp. 185-87.

54. See Jacobsen, *Thinking in the Spirit*, pp. 8-12 and 16-18.

ware of adopting ad hoc some pessimistic theology of religions schema simply inherited from another movement that may contain elements contrary to our own inherent identity. Right now the most relevant advice may be that of making sure we have made ourselves fully aware of the entire Pentecostal frame of reference.

Becoming aware of our optimistic heritage on theology of religions is only the beginning. We also need to express ownership. On this point Pentecostals can confess that we may have been unintentionally unfaithful to elements of our original impulse from the early days of the revival. When pessimism on the religions is the norm for judging the Pentecostal position, then we are failing to face our past faithfully. True, just because Pentecostal optimism toward religious others can be traced to the Azusa era does not make it either plausible or preferable. We, like most religious movements, have skeletons in our closet that we do not wish to resurrect, for some quite good reasons. But when someone as sensible as J. H. King, a solid and a stalwart figure, makes optimism on the religions a significant part of his life and thought, his spiritual heirs ought to pay attention. At the very least we ought to admit ownership of the tradition of an optimistic openness on the issue of theology of religions.[55]

Our restorationist heritage as Pentecostals compels us to at least consider whether we should actively attempt to develop a Pentecostal theology of religions along the optimistic lines exemplified by J. H. King and others. Once Pentecostals have accurately understood that an optimistic and positive approach to theology of religions is not a sop to politically correct ideology or liberal theology, and is not a detour inevitably taking us toward a philosophy of religious pluralism but is actually a component of early Pentecostalism, perhaps we can then begin to ask ourselves if constructing a contemporary Pentecostal optimistic theology of religions might be appropriate and attractive. Certainly since 9/11 contemporary classical Pentecostalism is being called upon, with the rest of the world — religious and otherwise — to address the existence of and relations among religious others.[56] Let us look to our own roots to grow a Pentecostal theology of religions.

Of course, though we can and should, in my opinion, draw on the in-

55. Significantly, Yong refers to an "almost unnoticed . . . strand of openness displayed by Pentecostals in their relationships with those in other faiths," *Discerning the Spirit(s)*, p. 187.

56. Tony Richie, "John Wesley and Mohammed: A Contemporary Inquiry Concerning Islam," *Asbury Theological Journal* (Fall 2003): 79-99.

sights of our original optimistic vision, the contemporary challenge includes developing a mature, moderate Pentecostal theology of religions
constructed to equip our movement for ministry and mission in today's
context.[57] In addition to exploring more in-depth the elements outlined
above in Bishop King's optimistic theology of religions, I suggest several
other ideas that need to be addressed in our developing theology of religions paradigm. First of all, Christian ecumenism cannot and should not
be assiduously avoided. This is a project calling for cooperation from the
whole household of faith. Second, interfaith dialogue and Christian evangelism and missions must be properly defined and practiced. Third, the
political, economical, social, and ecological global rights and responsibilities of religions and their adherents require responsible articulation and
oversight. Fourth, the practical ramifications of being a religious believer
in a world of science/scientism and modern/postmodern ambivalences,
which affect religious understanding and interaction, also demand attention. Fifth, and perhaps most pressing, we need to discuss how religious
organizations and individuals from different traditions can work together
in dealing with the extremists we all have in our midst — those who probably cause most of the trouble.[58]

An overarching assumption in this section has been that contemporary Pentecostal theology of religions calls for approbation and integration
of values of *continuity* and *creativity*.[59] Hereby faithfulness to our movement's conception joins forces with a vision for our maturation.[60] A

57. Tony Richie, "God's Fairness to People of All Faiths: A Respectful Proposal to Pentecostals for Discussion Regarding World Religions," *Pneuma: The Journal of the Society for
Pentecostal Studies* 28, no. 1 (Spring 2006): 105-19.

58. On the third anniversary of September 11, 2001, I was part of a group including Jewish, Christian, and Muslim, Hindu, Buddhist, and Sikh representatives. We met in New York
City and hammered out a statement for a joint press release condemning religion-related violence. Such events are admittedly a small start, but they are a step in the right direction.

59. Paul Tillich speaks of progress as a maturing of existing potentiality coupled with a
new moment of fresh opportunity, a *kairos* time; cf. P. Tillich, "The Decline and Validity of
the Idea of Progress," in *The Future of Religions* (New York: Harper & Row, 1966), pp. 64-79
(75-79). Hans Küng, *Theology for the Third Millennium: An Ecumenical View* (New York: An-
chor Books, 1990), talks about a *"double movement"* involving *"centripetal"* or "back to the
sources" and *"centrifugal"* or "out to open sea" orientations or *"a theology from the perspective of Christian origins and the Christian center, against the horizon of today's world"* (pp. 105-
6; original italics).

60. An intriguing use of a developmental metaphor for the maturation of the Pente-

Pentecostalism that recklessly rushes off after the latest theological fad runs the risk of losing the living impulse that birthed it. Constantly critiquing ourselves in view of the vitality of our fathers and mothers in the faith can help safeguard against dying a slow death of encroaching compromise. That does not mean we should see the past as sacrosanct. A Pentecostalism that avoids keeping abreast of current dilemmas or developments contrariwise loses its integrity in the eyes of its own constituents — much less nonconstituents. A movement without continuing relevance is a movement without relevant continuance. An optimistic Pentecostal theology of religions is congruous with principles of continuity and creativity. Optimism on possibilities of at least some divine presence and influence among the nonevangelized or adherents of non-Christian religions is continuous with an early Pentecostal ethos. Such optimism also allows us to creatively address the challenges of religious pluralism so prevalent today (see below).

Conclusion

Pentecostals might appropriately applaud God-enabled achievements and Spirit-guided progress since the Azusa Street revival. We must also rise to the occasion in accepting the serious responsibilities of life in Christ today. One of the most pressing issues confronting today's Bible-believing, Spirit-filled Christians has to do with how to handle the world religions crisis gripping the globe.[61] As observed earlier, Jacobsen says King's theology is at its core "deeply and consistently optimistic," with "an air of graciousness and patience."[62] Is not that description a beautiful and desirable prescription for Pentecostal theology today? So what does an optimistic, gracious, and patient Pentecostal theology of religions *do?* First of all, it does *not* compromise commitment to the unique and absolute character

---

costal movement may be seen in Cheryl Bridges Johns, "The Adolescence of Pentecostalism," *Pneuma: Journal of the Society for Pentecostal Studies* 17 (Spring 1995): 3-18.

61. Amos Yong suggests dialogue between the Christian faith and the world's religious traditions is "one of two essential conversations" for Pentecostals and other Christians today (the other being between religion and science), "Academic Glossolalia? Pentecostal Scholarship, Multi-Disciplinarity, and the Science-Religion Conversation," *Journal of Pentecostal Theology* 14, no. 1 (2005): 61-80 (65 n. 7).

62. See Jacobsen, *Thinking in the Spirit*, pp. 192-93.

of the person and work of Christ or other essential Christian convictions. Second, it does *not* drain Christian evangelism, missions, or witness of their energy and enthusiasm. Third, it *does* add meaning and momentum to relationships among individual and institutional religious participants, that is, all people of faith, presently sharing planet earth. Fourth, and for me personally perhaps most importantly, it *does* place all people in a just relation to the providential plan and purpose of the "God of the spirits of all mankind" (Num. 16:22; 27:16 NIV). When I read the scriptures, pray and worship, and as I sense the Spirit of my Lord Jesus moving upon and within me, I cannot consistently conceive of God as ignoring the cries of the vast mass of humankind to arbitrarily favor a few. Therefore, my personal position unreservedly affirms Jesus Christ the Son of God as the only absolute and universal Savior and Lord whose gracious presence and influence reaches into the whole world by the Holy Spirit (see Acts 4:12; Ps. 139:7). Fifth, optimism *does* avoid the extreme ideologies of narrow fundamentalism on the one hand, and naïve pluralism on the other, to bring balance and poise to a Pentecostal approach to Christian theology of religions.[63] That is what an optimistic, gracious, and patient Pentecostal theology of religions in the tradition of Azusa-era pioneer Bishop J. H. King does for me and what I believe it could and should do for our entire movement.

63. Tony Richie, "Neither Naïve nor Narrow: A Balanced Pentecostal Approach to Christian Theology of Religions," see *Cyberjournal for Pentecostal/Charismatic Research*, February 2006; http://www.pctii.org/cyberj/cyberj15/richie.html.

Contributors

Deidre Helen Crumbley (Ph.D., Northwestern University) is Associate Professor in the Africana Studies Program at North Carolina State University. Her research focuses on religion, gender, and power in Africa and its diaspora, as reflected in her two books currently under contract: *Spirit, Structure, and Flesh: Gender and Power in African Instituted Churches* and *Divine Mother — Holy Saints: Race, Gender, and Migration in the Rise of a Storefront Sanctified Church*, the latter being a historically embedded ethnography of her home church.

Ogbu U. Kalu (Ph.D., University of Toronto; died 2009) was awarded Doctor of Divinity *honoris causa* by Presbyterian College, Montreal, Canada, in 1997. A native of Nigeria, Dr. Kalu served with the West African Association of Theological Institutions, Conference of African Theological Institutions, and the Commission on the History of the Church in the Third World, and taught and acted as Dean at the University of Nigeria, Nsukka. Appointed the Henry Winters Luce Professor of World Christianity and Mission at McCormick Theological Seminary in Chicago in 2001, he served as a visiting professor in several universities. Author of sixteen books, including *African Church Historiography: An Ecumenical Perspective* (1988) and *African Christianity: An African Story* (2005), he also published over 180 articles, as well as the forthcoming Oxford University Press title *African Pentecostalism*.

Veli-Matti Kärkkäinen (Dr.Theol.Habil., University of Helsinki) is Professor of Systematic Theology at Fuller Theological Seminary and Docent of Ecumenics at the University of Helsinki. A native of Finland, he has also lived with his family and taught theology in Thailand. Author of eleven scholarly books, among others *The Trinity: Global Perspectives* (WJKP) and more than one hundred articles that have appeared in several languages, Dr. Kärkkäinen is also co-editor of *Global Dictionary of Theology* (with William Dyrness; IVP, 2008). He has participated widely in the theological, missiological, and interfaith work of the World Council of Churches and Faith and Order as well several bilateral ecumenical dialogues.

Wonsuk Ma (Ph.D., Fuller Theological Seminary) is Executive Director of Oxford Centre for Mission Studies and Research Tutor at Oxford Centre for Mission Studies, Oxford, England. As a Korean Pentecostal missionary in the Philippines (1979-2006), he served as the founding editor of *Asian Journal of Pentecostal Studies* (1998) and *Journal of Asian Mission* (1999), and the founding president of the Asian Pentecostal Society (1998). He is responsible for six authored and edited books.

Frank D. Macchia (D.Theol., University of Basel) is Professor of Theology at Vanguard University of Southern California. He is past president of the Society for Pentecostal Studies and is currently editor of the Society's journal, *Pneuma*. He serves on the International Reformed/Pentecostal dialogue and the Faith and Order Commission of the National Council of Churches. He has published numerous papers, essays, and articles dealing with issues of Pentecostalism, pneumatology, and ecumenism, among other topics. He has recently published *Baptized in the Spirit: A Global Pentecostal Theology* (Zondervan, 2005). His most recent book, *Justified in the Spirit: Towards a Trinitarian Soteriology,* is forthcoming from Eerdmans.

Jürgen Moltmann, professor emeritus at the University of Tübingen, Germany, is widely regarded as the leading living systematic and constructive theologian and pneumatologist at the international and ecumenical level. Among a number of bestselling and theologically groundbreaking constructive theological works, he is the author of the widely acclaimed *The Spirit of Life: A Universal Affirmation* (1992). Professor Moltmann has participated and given presentations in Pentecostal and charismatic theological settings as well as contributed to publications and topics dealing with Pentecostal theology.

Opoku Onyinah (Ph.D., University of Birmingham) is the Rector of Pentecost University College in Accra, Ghana. Rev. Opoku Onyinah is an executive member of the Church of Pentecost and served as the first International Missions Director. He has spoken at many conferences. In the field of Theology and Mission, he has shown particular interest in deliverance, exorcism, healing, African diaspora, and African Christianity. Dr. Opoku Onyinah actively participates in interfaith work of the WCC and is a member of the Commission on World Mission and Evangelism (CWME). He has authored eight books and written many articles.

Douglas Petersen (Ph.D., Oxford Centre for Mission Studies, Oxford, England) is the Margaret S. Smith Professor of World Mission and Intercultural Studies and Director of the Judkins Institute for Leadership at Vanguard University. In 1977 Petersen co-founded Latin America ChildCare (LACC) and served as its International Coordinator and President for twenty-three years. Dr. Petersen is an experienced practitioner and research scholar in the development and leadership of faith-based community organizations. He is the author of several books, including *Not by Might Nor by Power: A Pentecostal Theology of Social Concern,* and numerous scholarly journal articles on ethics, politics, and Pentecostalism.

Margaret M. Poloma (Ph.D., Case Western Reserve University), professor emerita of sociology at the University of Akron, has also served as a visiting professor in several theological schools. She has written extensively about religious experience in contemporary American society, including pioneering studies of prayer and divine healing. Many of her publications have focused on Pentecostal spirituality, including *Main Street Mystics: The Toronto Blessing and Reviving Pentecostalism* (2003). Dr. Poloma is currently working with two books, one (with Ralph W. Hood Jr.) on the *charismata* and spiritual empowerment in an emerging church and the other (with John C. Green), revisiting her 1989 book, titled *Assemblies of God on the Cross-Roads: Charisma and Institutional Dilemmas.*

Paulson Pulikottil (Ph.D., Sheffield University) is Head of the Department of Biblical Studies and the Dean of Academic Affairs at Union Biblical Seminary, Pune, India. He has been associate editor of the *Dictionary of Classical Hebrew Project* (University of Sheffield). His published works include *Transmission of Biblical Texts in Qumran* (2001). He is also pastor of the "Community of the Redeemed," a Full Gospel congregation, and has contributed to the academic study of Pentecostalism in the majority world through various published articles. He is also a member of the World Council of Churches Joint Consultative Group with Pentecostals.

Tony Richie (D.Min., Asbury Theological Seminary), currently a Ph.D. student at Asbury Theological Seminary and missionary teacher at SEMISUD (Quito, Ecuador), does adjunct teaching at the Church of God Theological Seminary and Lee University (Cleveland, TN) and is also an ordained bishop and senior pastor at New Harvest Church of God, Knoxville, TN. He serves the Society for Pentecostal Studies as liaison in interfaith issues to the NCCC (USA) and World Council of Churches. Previous publications include several journal articles and book chapters on Pentecostal theology and experience.

Amos Yong (Ph.D., Boston University) is Professor of Theology at Regent University School of Divinity, Virginia Beach, Virginia, and director of the School of Divinity's Ph.D. program in Renewal Studies. He has edited three books, including *Philip's Daughters: Women in Pentecostal-Charismatic Leadership* (Pickwick Press, 2008), and authored almost one hundred scholarly articles and six other volumes, most recently, *Hospitality and the Other: Pentecost, Christian Practices, and the Neighbor,* in Orbis Books' Faith Meets Faith series (2008).

Koo Dong Yun (Ph.D., The Graduate Theological Union, Berkeley, CA) is Professor of Systematic Theology at Bethany University, Santa Cruz, California. A native of South Korea, he also serves the Korea Institute for Advanced Theological Studies as Associate Editor of *KIATS Theological Journal.* He is an expert in Pentecostal and Asian contextual theologies including *minjung* and various Asian revival movements. He is the author of *Baptism in the Holy Spirit: An Ecumenical Theology of Spirit Baptism.*